THE SIERRA CLUB
WETLANDS READER

THE SIERRA CLUB

WETLANDS

READER

A LITERARY COMPANION

EDITED BY

SAM WILSON

AND TOM MORITZ

SIERRA CLUB BOOKS   SAN FRANCISCO

The Sierra Club, founded in 1892 by John Muir, has devoted itself to the study and protection of the earth's scenic and ecological resources—mountains, wetlands, woodlands, wild shores and rivers, deserts and plains. The publishing program of the Sierra Club offers books to the public as a nonprofit educational service in the hope that they may enlarge the public's understanding of the Club's basic concerns. The point of view expressed in each book, however, does not necessarily represent that of the Club. The Sierra Club has some sixty chapters coast to coast, in Canada, Hawaii, and Alaska. For information about how you may participate in its programs to preserve wilderness and the quality of life, please address inquiries to Sierra Club, 730 Polk Street, San Francisco, CA 94109.

LIBRARY OF CONGRESS CATALOGING-IN-PUBLICATION DATA

The Sierra Club wetlands reader : a literary journey / edited by Sam Wilson and Tom Moritz.
 p. cm.
 Includes bibliographical references (p.).
 ISBN 0-87156-425-4 (pbk.)
 1. Wetland conservation—United States. 2. Wetlands—United States. I. Wilson, Sam, 1946– . II. Moritz, Tom. III. Sierra Club.
QH76.S58 1995
333.91'8'0973—dc20

95-5602
CIP

Pages 259–261 constitute an extension of this copyright page.

Production by Robin Rockey
Cover design by Christine Taylor
Book design by Christine Taylor
Composition by Wilsted & Taylor

Printed in the United States on acid-free paper containing
a minimum of 50% recovered waste paper of which at least
10% of the fiber content is post-consumer waste.

10 9 8 7 6 5 4 3 2 1

SAM WILSON:

For the ones who sustain me, Lucy and Amber.

TOM MORITZ:

To Margaret Moritz who has provided love and support
and Bill Wilson who has offered hope and wisdom.

CONTENTS

CONTENTS

PREFACE

If there were Druids whose temples were the oak groves,
my temple is the swamp.
Henry David Thoreau

Even in our time of widespread reverence for natural environments, Thoreau's worshipful sentiment might seem a little misplaced. But to most people of his own time he must have sounded downright crazy.

Thoreau's was a vigorously expansionist America, whose frontiers had yet to be defined and whose natural settings were there to be tamed or, in the case of the swamp, eradicated. The prevailing attitude of his era was typified by the Federal Swamp Lands Act of 1849, which virtually gave away wetland areas to those who drained them.

Apprehension of and disdain for inundated areas have deep roots in American history and Western culture. Psalm 40:2, for example, tells of divine rescue "from the mud of the mire." John Bunyan's *The Pilgrim's Progress*, published in 1678, took this passing metaphor and turned it into an allegory of victory over sin and corruption. Perhaps the most influential book of colonial times apart from the Bible, it told of a man called Christian whose life and adventures were portrayed as a quest for salvation. The story opens with Christian fleeing from impending doom in the city of Destruction, but he doesn't get far before tumbling into the swamp of Despond. Fortunately, Help arrives in time to rescue him and to explain why such a foul trap lies in the path to redemption:

This miry slough is such a place as cannot be mended. It is the descent whither the scum and filth that attend conviction of sin do continually run, and therefore it is called the slough of Despond. . . . It is not the pleasure of the King that this place should remain so bad. His labourers also have, by the directions of his Majesty's surveyors, been for above these sixteen hundred years employed about this patch of ground, if perhaps it might be mended; yea, and to my knowledge, said he, here have been swallowed up at least twenty thousand cartloads, yea, millions of wholesome instructions . . . but it is the slough of Despond still, and so will be when they have done what they can.

Imagine Bunyan's surprise were he to learn that wetlands are, in fact, vital to cleansing the offal of humanity. Or, picture Help's incredulity were he informed that even the King had to comply with Section 404 of the Clean Water Act. Despond might be filled, but only after an arduous permit process requiring mitigation—restoration or creation of another wetland—and commission of the King's own army of surveyors to enforce it.

As a culture, we've finally come around to valuing natural areas of shallow waters and saturated lands, but even now we tend to view them with less than admiration. Peter Fritzell, who has written about the place of wetlands in American culture, put it this way: "One's Salem-springtime lover, after all, does not recline in marshy sedges or run trippingly, in flowing skirts, over squishy, cedar-shadowed mosses. One's rugged Marlboro-Viceroy-Camel man is found riding in the foothills of the Rockies or splitting timber in bright, dry forests; not mucking about in backwaters or sliding through beds of wild rice."

Are wetlands a case of the good not necessarily being the beautiful? Frederick Law Olmsted, America's "founder of landscape architecture," saw them to be merely in need of a little cosmetic work. At a time when massive canal-building and drainage projects were obliterating vast areas of American wetlands, Olmsted was fashioning them into elements of such definitive works of landscape design as New York's Central Park and the site of the 1893 Chicago World's Fair. A tremendously prolific worker, he designed parks for many of America's largest cities and institutions. He often found himself working with swamps and marshes, since by the time a park became a civic priority, wetlands typically constituted much of what undeveloped land was left.

Olmsted preferred his swamps with "sparsely wooded shores," installing canals and berms designed to give distinct interfaces between watery and upland areas. Writing on what constituted a well-groomed wetland, he suggested: "The witness of the eye alone would persuade us that Nature unassisted had achieved the whole result. But beauty of so suave and perfect a sort as this is never a natural product. Nature's beauty is wilder, if only because it includes traces of mutation and decay which here are carefully effaced. Nature suggests the ideal beauty, and the artist realizes it by faithfully working out her suggestions."

Certainly Olmsted would find little support among modern environmental restorationists for some of his manipulations, which included introducing species of exotic birds and plants. Yet he often found himself in disputes with clients over his unwillingness to alter nature as much as they wanted. You may recognize Olmsted's touch in his proposals for citified wetlands to the park commissions of Boston, Chicago, and Buffalo, which are included in the Impressions section of this book.

Since Olmsted's time, with the Clean Water Act of 1972 marking a significant turning point, popular sentiment has turned toward keeping certain areas of wetlands as pristine as possible, complete with mutation and decay. "No net loss" of wetland function has become a national priority, although we are far from consensus even on what constitutes a wetland.

Marjory Stoneman Douglas was an eloquent prophet of the shift in popular perception of wetlands. Much as Rachel Carson later alerted the nation to chemical threats, Douglas wrote of the Everglades with a compelling vision of admiration and sense of impending loss. And her style of activism set the tone for generations to come. Publication of her book *The Everglades: River of Grass* in 1947 coincided with the opening of Everglades National Park, for which she had lobbied for twenty years.

We have included excerpts from *River of Grass* in the Impressions section of this book, although Douglas's influence certainly extends into the subject of the second section, Impacts and Compensations. This series of readings is concerned with America's cultural about-face regarding wetlands, from historical policies that rewarded destruction to today's attempts at preservation and restoration. Beginning with the Swamp Lands Act of 1849, it includes excerpts from significant government documents as well as literary, legal, ecological, and social commentary—from Mark Twain's Uncle Mumford lambasting the precursor of the Army Corps of Engineers to an on-line debate over the definition of "wetland" gleaned from the Internet.

Because of the direct effects of wetland regulations on so many people, perhaps no other environmental issue has so polarized public opinion. As this book is about to go to press in the spring of 1995, the 104th Congress, in keeping with the conservative majority's "Contract with America," is taking up several bills that could significantly curtail existing wetland protection policies. Among the proposals is legislation that would require cost-benefit analyses of environmental programs as well as compensation for "takings" of private property where development permits have been denied or are perceived to be overly restrictive. Moreover, such basic environmental legislation as the Endangered Species Act and the Clean Water Act are threatened with drastic, potentially debilitating revisions.

A more insidious threat may lie in the unwillingness of the agencies mandated with protecting wetlands to follow through. The Army Corps of Engineers has been subject to particular criticism. According to an article by environmental writer Ted Williams in the March-April 1995 issue of *Audubon* magazine, "After a promising start, Section 404 [of the Clean Water Act] has mutated into a fast track for wetland wreckers and a hoax on the American public. It is a hoax perpetrated and perpetuated by a wasteful, bloated bureaucracy that is efficient only at finding ways to shirk its obligations and that when beaten on by developers, spews wetland-destruction permits as if it were a piñata." In the March-April 1995 issue of the Environmental Law Institute's *National Wetlands Newsletter*, David E. Ortman, director of Friends of the Earth's Northwest office, dissected the Corps' methods: "Like physicists deconstructing the universe with quarks, bosons, and other strange discoveries, the Corps has been busy deconstructing the wetland universe with similar strange inventions, such as alternative permit procedures, regional general permits, and letters of permission. The Corps, it seems, is willing to go to great lengths to avoid the individual permit application process."

Although the cause of wetlands protection in America is on the defensive on the legislative and regulatory fronts, the outlook isn't entirely bleak, particularly when accomplishments outside the Section 404 mitigation scheme are considered. In California's Great Central Valley, for example, rice farming and waterfowl have entered into a symbiotic relationship. Encompassing an area about half the size of New York state, "the Valley," as it is known to the people who farm it, is the richest agricultural region in the world. And it once supported one of the planet's greatest assemblages of wintering migratory waterfowl. A plan to restore waterfowl habitat centers on the 500,000-plus acres of rice fields in the Valley's northern lobe, and it has brought together a coalition that includes the California Rice Industry Association, Ducks Unlimited, the California Waterfowl Association, The Nature Conservancy, and author Marc Reisner. "We are strange bedfellows," says Reisner of the California Ricelands Habitat Partnership, "but it's a great alliance." Reisner made his reputation as an environmental writer with well-documented criticism of western agriculture's wasteful ways with water, but he's now happy to say he's changed his mind about the "monsoon crop grown in a desert state."

Due to a fortunate convergence of circumstances, which includes an air-quality law passed in 1991 that phases out the practice of burning rice stubble after fall harvest by the year 2000, rice farmers are beginning to leave water on their fields after fall harvest in order to decompose the coarse plant residues. Foraging birds help to break up the stubble and their droppings fertilize the following year's crop. An added benefit is floodwater catchment during the rainy season.

Of course, such serendipity can't sustain a comprehensive approach to wetlands preservation. Yet many farmers and other large-scale landowners have shown they are willing to restore and conserve wetlands, provided they are given a measure of technical and financial assistance. Landowners have voluntarily restored a half-million acres of wetlands in the last decade, assisted by programs like the U.S. Fish and Wildlife Service's Partners for Wildlife, and the Natural Resources Conservation Service's Wetland Reserve, which provide expertise and funds to cover all or part of the earth-moving costs. But the funding is limited, and waiting lists are growing.

Other options for property owners concerned with preserving or enhancing wetland areas include working with conservation district employees or local environmental organizations. In some cases property owners might find tax-reduction or other financial incentives by entering into rights transfers such as conservation easements. Since more than 75 percent of the remaining wetlands in the lower forty-eight states are privately owned, and many are partially drained or filled, the potential for restoration is enormous.

That potential includes a vital element of willingness and sometimes aspirations toward stewardship, attributes essential to sustaining efforts to preserve natural environments. Granted, the human inclination toward avarice being what it is, there probably always will be a need for wetland regulations and enforcement. But perhaps the future of wetlands preservation in America lies not so much in coercion as in cooperation.

Acknowledgments

We gratefully acknowledge the assistance of the staff of the Library at the California Academy of Sciences in San Francisco, particularly Library Assistant Patricia Shea Diner who acquired most of the literature reviewed for this collection. Anne Marie Malley of the Academy's Biodiversity Resource Center assisted with on-line resources, Lesley Segedy provided managerial assistance, and Susan Sevieri helped with retrievals and photocopies.

Thanks also to the staff of Dominican College's library, Louise Gratton for her input on the wetlands of Canada, Chuck James for several fruitful leads, and Jim Cohee of Sierra Club Books.

INTRODUCTION

Wetlands of North America

William A. Niering

What is a "wetland"? Because the term is loaded with political and
regulatory implications, even the experts have a hard time agreeing. But
they do agree on some descriptive words—such as "swamp," "marsh,"
and "bog"—which most people only vaguely understand as representing
places that are more or less soggy. In this introduction, borrowed from an
excellent survey of the natural history of North American wetlands,
William Niering explains the basic terminology and habitat characteristics
of the continent's various wetland types and sums up why they're worth
saving.

Niering is on the faculty of Connecticut College.

Not so long ago, Americans believed their marshes, swamps, and
bogs were wastelands. These wetlands couldn't be farmed, and they
harbored mosquitoes, cottonmouths, alligators, and other disagreeable creatures, to say nothing of malaria. Clearly, the best thing to do
was drain them, clear them, plow them, and control them.

With the help of congressional bills like the Swamp Land Act of
1849, which virtually gave away vast tracts of submerged acreage to

anyone who would reclaim them, Americans began to destroy their wetlands at a pace which has accelerated through the 20th century. When the United States was founded, the nation had 215 million acres of wetlands. Today, fewer than 99 million acres remain, and each year at least another 300,000 acres are lost.

The destruction has slowed, perhaps just in time, because we've discovered how valuable our wetlands actually are. As ecologists have come to understand the biochemical pathways by which living creatures transfer energy to one another, we've learned that wetlands, far from being waste places, sustain more life than almost any other ecosystems—as much as many tropical rain forests, and more than most good farmland.

Moreover, ecologists have shown that wetlands, which comprise no more than six percent of the earth's surface, play a disproportionately large role in maintaining the stability of the global environment. Wetlands retain and gradually release large quantities of water which otherwise would flow more quickly to the sea, and their dense vegetation traps sediments and consumes pollutants. Above water, the same abundance of plant life takes in large amounts of carbon dioxide and releases great quantities of oxygen, much the way rain forests do. And like rain forests, wetlands with their ample food supplies encourage and sustain a multitude of species, adding greatly to the planet's biotic diversity.

Wetlands act as "carbon sinks": places where the carbon in dead plant and animal tissues accumulates without being released into the atmosphere as carbon dioxide. Retaining carbon and producing oxygen, wetlands over the millennia have helped to stabilize global temperatures by offsetting the build-up of CO_2 in the atmosphere—the main cause of global warming.

Fortunately, we still have many kinds of wetlands in North America. Salt and brackish coastal marshes fringe the sandy, gently sloping Eastern Seaboard and the Gulf of Mexico, yielding to mangrove swamps in the subtropical heat of south Florida. The West has coastal marshes too, but the steepness and rockiness of much of the coastline make them far less extensive.

Freshwater wetlands occur in every region and climate of the continent. Florida's Everglades, a sea of grass which once covered more than one million acres, is the largest marsh complex in the United States, and certainly the best known. Throughout the Southeast, bald cypress and other hardwoods, standing in water year-round, grow in deep swamps like Georgia's Okefenokee. Along the flood plains of the Mississippi, the Arkansas, the Missouri, and dozens of other major rivers, hardwood swamp forests—much diminished by damming, draining, and logging—sustain oaks and gums which grow to impressive heights. The grasslands of the upper Midwest and south-central Canada are dotted with thousands of prairie pothole marshes, created 10,000 years ago by glacial gouging. In the Northeast, red maple swamp forests flourish both in the lowlands and on high plateaus, turning scarlet in early autumn. Peatlands or bogs dot the spruce forests in the north, especially in Canada. Many occupy what were once glacial lakes.

Canada has about one-fourth of the world's wetlands, and most of that is peatlands. So far, Canadian ecologists have mapped approximately 20 percent of their wetlands by location and type.

When ecologists speak of marshes, swamps, and bogs, they are making a distinction among three of the broadest categories of wetland ecosystems. Since these terms are often not too precise, the U.S. Fish and Wildlife Service has introduced new terms for its wetlands mapping project. It recognizes wetlands as occurring in marine, estuarine, lacustrine (associated with lakes), riverine (along rivers and streams), and palustrine systems. Palustrine systems represent freshwater marshes, swamps, and bogs not associated with lakes or rivers. Marshes are defined as emergent wetlands, and swamps as forested wetlands.

Water chemistry, frequency and degree of flooding, soil types, and other factors further define the nature of each wetland and the vegetation it supports—so much so, in fact, that in detailed mapping surveys, the terms *marsh*, *swamp*, and *bog* tend to disappear. For an overview, however, these traditional designations remain the clearest.

From the vast Everglades to the smallest prairie pothole or reed-fringed farm pond, marsh ecosystems are dominated by emergents, soft-stemmed, grasslike plants such as cattails, bulrushes, and pickerelweeds, which grow partly in and partly out of the water. Shallow marshes are usually thickly vegetated, with little open water. In freshwater marshes with three or more feet of water, broader open areas sustain floating and submerged aquatic plants such as water lilies, pondweeds, and carnivorous bladderworts.

While freshwater marshes depend on rainfall, rivers, and springs, tides flush through salt marshes every day. The salinity of the water and the duration and frequency of tidal flooding in a particular part of a salt marsh dictate, to a large extent, the species that are found there. In a typical estuary, the salt marsh ecosystem is composed of a mosaic of habitats bounded by salt seawater and fresh river water.

Swamps are wetlands that are dominated by flood-tolerant trees or shrubs. Climate plays a large role in determining the dominant trees in swamps throughout the United States; the red maples of northeastern swamps are replaced to the south by cypress and bottomland hardwoods like water gum and water oak. Wetlands often represent a temporal and spatial transition from open water to dry land, and some wetland species can bridge the difference between aquatic and terrestrial conditions. Many of the shrubs and trees growing in shallow or intermittent swamps are also found on drier soils nearby. In the Northeast and Midwest, flood plain forests of silver maple, cottonwood, and sycamore border rivers that flood their banks during the spring snow melt or heavy rains. In rich alluvial sediments, these trees often attain impressive diameters as they mature.

Shrub swamps of willow, alder, buttonwood, or mixed species often take over poorly drained depressions. Some are relatively stable; in others, wetland trees may colonize and create a forest swamp. All wetlands are highly dynamic ecosystems where a change in water level or rainfall can bring about changes in the plant and animal populations.

From high branches to underwater hollows, the range of living spaces in a forest swamp shelters a fascinating variety of species. A walk along the boardwalk in Corkscrew Swamp, where 500-year-old cypress trees are draped with Spanish moss, can be full of surprises. Look up, and a barred owl might be sitting on a branch just above your head. Look down, and you are likely to see a lush, floating mat of vegetation where baby alligators silently wait to gulp an insect or a frog. Spectacular wading birds, especially herons, stalk their prey in the rich swamp soup. *Tillandsia*, pineapple-shaped air plants with showy reddish blooms, hang from trees. A closer look reveals tiny epiphytic orchids attached to the tree branches.

Producing so much life, wetlands also produce a lot of dead organic matter. In bogs, where high acidity and poor drainage inhibit decomposers, dead matter collects much faster than it is broken down, and peat builds up. Over thousands of years, this process may transform a glacial lake into a peat bog 50 feet deep. Shrubs or trees grow on the surface, anchored in a matrix of sphagnum moss, the main component in commercial peat moss.

Floating mats of vegetation also form in peat bogs. Walking on these spongy, quaking mats can be an unforgettable experience. If you happen to fall through, your body will be perfectly preserved, since there is little or no oxygen to support the microorganisms which cause decay or decomposition. Preserved bodies thousands of years old have been found in European bogs.

As ecologists have added to our understanding of the wetlands' natural role, we've also learned that wetlands can play a part in the intensely manipulated human environment. For example, in the natural landscape, wetlands help minimize flood damage by storing flood water, reducing flood peaks, slowing flood waters, and increasing the duration of the flow after floods. A mere one-foot rise in water level over a one-acre wetland places 300,000 gallons of water in temporary storage without harming any plant and animal life.

Driving around the Pocono Mountains of Pennsylvania after the great flood of 1955, I saw dozens of bridges that had washed out. But every bridge on the roads below the Tannersville Bog Preserve, a northern spruce bog now owned by The Nature Conservancy, was intact. Clearly, the bog and the surrounding wetlands had detained much of the overflow—with no damage to their own inhabitants.

When considering how to control flood damage along the Charles River in Massachusetts, the U.S. Army Corps of Engineers concluded that saving the wetlands was the solution. Losing 40 percent of the basin's wetlands would increase flood damage by at least $3 million annually, and losing all the wetlands would incur annual flood damages of $17 million.

Rather than constructing dams, the Corps of Engineers acquired or protected by easements 8,000 acres of wetlands along the river. The average annual cost was $617,000, and annual benefits have averaged $2.4 million—obviously a sound economic and ecological investment.

Many wetlands are integrally linked to our water supplies, replenishing groundwater in the aquifers our wells draw on. In Massachusetts, the 2,700-acre Lawrence Swamp recharges the shallow aquifer under it at a rate of eight million gallons of water daily. This wetland recharges a 10,000-acre area and is the main water source for the city of Amherst. Prairie potholes, midwestern and southern swamps, and northeastern bogs also replenish local groundwater.

Wetlands contribute to water quality. Their dense vegetation can act as a nutrient trap, absorbing phosphates and nitrates from agricultural run-off and sewage. Some wetlands can also accumulate pollutants, including heavy metals. Many well-documented cases describe water quality improving downstream after nutrient-rich polluted water has flowed through a wetland.

In the Tinicum Marshes along the Delaware River near Philadelphia, the quality of sewage effluent improved dramatically as it flowed over the 500-acre freshwater tidal marsh. Researchers found a 57 percent reduction in the biological oxygen demand, a 63 percent reduction in nitrates, and a 57 percent reduction in phosphates. In Georgia, bottomland swamps along the Flint and Alcovy rivers have demonstrated a similar capacity. Some southern cypress swamps have been serving as pollution filters for decades; in others, especially cypress domes near Gainesville, Florida, sewage effluent has enhanced plant growth and productivity, and the swamps retain 97 percent of the coliform bacteria, heavy metals, and nutrients found in sewage. The underlying wetland soils can also play a major role in absorbing these contaminants.

In Michigan, a 1,700-acre experimental peat bog has been receiving sewage for over a decade. Although the vegetation has changed, it is still a highly functional system. In Arcata, California, the town has restored or created more than 100 acres of marsh which now filter sewage waste water before it enters Humboldt Bay. The water is cleaner than it would have been if a conventional sewage treatment plant had been used. More than 200 species of birds have been sighted in the area, and more than 100,000 people visit there each year.

Despite these successful experiments, we must be careful not to overload wetlands with sewage or other wastes. Although some wetlands can function quite well as pollution filters, others have a more limited capacity. In most cases, biological changes will occur, and some will not be positive. It would be particularly unwise to use wetlands for pollution control where endangered species live.

Of all the benefits we gain from wetlands, the most difficult to quantify are aesthetic and recreational. As development intensifies, wetlands still offer some of the best remaining open spaces for relaxation and renewal. For some people, hunting wetland game birds is a cherished pastime; others hunt with binoculars and cameras, tracking a variety of waterfowl, water birds, and other wildlife.

For environmental scientists, wetlands provide invaluable outdoor laboratories for teaching basic ecological concepts. Energy flow, recycling, and the limited carrying capacities that govern all living organisms are researched there. Scientists are only beginning to understand how these complex ecosystems function and what factors maintain them as productive communities. We have much to learn about how wetlands maintain our planet's life-support system. If we preserve our wetlands, we will certainly help to keep the earth habitable for its millions of life forms, including humankind.

THE SIERRA CLUB
WETLANDS READER

Part One

IMPRESSIONS

Travels

William Bartram *1739–1823*

William Bartram's fascination with life was deeply rooted in science and spirituality. He explored the waterways of southern Georgia and Florida at the time of the American Revolution, documenting the region's botany and the ways of the native "Siminoles." This excerpt recounts a trip up the St. Johns River in northeastern Florida to Lake George.

About the middle of May, every thing being in readiness to proceed up the river, we set sail. The traders with their goods in a large boat went a-head, and myself in my little vessel followed them; and as their boat was large, and deeply laden, I found that I could easily keep up with them, and, if I chose, out-sail them; but I preferred keeping them company, as well for the sake of collecting what I could from conversation, as on account of my safety in crossing the great lake, expecting to return alone, and descend the river at my own leisure.

We had a pleasant day, the wind fair and moderate, and ran by Mount Hope, so named by my father John Bartram, when he ascended this river, about fifteen years ago. It was a very high shelly bluff, upon the little lake. It was at that time a fine orange grove, but now cleared and converted into a large indigo plantation, the property of an English gentleman, under the care of an agent. In the evening we arrived at Mount Royal, where we came to, and stayed all night: we were treated with great civility, by a gentleman whose name was ——— Kean, and who had been an Indian trader.

From this place we enjoyed a most enchanting prospect of the great Lake George, through a grand avenue, if I may so term this narrow reach of the river, which widens gradually for about two miles, towards its entrance into the lake, so as to elude the exact rules of perspective, and appears of an equal width.

At about fifty yards distance from the landing place, stands a magnificent Indian mount. About fifteen years ago I visited this place, at which time there were no settlements of white people, but all appeared wild and savage; yet in that uncultivated state it possessed an almost inexpressible air of grandeur, which was now entirely changed. At that time there was a very considerable extent of old fields round about the mount; there was also a large orange grove, together with palms and live oaks, extending from near the mount, along the banks, downwards, all of which has since been cleared away to make room for planting ground. But what greatly contributed towards completing the magnificence of the scene, was a noble Indian highway, which led from the great mount, on a straight line, three quarters of a mile, first through a point or wing of the orange grove, and continuing thence through an awful forest of life oaks, it was terminated by palms and laurel magnolias, on the verge of an oblong artificial lake, which was on the edge of an extensive green level savanna. This grand highway was about fifty yards wide, sunk a little below the common level, and the earth thrown up on each side, making a bank of about two feet high. Neither nature nor art could any where present a more striking contrast, as you approached this savanna. The glittering water pond played on the sight, through the dark grove, like a brilliant diamond, on the bosom of the illumined savanna, bordered with various flowery shrubs and plants; and as we advanced into the plain, the sight was agreeably relieved by a distant view of the forests, which partly environed the green expanse on the left hand, whilst the imagination was still flattered and entertained by the far distant misty points of the surrounding forests, which projected into the plain, alternately appearing and disappearing, making a grand sweep round on the right, to the distant banks of the great lake. But that venerable grove is now no more. All has been cleared away and planted with indigo, corn, and cotton, but since deserted: there was now scarcely five acres of ground under fence. It appeared like a desert to a great extent, and terminated, on the land side, by frightful thickets, and open pine forests.

It appears, however, that the late proprietor had some taste, as he has preserved the mount and this little adjoining grove inviolate. The prospect from this station is so happily situated by nature, as to comprise at one view the whole of the sublime and pleasing.

At the reanimating appearance of the rising sun, nature again revives; and I obey the cheerful summons of the gentle monitors of the meads and groves.

Ye vigilant and faithful servants of the Most High! ye who worship the Creator morning, noon, and eve, in simplicity of heart! I haste to join the universal anthem. My heart and voice unite with yours, in sincere homage to the great Creator, the universal Sovereign.

O may I be permitted to approach the throne of mercy! May these my humble and penitent supplications, amidst the universal shouts of homage from thy creatures, meet with thy acceptance!

And although I am sensible, that my service cannot increase or diminish thy glory, yet it is pleasing to thy servant to be permitted to sound thy praise; for, O sovereign Lord! we know that thou alone art perfect, and worthy to be worshipped. O universal Father! look down upon us, we beseech thee, with an eye of pity and compassion, and grant that universal peace and love may prevail in the earth, even that divine harmony which fills the heavens, thy glorious habitation!

And, O sovereign Lord! since it has pleased thee to endue man with power and pre-eminence here on earth, and establish his dominion over all creatures, may we look up to thee, that our understanding may be so illuminated with wisdom, and our hearts warmed and animated with a due sense of charity, that we may be enabled to do thy will, and perform our duty towards those submitted to our service and protection, and be merciful to them, even as we hope for mercy.

Thus may we be worthy of the dignity and superiority of the high and distinguished station in which thou has placed us here on earth.

The morning being fair, and having a gentle favourable gale, we left our pleasant harbour, in pursuit of our desired port.

Now as we approach the capes, behold the little ocean of Lake George, the distant circular coast gradually rising to view, from his misty fringed horizon. I cannot entirely suppress my apprehensions of danger. My vessel at once diminished to a nut-shell on the swelling seas, and at the distance of a few miles, must appear to the surprised observer as some aquatic animal, at intervals emerging from its surface. This lake is a large and beautiful piece of water; it is a dilatation of the river St. Juan, and is about fifteen miles wide, and generally about fifteen or twenty feet deep, excepting at the entrance of the river, where lies a bar, which carries eight or nine feet of water. The lake is beautiful with two or three fertile islands. The first lies in the bay, as we ascend into the lake, near the west coast, about S.W. from Mount Royal, from whence it appears to form part of the west shore of the bay. The second island seems to ride on the lake before us as we enter, about a mile within it. This island is about two miles in breadth, and three quarters of a mile where broadest, mostly high land, well timbered, and fertile. The third and last lies at the south end of the lake, and near the entrance of the river; it is nearly circular, and contains but a few acres of land, the earth high and fertile, and almost an entire orange grove, with grand magnolias and palms.

Soon after entering the lake, the wind blew so briskly from the west, with thunder-clouds gathering upon the horizon, that we were obliged to seek a shelter from the approaching tempest, on the large beautiful island before mentioned; where, having gained the south promontory, we met with an excellent harbour, in which we continued the remaining part of the day and the night. This circumstance gave me an opportunity to explore the greatest part of it.

The island appears, from obvious vestiges, to have been once the chosen residence of an Indian prince, there being to this day evident remains of a large town of the Aborigines. It was situated on an eminence near the banks of the lake, and commanded a comprehensive and charming prospect of the waters, islands, east and west shores of the lake, the capes, the bay, and Mount Royal; and to the south, the view is in a manner infinite, where the skies and waters seem to unite. On the site of this ancient town, stands a very pompous Indian mount, or conical pyramid of earth, from which runs in a straight line a grand avenue or Indian highway, through a magnificent grove of magnolias, live oaks, palms, and orange trees, terminating at the verge of a large green level savanna. This island appears to have been well inhabited, as is very evident, from the quantities of fragments of Indian earthen ware, bones of animals and other remains, particularly in the shelly heights and ridges all over the island. There are no habitations at present on the island, but a great number of deer, turkeys, bears, wolves, wild cats, squirrels, raccoons, and opossums. The bears are invited here to partake of the fruit of the orange tree, which they are immoderately fond of; and both they and turkeys are made extremely fat and delicious, from their feeding on the sweet acorns of the live oak. . . .

There are some rich swamps on the shores of the island, and these are verged on the outside with large marshes, covered entirely with tall grass, rushes, and herbaceous plants; amongst these are several species of Hibiscus, particularly the hibiscus coccineus. This most stately of all herbaceous plants grows ten or twelve feet high, branching regularly, so as to form a sharp cone. These branches also divide again, and are embellished with large expanded crimson flowers. I have seen this plant of the size and figure of a beautiful little tree, having at once several hundred of these splendid flowers, which may be then seen at a great distance. They continue to flower in succession all summer and autumn, when the stems wither and decay; but the perennial root sends forth new stems the next spring, and so on for many years. . . .

Having finished my tour on this princely island, I prepared for repose. A calm evening had succeeded the stormy day. The late tumultuous winds had now ceased, the face of the lake had become placid, and the skies serene; the balmy winds breathed the animating odours of the groves around me; and as I reclined on the elevated banks of the lake, at the foot of a live oak, I enjoyed the prospect of its wide waters, its fringed coasts, and the distant horizon.

The squadrons of aquatic fowls, emerging out of the water, and hastening to their leafy coverts on shore, closed the varied scenes of the past day. I was lulled asleep by the mixed sounds of the wearied surf, lapping on the hard beaten shore, and the tender warblings of the painted nonpareil and other winged inhabitants of the grove.

At the approach of day the dread voice of the alligators shook the isle, and resounded along the neighbouring coasts, proclaiming the appearance of the glorious sun. I arose, and prepared to accomplish my daily task. A gentle favourable gale led us out of the harbour: we sailed across the lake, and towards evening entered the river on the opposite south coast, where we made a pleasant and safe harbour, at a shelly promontory, the east cape of the river on that side of the lake. It is a most desirable situation, commanding a full view of the lake. The cape opposite to us was a vast cypress swamp, environed by a border of grassy marshes, which were projected farther into the lake by floating fields of the bright green pistia stratoites, which rose and fell alternately with the waters. Just to leeward of this point, and about half a mile in the lake, is the little round island already mentioned. But let us take notice of our harbour and its environs: it is a beautiful little cove, just within the sandy point, which defends it from the beating surf of the lake. From a shelly bank, ten or twelve feet perpendicular from the water, we entered a grove of live oaks, palm, magnolia, and orange trees, which grow amongst shelly hills, and low ridges, occupying about three acres of ground, comprehending the isthmus, and a part of the peninsula, which joins in to the grassy plains. This enchanting little forest is partly encircled by a deep creek, a branch of the river, that has its source in the high forests of the main, south east from us; and winds through the extensive grassy plains which surround this peninsula, to an almost infinite distance, and then unites its waters with those of the river, in this little bay which formed our harbour. This bay, about the mouth of the creek, is almost covered with the leaves of the nymphæa nelumbo: its large sweet-scented yellow flowers are lifted up two or three feet above the surface of the water, each upon a green starol, representing the cap of liberty.

The evening drawing on, and there being no convenient landing place for several miles higher up the river, we concluded to remain here all night. Whilst my fellow travellers were employing themselves in collecting fire-wood, and fixing our camp, I improved the opportunity in reconnoitring our ground; and taking my fusee with me, I penetrated the grove, and afterwards entered some almost unlimited savannas and plains, which were absolutely enchanting; they had been lately burnt by the Indian hunters, and had just now recovered their vernal verdure and gaiety.

How happily situated is this retired spot of earth! What an elysium it is! where the wandering Siminole, the naked red warrior, roams at large, and after the vigorous chase retires from the scorching heat of the meridian sun. Here he reclines, and reposes under the odoriferous shades of Zanthoxylon, his verdant couch guarded by the Deity; Liberty, and the Muses, inspiring him with wisdom and valour, whilst the balmy zephyrs fan him to sleep. . . .

• • •

We will now take a view of the Lower Creeks or Siminoles, and the natural disposition which characterises this people; when, from the striking contrast, the philosopher may approve or disapprove, as he may think proper, from the judgment and opinion given by different men.

The Siminoles are but a weak people with respect to numbers. All of them, I suppose, would not be sufficient to people one of the towns in the Muscogulge; for instance, the Uches on the main branch of the Apalachucla river, which alone contains near two thousand inhabitants. Yet this handful of people possesses a vast territory; all East Florida and the greatest part of West Florida, which being naturally cut and divided into thousands of islets, knolls, and eminences, by the innumerable rivers, lakes, swamps, vast savannas and ponds, form so many secure retreats and temporary dwelling places, that effectually guard them from any sudden invasions or attacks from their enemies; and being such a swampy, hommocky country, furnishes such a plenty and variety of supplies for the nourishment of varieties of animals, that I can venture to assert, that no part of the globe so abounds with wild game or creatures fit for the food of man.

Thus they enjoy a superabundance of the necessaries and conveniences of life, with the security of person and property, the two great concerns of mankind. The hides of deer, bears, tigers, and wolves, together with honey, wax and other productions of the country, purchase their cloathing, equipage, and domestic utensils from the whites. They seem to be free from want or desires. No cruel enemy to dread; nothing to give them disquietude, but the gradual encroachments of the white people. Thus contented and undisturbed, they appear as blithe and free as the birds of the air, and like them as volatile and active, tuneful and vociferous. The visage, action, and deportment of the Siminoles, form the most striking picture of happiness in this life; joy, contentment, love, and friendship, without guile or affectation, seem inherent in them, or predominant in their vital principle, for it leaves them but with the last breath of life. It even seems imposing a constraint upon their ancient chiefs and senators, to maintain a necessary decorum and solemnity, in their public councils; not even the debility and decrepitude of extreme old age, is sufficient to erase from their visages this youthful, joyous simplicity; but, like the gray eve of a serene and calm day, a gladdening, cheering blush remains on the Western horizon after the sun is set.

I doubt not but some of my countrymen who may read these accounts of the Indians, which I have endeavoured to relate according to truth, at least as they appeared to me, will charge me with partiality or prejudice in their favour.

I will, however, now endeavour to exhibit their vices, immoralities, and imperfections, from my own observations and knowledge, as well as accounts from the white traders, who reside amongst them.

The Indians make war against, kill, and destroy their own species, and their motives spring from the same erroneous source as they do in all other nations of mankind; that is, the ambition of exhibiting to their fellows a superior character of personal and national valour, and thereby immortalizing themselves, by transmitting their names with honour and lustre to posterity; or revenge of their enemy, for public or personal insults; or, lastly, to extend the borders and boundaries of their territories. But I cannot find, upon the strictest inquiry, that their bloody contests at this day are marked with deeper stains of inhumanity or savage cruelty, than what may be observed amongst the most civilized nations: they do indeed scalp their slain enemy, but they do not kill the females or children of either sex: the most ancient traders, both in the Lower and Upper Creeks, assured me they never saw an instance of either burning or tormenting their male captives; though it is said they used to do it formerly. I saw in every town in the Nation and Siminoles that I visited, more or less male captives, some extremely aged, who were free and in as good circumstances as their masters; and all slaves have their freedom when they marry, which is permitted and encouraged, when they and their offspring are every way upon an equality with their conquerors. They are given to adultery and fornication, but, I suppose, in no greater excess than other nations of men. They punish the delinquents, male and female, equally alike, by taking off their ears. This is the punishment for adultery. Infamy and disgrace is supposed to be a sufficient punishment for fornication, in either sex.

They are fond of games and gambling, and amuse themselves like children, in relating extravagant stories, to cause surprise and mirth.

They wage eternal war against deer and bear, to procure food and cloathing, and other necessaries and conveniences; which is indeed carried to an unreasonable and perhaps criminal excess, since the white people have dazzled their senses with foreign superfluities.

The Everglades: River of Grass

Marjory Stoneman Douglas

Marjory Stoneman Douglas found inspiration in the Everglades, and mid-twentieth-century conservationists found a call to action in her writing. Publication of *River of Grass* in 1947 coincided with the opening of Everglades National park, for which she had lobbied for twenty years. Two decades later, she rallied the vanguard of the environmental movement to block a proposed jetport at the heart of the interface of Big Cypress Swamp and the Everglades. Today, at the age of 105, Marjory Stoneman Douglas is a living national treasure.

There are no other Everglades in the world.

They are, they have always been, one of the unique regions of the earth, remote, never wholly known. Nothing anywhere else is like them: their vast glittering openness, wider than the enormous visible round of the horizon, the racing free saltness and sweetness of their massive winds, under the dazzling blue heights of space. They are unique also in the simplicity, the diversity, the related harmony of the forms of life thcy enclose. The miracle of the light pours over the green and brown expanse of saw grass and of water, shining and slow-moving below, the grass and water that is the meaning and the central fact of the Everglades of Florida. It is a river of grass.

The great pointed paw of the state of Florida, familiar as the map of North America itself, of which it is the most noticeable appendage, thrusts south, farther south than any other part of the mainland of the United States. Between the shining aquamarine waters of the Gulf of Mexico and the roaring deep-blue waters of the north-surging Gulf Stream, the shaped land points toward Cuba and the Caribbean. It points toward and touches within one degree of the tropics.

More than halfway down that thrusting sea-bound peninsula nearly everyone knows the lake that is like a great hole in that pawing shape, Lake Okeechobee, the second largest body of fresh water, it is always said, "within the confines of the United States." Below that lie the Everglades.

They have been called "the mysterious Everglades" so long that the phrase is a meaningless platitude. For four hundred years after the discovery they seemed more like a fantasy than a simple geographic and historic fact. Even the men who in the later years saw them more clearly could hardly make up their minds what the Everglades were or how they could be described, or what use could be made of them. They were mysterious then. They are mysterious still to everyone by whom their fundamental nature is not understood.

Off and on for those four hundred years the region now called "The Everglades" was described as a series of vast, miasmic swamps, poisonous lagoons, huge dismal marshes without outlet, a rotting, shallow, inland sea, or labyrinths of dark trees hung and looped about with snakes and dripping mosses, malignant with tropical fevers and malarias, evil to the white man. . . .

The truth of the river is the grass. They call it saw grass. Yet in the botanical sense it is not grass at all so much as a fierce, ancient, cutting sedge. It is one of the oldest of the green growing forms in this world.

There are many places in the South where this saw grass, with its sharp central fold and edges set with fine saw teeth like points of glass, this sedge called *Cladium jamaicensis,* exists. But this is the greatest concentration of saw grass in the world. It grows fiercely in the fresh water creeping down below it. When the original saw grass thrust up its spears into the sun, the fierce sun, lord and power and first cause over the Everglades as of all the green world, then the Everglades began. They lie wherever the saw grass extends: 3,500 square miles, hundreds and thousands and millions, of acres, water and saw grass.

The first saw grass, exactly as it grows today, sprang up and lived in the sweet water and the pouring sunlight, and died in it, and from its own dried and decaying tissues and tough fibers bright with silica sprang up more fiercely again. Year after year it grew and was fed by its own brown rotting, taller and denser in the dark soil of its own death. Year after year after year, hundreds after hundreds of years, not so long as any geologic age but long in botanic time, far longer than anyone can be sure of, the saw grass grew. Four thousand years, they say, it must at least have grown like that, six feet, ten feet, twelve feet, even fifteen in places of deepest water. The edged and folded swords bristled around the delicate straight tube of pith that burst into brown flowering. The brown seed, tight enclosed after the manner of sedges, ripened in dense brownness. The seed was dropped and worked down in the water and its own ropelike mat of roots. All that decay of leaves and seed covers and roots was packed deeper year after year by the elbowing upthrust of its own life. Year after year it laid down new layers of virgin muck under the living water.

There are places now where the depth of the muck is equal to the height of the saw grass. When it is uncovered and brought into the sunlight, its stringy and grainy dullness glitters with the myriad un-rotted silica points, like glass dust. . . .

In the Everglades one is most aware of the superb monotony of saw grass under the world of air. But below that and before it, enclosing and causing it, is the water.

It is poured into Lake Okeechobee from the north and west, from that fine chain of lakes which scatter up and down the center of Florida, like bright beads from a string. They overflow southward. The water is gathered from the northwest through a wide area of open savannas and prairies. It swells the greatest contributing streams, the Kissimmee River, and the Taylor River and Fisheating Creek, and dozens of other smaller named and unnamed creeks or rivulets, and through them moves down into the great lake's tideless blue-misted expanse.

The water comes from the rains. The northern lakes and streams, Okeechobee itself, are only channels and reservoirs and conduits for a surface flow of rain water, fresh from the clouds. A few springs may feed them, but no melting snow water, no mountain freshets, no up-gushing from caverns in ancient rock. Here the rain is everything.

Here the rain falls more powerfully and logically than anywhere else upon the temperate mainland of the United States. There are not four sharply marked seasons, as in the North. Here winter and spring and summer and fall blend into each other subtly, with nothing like such extremes of heat and cold. Here, actually, there are only two seasons, the wet and the dry, as there are in the tropics. The rains thunder over all this long land in their appointed season from the low clouds blowing in from the sea, or pour from clouds gathered all morning from the condensation of the wet below. Then for months it will not rain at all, or very little, and the high sun glares over the drying saw grass and the river seems to stand still.

This land, by the maps, is in the temperate zone. But the laws of the rain and of the seasons here are tropic laws.

History of Okefenokee Swamp

A. S. McQueen and Hamp Mizell

To entrepreneurs of the late nineteenth century, the cypress forests of southern Georgia's Okefenokee Swamp looked like a bonanza of timber, if only they could get the water out of the way. The first two of the following excerpts from a history published in 1926 tell of the failed first and the successful second attempt. Although the authors, lifelong residents of the area, are full of praise for the outfit that figured out how to penetrate and largely devastate the swamp without moving the water, elsewhere in the book they speak of "the advisability of the U.S. Government taking over the Okefenokee Swamp area as a sanctuary for the fast disappearing wild life."

The third excerpt concerns the Seminole chief Billy Bowlegs, who was prominent in the uprising that resulted when President Andrew Jackson banished the Indians of the Southeast to territories west of the Mississippi. Jackson's policy was declared unconstitutional by the U.S. Supreme Court, but he enforced it anyway. Billy Bowlegs was among those who refused to travel the "trail of tears" and found refuge to the south, in the Everglades.

Jackson's Folly

It seems that several members of the Legislature thought that the Okefenokee Swamp could be drained and reclaimed, and that it would be a wonderfully rich, productive area, and determined to see it well done. As a consequence a bill was introduced in the Legislature at the 1889 session incorporating "The Suwannee Canal Company," which also provided that the Governor sell the Okefenokee Swamp to certain named incorporators. It was a wonderfully constructed Act, and I wish every lawyer who reads this will take the pains to look it up and read it. It provided that the land should not be sold at less than 12½ cents per acre. It, however, named Frank W. Hall, Marshall A. Phillips, and their associates (unnamed) as the Suwannee Canal Company, but also provided that the Governor should advertise for bids sixty days in the Atlanta Constitution, Macon Telegraph, Savannah Morning News, and one paper in each of the states of New York and Florida.

The capital stock of the corporation was authorized at one million dollars, and with the privilege of increasing the same to five million dollars. The unique feature of this Act, selling, as developed later, millions of dollars worth of timber, was that if the named parties, as the incorporators of the Suwannee Canal Company, should not be the highest bidders, then, in that event, the successful bidders should have the right to the corporation "Suwannee Canal Co." The exact language follows: "The bids shall be sealed and sent to the Governor, who shall open the same after the expiration of the time for advertising, and the highest bidder shall be incorporated under the provisions of this Act as the Suwannee Canal Co., instead of the incorporators herein named."

The Act further states "That this Act shall be taken and deemed as a public Act, and shall be liberally construed for the carrying of the aforesaid purposes into effect." It also reserves to the State of

Georgia a royalty of one dollar per ton for all phosphate rock that might be discovered and mined in this great, boggy swamp of disappearing lakes and islands that the Indians so aptly called "Quivering Earth."

The Act was finally carried into effect, and the purchase price named in the deed from Governor N. J. Northern was $62,101.80, and the acreage thought to be conveyed was 219,500 acres, but a later deed between the parties themselves conveyed 430,000 acres. The $62,101.80 would about pay two months pay-roll for the Hebard Cypress Company, present owners of the Swamp, for the workmen engaged in getting out cypress timber and manufacturing it into lumber.

Be that as it may, it developed that the proposition of drainage and reclamation was a stupendous task, and the people (not engineers or scientists) who know most about the Swamp say that it cannot be done, and they advance very plausible reasons—the main reason being that in places there is apparently no bottom, and in other places it is known that a very few feet of muck and earth surface separates the apparent ground surface from the water underneath.

Now follows the tale known in the section around the Swamp as "Jackson's Folly." Captain Harry Jackson, a prominent Atlanta capitalist, became interested in the venture and either acquired an interest with the original incorporators, or was one of the "associates" named in the Act. In any event, he was the prime mover and financial agent for the great venture of draining the Swamp and also using the water to float the millions of feet of timber to the outside for manufacture.

The work started some time during the year 1891, and thousands of dollars were spent during the next few years. A main canal was dug on the Charlton County side from the nearest point to the St. Marys River which penetrates the Swamp for approximately 14 miles. The idea was to drain the Swamp into the St. Marys River, and the nearest line between the two was selected as the route for the canal. The canal was never completed to the St. Marys River, but the main canal of 14 miles and branch canals aggregating 8 miles were dug at a cost of many thousands of dollars. Captain Jackson did, however, succeed in towing out by the canal route quite a lot of timber, but too much money had been invested in the canals, mills, dredge boats, tram-roads, etc., and the venture was a failure to the loss of over a million dollars to Captain Jackson and his associates.

Captain Jackson died in 1895 and the operations ceased. However, much of the magnificent cypress of the finest quality had been secured from the Swamp and manufactured into lumber. The mill-site and living quarters of the superintendent and foremen, commissary and office was known as "Camp Cornelia" in honor of Captain Jackson's daughter, and the site is still known by this name. The last remaining house, a large two-story wood structure, was destroyed by fire during the year 1923.

All that now remains of Jackson's Folly are the canals, now lined with lily-pads and overhung by trees, and the fast rotting dredge boats all along the abandoned canals. It was, however, a God-send to the disciples of Isaac Walton, for when the water becomes low in the Swamp the fish leave the so-called prairies and congregate in the canals, where they are caught in great numbers.

Hon. John T. Boifeuillet recently wrote: "The State of Georgia employed Colonel R. L. Hunter, an engineer, to make a survey of the Swamp to ascertain if it were practicable to drain the territory. He performed the work in 1856–57, at a cost of $3,260.00. His report to the Governor, accompanied by a map, was filed away in the archives of the state, where it remained until 1875, when the late Colonel E. Y. Clarke, of Atlanta, discovered it, and he formed an expedition to explore the Swamp, in connection with the state Geological Survey. Specimens of timber obtained in the Swamp by the exploring party were exhibited at the Paris Exposition in 1878.

"Engineer Hunter estimated that the Swamp could be drained for $1,067,250, but Captain Jackson, so I have read, soon after the operations of his company began, gave it as his opinion that 300 miles of canal would be necessary to accomplish thorough drainage. The cost of this would be enormous."

I have made diligent inquiry to ascertain the real reason for the abandonment of the project as a drainage proposition, and no one could tell me. I talked to scores of white men employed in the work and none could give any reason except that it was "evidently too large a venture for the finances involved." I remarked one day "that I would certainly like to know the real reason for the abandonment of this drainage project," and an old negro overheard the remark and replied, "Boss, I can certainly tell you." I told him to "shoot," and he began by telling me that he was the cook on the first dredge boat and cooked for the steam shovel crew, and that he was "right there and knew." His explanation was that when the canal had been dug for about 8 miles into the swamp the "water started to run back the other way." Instead of towards the St. Marys River it wanted to run back clear through the Swamp to the Suwannee River, and he asked me to observe it the next time I went to the canal on a fishing trip. I did observe it, and the old negro is right, for the water does run back "the other way." Captain Jackson's engineer must have slipped a cog, for, quoting the old negro again "the further we went into the Swamp the faster the water run the other way," and that is the way it runs today, and most of the canal water now empties finally into the Suwannee River instead of into the St. Marys.

Commercial Operations

The Swamp, in its entirety, is owned in fee by the Hebard Lumber Company, composed of practically one family, and vast timber operations have been carried on by the Hebard Cypress Company, both being owned by practically the same persons, many of the stockholders of the Hebard Lumber Co., also being stockholders in the Hebard Cypress Co.

The Hebard Cypress Company began operations in the Swamp in the year 1908 and started saw-mill operations in the year 1909. It is stated by those who are in a position to know that fully a million dollars was spent in preparation before any timber was sawed. These people saw the opportunity from the distant North and acted upon this vision and foresight. Active operations have been maintained since the year 1909, and literally millions upon millions of feet of the finest cypress timber in the world have been manufactured into cypress lumber by these people.

A modern mill, with a capacity of 150,000 feet per day, was established at Hebardville, near the city of Waycross, and this mill-site has grown into a thriving little town of about 1000 inhabitants, with a modern school system, churches, lighting plant, etc. A railroad was chartered several years ago known as the Waycross & Western, running from Hebardville to Hopkins, a village on the edge of the Swamp. The logs are hauled over this railroad a distance of about 20 miles to the mill-site at Hebardville. In addition to this railroad these people have, at enormous expense, constructed about 35 miles of railroad into the very heart of the great Swamp, most of it being built upon piling. A small but powerful type of locomotive engine is used in the Swamp. It is really astonishing to see these small engines bring long strings of flats loaded with cypress logs. These small engines bring the logs from the interior of the Swamp to the village of Hopkins, where they are carried by the Waycross & Western railroad to Hebardville, the mill-site.

For several years the Hebardville mill only cut the cypress timber, the pine timber in and near the swamp being leased to another concern, the Twin-Tree Lumber Co., which operated a large mill in the village of Hopkins. At one time, while the Twin-Tree Lumber Company was in operation, together with the Hebard Cypress Company and various turpentine operations, there were employed in the Swamp and at the mills from 1600 to 2000 men. The interior camp of the Hebard Cypress Company was established on Billy's Island, which grew to a town of six hundred inhabitants, and despite the fact that this town is far in the interior of a great swamp the inhabitants have all the modern conveniences of towns of similar size anywhere. A moving picture show has been in operation for years; a public school has been maintained by Charlton County, and churches have been established. A large supply store has been operated by the company and a modern, well-equipped hotel and boarding house is run by the company for the use of the single men who work in the Swamp.

It is now possible to be on Billy's Island—cut off from the outside world except by the railroad—and not only go to see a good moving picture show, but by the use of that marvelous invention, the radio, to "tune in" with the commercial and art centers of the world, and it is demonstrative of the wonderful age in which we live that less than one hundred years ago this island was inhabited by a primitive race of Indians—the Seminoles.

The timber has about all been cut from this great Swamp, and within a few more months this busy island will again, no doubt, slip back to the primitive; the scream of the locomotive will again be supplanted by the scream of the panther and bob-cat; the wild deer will again roam over this spot as of yore; the alligators will again climb upon the sand banks to lay quietly and undisturbed in the warm sun-light; the turtle will come to deposit its eggs in the spring, and the ever-watchful black bear will be on the trail of the turtle eggs, and all that will be left to show the superiority of the white man over the red man who preceded him, will be the wreck and ruin left in the slaughter of the primeval forest, and the white man will have gold and silver—the price of the forest—whereas the red man left with his bows and arrows, tomahawks, his squaws and broods of young, leaving the mighty cypress and pine trees undisturbed and the Swamp itself in all the glorious beauty as designed by Nature. They expected to find a happier and better "hunting ground" further on—and so do we. After all, nothing but the Anglo-Saxon egotism supports us in so much assumed superiority.

Billy Bowlegs

Laura Singleton Walker

Ko-nip-ha-tco (Billy Bowlegs) was the youngest son of Seacoffee, the Indian who had in 1750 led the band of runaway Creeks, afterward called Seminoles, into Florida. Billy Bowlegs was one of the principal chiefs of the Seminoles and lived in "King Pain's Town," Florida. In his early life he was aggressive, inciting the Indians in their attacks on the frontiers. He and his warriors were subdued by Georgia Volunteers, which put an end to the Seminole raids in this state.

Billy developed into a progressive leader among his race, and became desirous of identifying himself with the white people. He lived among them as much as possible, imitating their ways and studying their language. Captain F. A. Hendry of Fort Myers, Florida, who taught him to read, stated he was apt, and delighted in clothing himself in our dress and "taking to the bed and table, instead of the ground and kettle, for sleep and food." He often boastfully asserted to Captain Hendry, "me all same white man."

The Florida Indians were not classed as Nomads. They had fixed habitations, in well defined districts, permanent camps and wigwams which remained from year to year, the abiding places of their families. There were times during the year when the Indians gathered into temporary camps for a few weeks, and one of their largest ones was located in the Okefenokee Swamp. Billy Bowlegs observed no time limit while in the Okefenokee Camp, and was there so often that the Seminoles in Florida regarded him as a member of a foreign community.

In 1838, under the orders of General Winfield Scott, troops were stationed at various points throughout the Cherokee and Creek countries, where stockade forts were erected for the purpose of collecting the Indians preparatory to removal from the State. The stockade fort built by a squad of soldiers in the Swamp did not escape the vigilant eyes of Billy, who safely retreated to the shades of the friendly Everglades of Florida, where he remained until the Georgia Creeks and Cherokee under "the lash" had passed out on the unknown trail.

Later, Billy made one of the islands in the Okefenokee Swamp his permanent home, and this island now is a progressive village lighted by electricity and has well graded side walks, planted in shade trees and is known as Billy's Island.

Turtle Ways

Allen Chesser

Early settlers of the Okefenokee Swamp were called "Crackers" by the British loyalists of the region, for whom the term meant "great boaster," "independent," and "democratical." The nickname persists to this day, but the swamp dwellers' unique culture and vernacular, which remained isolated and largely unchanged until the 1920s, has since essentially vanished.

Following is a description of the egg-laying habits of the soft-shelled turtle, as told by one of the last of the true Crackers. The bracketed notations are provided by Delma Presley, director of the Georgia Southern University Museum.

[**O**n warm June afternoons, the soft-shelled turtle likes to deposit its eggs in the soft earth. This distinctly aquatic species lays its complement of eggs, carefully fills up the hole with earth, and makes its way home in the water. However, before returning to the water, it pauses to vigorously scratch up the ground. Then it scatters the earth about, leaving a conspicuous trace of its presence. This shrewd act, known in the Okefenokee as "scuffling," effectively draws attention of some marauding animals away from the exact spot where eggs have been concealed.

Francis Harper noticed the turtle's unusual behavior on a June afternoon in 1921. Knowing Allen Chesser could explain matters thoroughly, Harper asked him about the "scuffling" episode.]

Yes, sir, they've got that knowledge. They're given that knowledge, or they wouldn't do it. Everything according to its time or its manner.

He wants to deceive whatever hunts the eggs; he don't want the eggs found. That's his mode.

Them yaller-bellied tarrapins [Florida terrapins], they just lay their eggs anywhere. Don't scuffle a-tall. Gophers [gopher turtles] are the same. The old soft-shell turtle is given sense. It's a sharp trick. One wouldn't catch on to it.

In the first outset, when they come out, they locate a place where they want to dig their hole. And they ain't like everything else. If I was going to dig a hole, I'd use my fore feet. But he digs with his hind feet. He takes one handful of dirt and throws it out *thataway*. Then he'll change and throw it out the other way. He gets his hole dug and lays his eggs, then kivers 'em with his hind feet. Then he starts off.

Come to the scuffling part now. He won't start to scuffle till he gets off ten or twelve feet. Then starts scuffling. Keeps moving along and scuffling. Then he'll stop that and go on to his home again in the water. I suppose he does that to save his eggs, to fool them that wants to eat 'em. I know it fooled me, till I got catched on to it.

Lots-a-times they bury themselves before they go to the water and stay there ten or twelve hours.

I seed a sight of them things one evening, just like a bunch of sheep. You could see them things, a dozen or two in a bunch, just a drift. It was a dry time. I seed them things a-feeding all over the prairie. It looked like they was feeding on grass, to the best of my judgment. It was in the summer season. They eat fish, crawfish, and things like that.

When I find where a turtle has scuffled, I don't dig for the eggs. I take me a stick and dig for the hole.

Now the jackdaw [fish crow, *Corvus ossifragus*] will sit around while the turtle's at work. He'll wait on him and fight up in the tree with each other, because they are all hungry and want to get there first.

Coon, he small feller, digs a small hole [to get to the eggs]. But the bear, with his paws he'll dig a hole. The old gip [female dog] finds pups [gives birth], and will be hungry and will range these woods digging turtle eggs.

The Great Dismal

Bland Simpson

The Great Dismal Swamp, a large "pocosin"—from the Algonquian term meaning "shallow place"—was viewed by the American colonists as anything but a valuable natural resource. Straddling the eastern border of Virginia and North Carolina, subject to peat fires that sometimes burned for years, it was seen as a hellish impediment to civilization. George Washington himself took up the task of taming it, first making a failed attempt at farming, then skirting it with a canal to join Chesapeake Bay with Albemarle Sound and the shipping corridor behind North Carolina's Outer Banks.

Writer Bland Simpson's fascination with the swamp dates back to childhood boat rides on the Pasquotank River with his father, who told him, "If we followed it all the way . . . we would disappear with the river in the Great Dismal Swamp."

Twenty years and the American Revolution separated George Washington from his time in the Swamp when Canal talk started up in the 1780s. Nothing had yet come of his Land Company adventure in the northwest quadrant of the Swamp, and when Hugh Williamson of North Carolina broached the notion of a ship canal to Washington in 1784, the future president was ambivalent.

On the one hand Washington felt the project "would in my opinion be tedious and attended with an expense which might prove discouraging." All the same, he wrote Williamson in late March of that year, "I have long been satisfied of the practicability of opening communication between the waters which empty into Albemarle Sound thro' Drummond's Pond and the Waters of Elizabeth or Nansemond Rivers."

Two weeks before Christmas 1784, Williamson wrote Thomas Jefferson in Paris, still pushing the Dismal Swamp Canal but worrying in print over political backlash in the Old North State: "People near Edenton are afraid that a canal from Pasquotank River, through Drummond's Lake, would deprive that town of its small remains of Trade, and the people of Pasquotank River who would be profitted by the canal have not Enterprise enough to go on with Work."

Jefferson was undaunted, replying two months later: "I am glad to find you think of me in the affair of the Dismal. It is the only speculation in my life I have decidedly wished to be engaged in."

Though the 1784 Nicholas Forster survey of "The course of the intended Canal thro' the Dismal Swamp" put the route several miles east of Drummond's Pond, bending westerly towards the Lake to avoid Balyhack Branch, headwaters of the Northwest River, George Washington warmed to the Canal idea. By late 1785 he was writing James Madison and expressing his pleasure that "our Assembly were in a way of adopting a mode for establishing the cut between Elizabeth River and Pasquotank."

With second-term Governor Patrick Henry pushing it in Virginia, and with North Carolina's Governor Caswell at least overcoming his reservations enough to present Virginia's proposal to the Carolina Assembly, the Dismal Swamp Canal plan moved forward in both legislatures. Virginia voted it in on the first of December, 1787, and North Carolina risked what one opponent predicted would be a "dwindling into fishing towns" because of the Canal and finally let the Canal Act get by on third reading in 1790. Both bodies had approved the Canal on a subscription basis, so now began the slow process of raising money to hire the shovels. George Washington bought two hundred shares, the state of Virginia seventy, and North Carolina none.

It was 1793 before digging began.

Three years later, when the Duke de la Rochefoucauld-Liancourt toured through the Great Dismal country, he was impressed with the five miles already dug in each of the two states. But he was even more impressed by the engineering procedures of the enterprise. "What must appear surprizing, is that, for this canal which already seems in such a state of forwardness, no levels have been taken. It is not yet known what number of locks may be necessary, and even whether any will be requisite. Consequently it is impossible to ascertain what may be the expense of completing it, or even whether the success of the undertaking can be depended on. It is thus almost all the public works are carried on in America, where there is a total want of men with talents in the arts."

Its construction was "a slow nibbling process," in the words of Canal Historian Alexander Crosby Brown, a process characterized by delays, by extensions of projected completion dates by the two legislatures, by lack of money, and by lack of labor. Though the worker had to show up with his own axe, spade, or shovel, an 1808 solicitation in the *Norfolk Gazette and Public Ledger* pledged to laborers "good wholesome food and the usual quantity of whisky per diem." The digging had gone on from both ends towards the middle, and when these two ditchings met each other and joined the Albemarle Sound with the Chesapeake Bay in 1805, four miles of the Canal were at half the prescribed width.

There was some grade of trouble all the time. The great 1806 fire in the Swamp clogged the Canal, both above and below water, with trees. And there was competition over water levels: those who were trying to float shingles out of the Swamp over the Canal needed more water than those who were still digging on it. An 1808 high water drove Samuel Proctor, the digging director in North Carolina, to "cut loose that lock at Mr. Spences in order to get the water off." Proctor reported to the Canal Company president: "But that man known by the name of Isaac Place—goes at the dead hour of the night & stops it—if some measure is not taken to prevent his meddling with that end of the canal it will never be done." Isaac Pleas, in his own report to the president, dismissed Proctor's hydraulic practices and claimed he was under personal attack: "Yet I did not think the spleen would be carri'd so far as to Injure me, until of lately there has appeared some striking features in the conduct of Samuel Proctor that shows he would wantonly do me what Injury lays in his power."

The Canal, though completed, was "little more than a muddy ditch," according to historian Brown. Only shingle flats floated over it in its earliest years, and one outraged shareholder declared to the company by open letter in an April 1808 *Norfolk Gazette and Public Ledger:* "You have marked the course of the canal it is true—you have made an indifferent road, and a boat can swim empty four or five miles in the center of the Dismal Swamp! All this you have performed in little more than sixteen years!"

The company had realized by 1804 that the Canal was going to require waters from Lake Drummond—an eventuality foreseen and legislated for by the Virginia Assembly in 1787—to float boats of any size and substance. On August 4, 1812, eighteen citizens of Norfolk County met with the sheriff and gazed Swampward at the 300-foot by three-and-a-half-mile strip of Dismal they were about to condemn, in order that a small canal—the Feeder Ditch—could drain Drummond into the main Canal. The sheriff's jury appraised the necessary lands at a penny an acre, and the Canal company paid its dollar and a quarter for the strip and cut the Feeder that year.

In June of 1814, James Smith's twenty-ton craft came down the Roanoke River from Scotland Neck, sailed out onto Albemarle Sound at Batchelor Bay, made it up the Pasquotank, rounding the Narrows at Elizabeth City and winding through the Moccasin Track, thence north to Deep Creek and the south branch of the Elizabeth River, a big Carolina boat now in Norfolk bearing bacon and brandy.

The first ship had made passage through the Dismal Swamp Canal. . . .

In 1929, the [federal] government bought the Swamp Canal . . . redredged and repaired it, and found it extremely useful strategically during the Atlantic Coast submarine threat of World War II. Postwar plans for the channel through the Swamp, as diverse as one to make the Canal an industrial corridor, an American Ruhr, and another to make of it an oddball botanical splendor, a twenty-two mile floral display, have come to naught. In the late 1950s, the Corps of Engineers began an effort to close the Canal down altogether, as commercial traffic had become nearly nonexistent and almost all the water-intensive lockages—a million and a quarter gallons each time—were for pleasure craft. That effort continues today, in the face of strong political pressure from northeastern North Carolina—my old hometown of Elizabeth City, particularly—to keep it open.

Fred Fearing, a spry retired mailman in Elizabeth City and old friend of my family, has in recent years with another man been meeting incoming sailboats and yachts down at the Elizabeth City docks and greeting them with flowers and champagne. When I asked him one night in August of 1985 about the Canal's being unnavigable and nearly dry, he exploded bitterly at the Corps, which had reported drought and leaky wickets at the locks as the cause of the Canal's low-water closing.

"The sonofabitches!" Fearing said. "The bastards! They're draining it down cause they want to shut it up for good. Oldest continuously used man-made waterway in American history, and this is how it ends up. Bastards!"

The Lake of the Dismal Swamp

Thomas Moore *1779–1852*

Wetlands have inspired some of the world's most maudlin poetry. In 1803
Irish poet Thomas Moore, who had been en route to Bermuda but found
himself stranded in Norfolk, Virginia, wrote "The Lake of the Dismal
Swamp" after an excursion there. It remains the best-known poem
associated with the Great Dismal Swamp and perhaps any wetland in
America.

"They made her a grave too cold and damp
   For a soul so warm and true;
And she's gone to the lake of the Dismal Swamp
Where all night long, by a firefly lamp,
   She paddles her white canoe.

"And her firefly lamp I soon shall see,
   And her paddle I soon shall hear;
Long and loving her life shall be,
And I'll hide the maid in a cypress tree,
   When the footstep of death is near!"

Away to the Dismal Swamp he speeds;
   His path was rugged and sore;
Through tangled juniper, beds of reeds,
Through many a fen, where the serpent feeds,
   And man never trod before.

And when on the earth he sank to sleep,
   If slumber his eyelids knew,

He lay where the deadly vine doth weep,
Its venomous tear and nightly steep,
   The flesh with blistering dew!

And near him the she-wolf stirred the brake,
   And the copper snake breathed in his ear,
Till he starting cried, from his dream awake,
"Oh, when shall I see the dusky lake,
   And the white canoe of my dear?"

He saw the lake and a meteor bright
   Quick over its surface played—
"Welcome!" he said; "my dear one's light";
And the dim shore echoed for many a night,
   The name of the death-cold maid.

Till he hollowed a boat of the birchen bark,
   Which carried him off from shore;
Far he followed the meteor spark;
The wind was high and the clouds were dark,
   And the boat returned no more.

But oft from the Indian hunter's camp,
   This lover and maid so true,
Are seen at the hour of midnight damp,
To cross the lake by a firefly lamp,
   And paddle their white canoe.

Dred: A Tale of the Great Dismal Swamp

Harriet Beecher Stowe   *1811–1896*

Harriet Beecher Stowe may be the least understood of America's most influential writers. Abraham Lincoln was purported to have called her "the little lady who wrote the book that made the big war." Yet the stage shows of *Uncle Tom's Cabin* that made her famous were melodramatic, often lurid, presentations of her work.

As for the literary merit of her writing, one can find critiques ranging from "brilliant expression" to "of conscious art there exists barely the microscopic drop indispensable for clinical analysis." She is said to have written in a trancelike state and to have revised little, so perhaps both views are correct.

In *Dred,* Stowe's second antislavery novel, the black protagonist finds refuge and spiritual release in the swamp.

Life in the Swamps.

There is a twilight ground between the boundaries of the sane and insane, which the old Greeks and Romans regarded with a peculiar veneration. They held a person whose faculties were thus darkened as walking under the awful shadow of a supernatural presence; and, as the mysterious secrets of the stars only become visible in the night, so in these eclipses of the more material faculties they held there was often an awakening of supernatural perceptions.

The hot and positive light of our modern materialism, which exhales from the growth of our existence every dewdrop, which searches out and dries every rivulet of romance, which sends an unsparing beam into every cool grotto of poetic possibility, withering the moss, and turning the dropping cave to a dusty den—this spirit, so remorseless, allows us no such indefinite land. There are but two words in the whole department of modern anthropology—the sane and the insane; the latter dismissed from human reckoning almost with contempt. We should find it difficult to give a suitable name to the strange and abnormal condition in which this singular being, of whom we are speaking, passed the most of his time.

It was a state of exaltation and trance, which yet appeared not at all to impede the exercise of his outward and physical faculties, but rather to give them a preternatural keenness and intensity, such as sometimes attends the more completely-developed phenomena of somnambulism.

In regard to his physical system there was also much that was peculiar. Our readers may imagine a human body of the largest and keenest vitality, to grow up so completely under the nursing influences of nature, that it may seem to be as perfectly *en rapport* with them as a tree; so that the rain, the wind, and the thunder, all those forces from which human beings generally seek shelter, seem to hold with it a kind of fellowship, and to be familiar companions of existence.

Such was the case with Dred. So completely had he come into sympathy and communion with nature, and with those forms of it which more particularly surrounded him in the swamps, that he moved about among them with as much ease as a lady treads her Turkey carpet. What would seem to us in recital to be incredible hardship, was to him but an ordinary condition of existence. To walk knee-deep in the spongy soil of the swamp, to force his way through thickets, to lie all night sinking in the porous soil, or to crouch, like the alligator, among reeds and rushes, were to him situations of as much comfort as well-curtained beds and pillows are to us.

It is not to be denied, that there is in this savage perfection of the natural organs a keen and almost fierce delight, which much excel the softest seductions of luxury. Anybody who has ever watched the eager zest with which the hunting-dog plunges through the woods, darts through the thicket, or dives into water, in an ecstasy of enjoyment, sees something of what such vital force must be.

Dred was under the inspiring belief that he was the subject of visions and supernatural communications. The African race are said by mesmerists to possess, in the fullest degree, that peculiar temperament which fits them for the evolution of mesmeric phenomena; and hence the existence among them, to this day, of men and women who are supposed to have peculiar magical powers. The grandfather of Dred, on his mother's side, had been one of these reputed African sorcerers; and he had early discovered in the boy this peculiar species of temperament. He had taught him the secret of snake-charming, and had possessed his mind from childhood with expectations of prophetic and supernatural impulses. That mysterious and singular gift, whatever it may be, which Highland seers denominate second sight, is a very common tradition among the negroes; and there are not wanting thousands of reputed instances among them to confirm belief in it. What this faculty may be, we shall not pretend to say. Whether there be in the soul a yet undeveloped attribute, which is to be to the future what memory is to the past, or whether in some individuals an extremely high and perfect condition of the sensuous organization endows them with something of that certainty of instinctive discrimination which belongs to animals, are things which we shall not venture to decide upon.

It was, however, an absolute fact with regard to Dred, that he had often escaped danger by means of a peculiarity of this kind. He had been warned from particular places where the hunters had lain in wait for him; had foreseen in times of want where game might be ensnared, and received intimations where persons were to be found in whom he might safely confide; and his predictions with regard to persons and things had often chanced to be so strikingly true, as to invest his sayings with a singular awe and importance among his associates.

It was a remarkable fact, but one not peculiar to this case alone, that the mysterious exaltation of mind in this individual seemed to run parallel with the current of shrewd, practical sense; and, like a man who converses alternately in two languages, he would speak now the language of exaltation, and now that of common life, interchangeably. This peculiarity imparted a singular and grotesque effect to his whole personality.

On the night of the camp-meeting, he was . . . in a state of the highest ecstasy. The wanton murder of his associate seemed to flood his soul with an awful tide of emotion, as a thunder-cloud is filled and shaken by slow-gathering electricity. And, although the distance from his retreat to the camp-ground was nearly fifteen miles, most of it through what seemed to be impassable swamps, yet he performed it with as little consciousness of fatigue as if he had been a spirit. Even had he been perceived at that time, it is probable that he could no more have been taken, or bound, than the demoniac of Gadara.

After he parted from Harry, he pursued his way to the interior of the swamp, as was his usual habit, repeating to himself, in a chanting voice, such words of prophetic writ as were familiar to him.

The day had been sultry, and it was now an hour or two past midnight, when a thunder-storm, which had long been gathering and muttering in the distant sky, began to develop its forces.

A low, shivering sigh crept through the woods, and swayed in weird whistlings the tops of the pines; and sharp arrows of lightning came glittering down among the darkness of the branches, as if sent from the bow of some warlike angel. An army of heavy clouds swept in a moment across the moon; then came a broad, dazzling, blinding sheet of flame, concentrating itself on the top of a tall pine near where Dred was standing, and in a moment shivered all its branches to the ground, as a child strips the leaves from a twig. Dred clapped his hands with a fierce delight; and, while the rain and wind were howling and hissing around him, he shouted aloud:

"Wake, O, arm of the Lord! Awake, put on thy strength! The voice of the Lord breaketh the cedars—yea, the cedars of Lebanon! The voice of the Lord divideth the flames of fire! The voice of the Lord shaketh the wilderness of Kadesh! Hail-stones and coals of fire!"

The storm, which howled around him, bent the forest like a reed, and large trees, uprooted from the spongy and tremulous soil, fell crashing with a tremendous noise; but, as if he had been a dark spirit of the tempest, he shouted and exulted.

The perception of such awful power seemed to animate him, and yet to excite in his soul an impatience that He whose power was so infinite did not awake to judgment.

"Rend the heavens," he cried, "and come down! Avenge the innocent blood! Cast forth thine arrows, and slay them! Shoot out thy lightnings, and destroy them!"

His soul seemed to kindle with almost a fierce impatience, at the toleration of that Almighty Being, who, having the power to blast and to burn, so silently endures. Could Dred have possessed himself of those lightnings, what would have stood before him? But his cry, like the cry of thousands, only went up to stand in waiting till an awful coming day!

Journal

Henry David Thoreau   *1817–1862*

Poet and philosopher Ralph Waldo Emerson wrote of Thoreau that
"his study of Nature was a perpetual ornament to him, and inspired his
friends with curiosity to see the world through his eyes, and to hear his
adventures." Emerson himself was a world traveler, but Thoreau rarely left
the environs of his home in Concord, Massachusetts.

To Thoreau, any time of year was a good time for a tramp through a
swamp. And he meticulously recorded what he found. The following
excerpts, from entries spanning 1840–1858, are a composite year in the
seasonal cycle of the wetlands of Concord.

JAN. 10. . . . I love to wade and flounder through the swamp
now, these bitter cold days when the snow lies deep on the ground,
and I need travel but little way from the town to get to a Nova Zembla
solitude,—to wade through the swamps, all snowed up, untracked
by man, into which the fine dry snow is still drifting till it is even with
the tops of the water andromeda and half-way up the high blueberry
bushes. I penetrate to islets inaccessible in summer, my feet slump-
ing to the sphagnum far out of sight beneath, where the alder berry
glows yet and the azalea buds, and perchance a single tree sparrow
or a chickadee lisps by my side, where there are few tracks even of
wild animals; perhaps only a mouse or two have burrowed up by the
side of some twig, and hopped away in straight lines on the surface
of the light, deep snow, as if too timid to delay, to another hole by the
side of another bush; and a few rabbits have run in a path amid the
blueberries and alders about the edge of the swamp. This is instead
of a Polar Sea expedition and going after Franklin. There is but little
life and but few objects, it is true. We are reduced to admire buds,
even like the partridges, and bark, like the rabbits and mice,—the

great yellow and red forward-looking buds of the azalea; the plump red ones of the blueberry, and the fine sharp red ones of the panicled andromeda, sleeping along its stem, the speckled black alder, the rapid-growing dogwood, the pale-brown and cracked blueberry, etc. Even a little shining bud which lies sleeping behind its twig and dreaming of spring, perhaps half concealed by ice, is object enough. I feel myself upborne on the andromeda bushes beneath the snow, as on a springy basketwork, then down I go up to my middle in the deep but silent snow, which has no sympathy with my mishap. Beneath the level of this snow how many sweet berries will be hanging next August! . . .

JAN. 30. P.M. —To Gowing's Swamp. I thought it would be a good time to rake in the mud of that central pool, and see what animal or vegetable life might be there, now that it is frozen. I supposed that tortoises and frogs might be buried in the mud. The pool, where there is nothing but water and sphagnum to be seen and where you cannot go in the summer, is about two rods long and one and a half wide, with that large-seeded sedge in a border a rod wide about it. Only a third of this (on one side) appears as water now, the rest a level bed of green sphagnum frozen with the water, though rising three or four inches above the general level here and there. I cut a hole through the ice, about three inches thick, in what alone appeared to be water, and, after raking out some sphagnum, found that I could not fairly reach the mud and tortoises,—if there are any there,—though my rake was five feet and nine inches long; but with the sphagnum I raked up several kinds of bugs, or insects. I then cut a hole through the frozen sphagnum nearer the middle of the pool, though I supposed it would be a mere mass of sphagnum with comparatively little water, and more mud nearer the surface. To my surprise, I found clear water under this crust of sphagnum to about five feet in depth, but still I could not reach the mud with my rake through the more decayed sphagnum beneath.

I returned to the thicket and cut a maple about eighteen feet long. This dropped down five or six feet, and then, with a very slight pressure, I put it down the whole length. I then went to the thicket again, searched a long while for a suitable pole, and at last cut another maple thirty feet long and between four and five inches thick at the butt, sharpened and trimmed and carried it on my shoulder to the spot, and, rough as it was, it went down with very little pressure as much as twenty feet, and with a little more pressure *twenty-six feet and one inch;* and there I left it, for I had measured it first. If the top had not been so small that it bent in my hands, I could probably have forced it much further. I suspect that the depth of mud and water under where I walk in summer on the water andromeda, *Andromeda Polifolia, Kalmia glauca,* sphagnum, etc., is about the same. The whole swamp would flow off down an inclined plane. Of course there is room enough for frogs and turtles, safe from frost. . . .

FEB. I . It seems . . . that there is, over this andromeda swamp, a crust about three feet thick, of sphagnum, andromeda (*calyculata* and *Polifolia*), and *Kalmia glauca,* etc., beneath which there is almost clear water, and, under that, an exceedingly thin mud. There can be no soil above that mud, and yet there were three or four larch trees three feet high or more between these holes, or over exactly the same water, and there were small spruces near by. For aught that appears, the swamp is as deep under the andromeda as in the middle. The two andromedas and the *Kalmia glauca* may be more truly said to grow in water than in soil there. When the surface of a swamp shakes for a rod around you, you may conclude that it is a network of roots two or three feet thick resting on water or a very thin mud. The surface of that swamp, composed in great part of sphagnum, is really floating. It evidently begins with sphagnum, which floats on the surface of clear water, and, accumulating, at length affords a basis for that large-seeded sedge (?), andromedas, etc. The filling up of a swamp, then, in this case at least, is not the result of a deposition of vegetable matter washed into it, settling to the bottom and leaving the surface clear, so filling it up from the bottom to the top; but the vegetation first extends itself over it as a film, which gradually thickens till it supports shrubs and completely conceals the water, and the under part of this crust drops to the bottom, so that it is filled up first at the top and the bottom, and the middle part is the last to be reclaimed from the water.

Perhaps this swamp is in the process of becoming peat. This swamp has been partially drained by a ditch.

I fathomed also two rods within the edge of the blueberry bushes, in the path, but I could not force a pole down more than eight feet five inches; so it is much more solid there, and the blueberry bushes require a firmer soil than the water andromeda.

This is a regular *quag*, or shaking surface, and in this way, evidently, floating islands are formed. I am not sure but that meadow, with all its bushes in it, would float a man-of-war. . . .

APRIL 9. WEDNESDAY. ANOTHER FINE DAY. . . . Leave behind greatcoat. The waters have stolen higher still in the night around the village, bathing higher its fences and its dry withered grass stems with a dimple. See that broad, smooth vernal lake, like a painted lake. Not a breath disturbs it. The sun and warmth and smooth water and birds make it a carnival of Nature's. I am surprised when I perceive men going about their ordinary occupations. I presume that before ten o'clock at least all the villagers will have come down to the bank and looked over this bright and placid flood,—the child and the man, the housekeeper and the invalid,—even as the village beholds itself reflected in it. How much would be subtracted from the day if the water was taken away! This liquid transparency, of melted snows partially warmed, spread over the russet surface of the earth! It is certainly important that there be some priests, some worshippers of Nature. I do not imagine anything going on to-day away from and out of sight of the waterside. . . .

[MAY 12.] I have been surprised to discover the amount and the various kinds of life which a single shallow swamp will sustain. On the south side of the pond, not more than a quarter of a mile from it, is a small meadow of ten or a dozen acres in the woods, considerably lower than Walden, and which by some is thought to be fed by the former by a subterranean outlet,—which is very likely, for its shores are quite springy and its supply of water is abundant and unfailing,—indeed tradition says that a sawmill once stood over its outlet, though its whole extent, including its sources, is not more than I have mentioned,—a meadow through which the Fitchburg Railroad passes by a very high causeway, which required many a carload of sand, where the laborers for a long time seemed to make no progress, for the sand settled so much in the night that by morning they were where they were the day before, and finally the weight of the sand forced upward the adjacent crust of the meadow with the trees on it many feet, and cracked it for some rods around. It is a wet and springy place throughout the summer, with a ditch-like channel, and in one part water stands the year round, with cat-o'-nine-tails and tussocks and muskrats' cabins rising above it, where good cranberries may be raked if you are careful to anticipate the frost which visits this cool hollow unexpectedly early. Well, as I was saying, I heard a splashing in the shallow and muddy water and stood awhile to observe the cause of it. Again and again I heard and saw the commotion, but could not guess the cause of it,—what kind of life had its residence in that insignificant pool. We sat down on the hillside. Ere long a muskrat came swimming by as if attracted by the same disturbance, and then another and another, till three had passed, and I began to suspect that they were at the bottom of it. Still ever and anon I observed the same commotion in the waters over the same spot, and at length I observed the snout of some creature slyly raised above the surface after each commotion, as if to see if it were observed by foes, and then but a few rods distant I saw another snout above the water and began to divine the cause of the disturbance. Putting off my shoes and stockings, I crept stealthily down the hill and waded out slowly and noiselessly about a rod from the firm land, keeping behind the tussocks, till I stood behind the tussock near which I had observed the splashing. Then, suddenly stooping over it, I saw through the shallow but muddy water that there was a mud turtle there, and thrusting in my hand at once caught him by the claw, and, quicker than I can tell it, heaved him high and dry ashore; and there came out with him a large pout just dead and partly devoured, which he held in his jaws. It was the pout in his flurry and the turtle in his struggles to hold him fast which had created the commotion. There he had lain, probably buried in the mud at the bottom up to his eyes, till the pout came sailing over, and then this musky lagune had put forth in the direction of his ventral fins, expanding suddenly under the influence of a more than vernal heat,—there are sermons in stones, aye and mud turtles at the bottoms of the pools,—in the direction of his ventral fins, his tender white belly, where he kept no eye; and the minister squeaked his last. Oh, what an eye was there, my countrymen! buried in mud up to the lids, meditating on what? sleepless at the bottom of the pool, at the top of the bottom, directed heavenward, in no danger from motes. Pouts expect their foes not from below. Suddenly a mud volcano swallowed him up, seized his midriff; he fell into those relentless jaws from which there is no escape, which relax not their hold even in death. There the pout might calculate on remaining until nine days after the head was cut off. Sculled through Heywood's shallow meadow, not thinking of foes, looking through the water up into the sky. I saw his [the turtle's] brother sunning and airing his broad back like a ship bottom up which had been scuttled,—foundered at sea. I had no idea that there was so much going on in Heywood's meadow. . . .

JULY 17. SATURDAY. . . . I love to see a clear crystalline water flowing out of a swamp over white sand and decayed wood, spring-like. The year begins to have a husky look or scent in some quarters. I remark the green coats of the hazelnuts, and hear the permanent jay. Some fields are covered now with tufts or clumps of indigoweed, yellow with blossoms, with a few dead leaves turned black here and there.

Beck Stow's Swamp! What an incredible spot to think of in town or city! When life looks sandy and barren, is reduced to its lowest terms, we have no appetite, and it has no flavor, then let me visit such a swamp as this, deep and impenetrable, where the earth quakes for a rod around you at every step, with its open water where the swallows skim and twitter, its meadow and cotton-grass, its dense patches of dwarf andromeda, now brownish-green, with clumps of blueberry bushes, its spruces and its verdurous border of woods imbowering it on every side. The trees now in the rain look heavy and rich all day, as commonly at twilight, drooping with the weight of wet leaves. . . .

[AUG. 30.] I found these cunning little cranberries lying high and dry on the firm uneven tops of the sphagnum,—their weak vine considerably on one side,—sparsely scattered about the drier edges of the swamp, or sometimes more thickly occupying some little valley a foot or two over, between two mountains of sphagnum. They were of two varieties, judging from the fruit. The one, apparently the ripest, colored most like the common cranberry but more scarlet, *i.e.* yellowish-green, blotched or checked with dark scarlet-red, commonly pear-shaped; the other, also pear-shaped, or more bulged out in the middle, thickly and finely dark-spotted or peppered on yellowish-green or straw-colored or pearly ground,—almost exactly like the smilacina and convallaria berries now, except that they are a little larger and not so spherical,—and with a tinge of purple. A singular difference. They both lay very snug in the moss, often the whole of the long (an inch and a half or more) peduncle buried, their vines very inobvious, projecting only one to three inches, so that it was not easy to tell what vine they belonged to, and you were obliged to open the moss carefully with your fingers to ascertain it; while the common large cranberry there, with its stiff erect vine, was commonly lifted above the sphagnum. . . .

I waded quite round the swamp for an hour, my bare feet in the cold water beneath, and it was a relief to place them on the warmer surface of the sphagnum. I filled one pocket with each variety, but sometimes, being confused, crossed hands and put them into the wrong pocket.

I enjoyed this cranberrying very much, notwithstanding the wet and cold, and the swamp seemed to be yielding its crop to me alone, for there are none else to pluck it or to value it. I told the proprietor once that they grew here, but he, learning that they were not abundant enough to be gathered for the market, has probably never thought of them since. I am the only person in the township who regards them or knows of them, and I do not regard them in the light of their pecuniary value. I have no doubt I felt richer wading there with my two pockets full, treading on wonders at every step, than any farmer going to market with a hundred bushels which he has raked, or hired to be raked. I got further and further away from the town every moment, and my good genius seemed [to] have smiled on me, leading me hither, and then the sun suddenly came out clear and bright, but it did not warm my feet. I would gladly share my gains, take one, or twenty, into partnership and get this swamp with them, but I do not know an individual whom this berry cheers and nourishes as it does me. When I exhibit it to them I perceive that they take but a momentary interest in it and commonly dismiss it from their thoughts with the consideration that it cannot be profitably cultivated. You could not get a pint at one haul of a rake, and Slocum would not give you much for them. But I love it the better partly for that reason even. I fill a basket with them and keep it several days by my side. If anybody else—any farmer, at least—should spend an hour thus wading about here in this secluded swamp, barelegged, intent on the sphagnum, filling his pocket only, with no rake in his hand and no bag or bushel on the bank, he would be pronounced insane and have a guardian put over him; but if he'll spend his time skimming and watering his milk and selling his small potatoes for large ones, or generally in skinning flints, he will probably be made guardian of somebody else. . . .

[OCT. 22.] A man at work on the Ledum Pool, draining it, says that, when they had ditched about six feet deep, or to the bottom, near the edge of this swamp, they came to old flags, and he thought that the whole swamp was once a pond and the flags grew by the edge of it. Thought the mud was twenty feet deep near the pool, and that he had found three growths of spruce, one above another, there. He had dug up a hard-pan with iron in it (as he thought) under a part of this swamp, and in what he cast out sorrel came up and grew, very rankly indeed. . . .

[NOV. 23.] Walked through Gowing's Swamp from west to east. You may say it is divided into three parts,—first, the thin woody; second, the coarse bushy or gray; and third, the fine bushy or brown.

First: The trees are larch, white birch, red maple, spruce, white pine, etc.

Second: The coarse bushy part, or blueberry thicket, consists of high blueberry, panicled andromeda, *Amelanchier Canadensis* var. *oblongifolia*, swamp-pink, choke-berry, *Viburnum nudum*, rhodora, (and probably prinos, holly, etc., etc., not distinguishable easily now), but chiefly the first two. Much of the blueberry being dead gives it a very gray as well as scraggy aspect. It is a very bad thicket to break through, yet there are commonly thinner places, or often opens, by which you may wind your way about the denser clumps. Small specimens of the trees are mingled with these and also some water andromeda and lambkill.

Third: There are the smooth brown and wetter spaces where the water andromeda chiefly prevails, together with purplish lambkill about the sides of them, and hairy huckleberry; but in the midst and wettest part the narrow revolute and glaucous (beneath) leaves of the *Andromeda Polifolia* and *Kalmia glauca* are seen, and in the sphagnum the *Vaccinium Oxycoccus*. In one of the latter portions occurs that open pool.

Spahgnum is found everywhere in the swamp.

First, there is the dark wooded part; second, the scraggy gray blueberry thicket; third, the rich brown water andromeda spaces.

The high blueberry delights singularly in these localities. You distinguish it by its gray spreading mass; its light-gray bark, rather roughened; its thickish shoots, often crimson; and its plump, roundish red buds. Think of its wreaths and canopies of cool blue fruit in August, thick as the stars in the Milky Way! The panicled andromeda is upright, light-gray, with a rather smoother bark, more slender twigs, and small, sharp red buds lying close to the twig. The blueberry is particularly hard to break through, it is so spreading and scraggy, but a hare can double swiftly enough beneath it. The ground of spahgnum is now thickly strewn with the leaves of these shrubs.

The water andromeda makes a still more uniformly dense thicket, which must be nearly impervious to some animals; but as man lifts his head high above it, [he] finds but little difficulty in making his way through it, though it sometimes comes up to his middle, and if his eye scans its surface it makes an impression of smoothness and denseness,—its rich brown, wholesome surface, even as grass or moss.

Ascending the high land on the south, I looked down over the large open space with its *navel* pool in the centre. This green stagnant pool, rayed with the tracks or trails of musquash and making but a feeble watery impression, reminded me of portions of the map of the moon.

This swamp appears not to have had any natural outlet, though an artificial one has been dug. The same is perhaps the case with the C. Miles Swamp. And is it so with Beck Stow's? These three are the only places where I have found the *Andromeda Polifolia.* The *Kalmia glauca* in Gowing's, C. Miles's, and Holden's swamps. The latter has no outlet of any kind.

I am interested in those plants, like panicled andromeda, shrub oak, etc., for which no use that I know has been discovered. The panicled andromeda, instead of the date tree, might be my coat-of-arms.

Life and Death of the Salt Marsh

John and Mildred Teal

Existing at the interface of land and sea, salt marshes are intimately linked to changes in global climate. This excerpt traces the evolution of the salt marsh habitat of the northeastern states since the time of the Ice Age.

John and Mildred Teal have studied salt marshes from Georgia to Nova Scotia. They both recently retired from the Woods Hole Oceanographic Institution on Cape Cod.

About fifty thousand years ago, a prodigious ice sheet, the Laurentide Glacier, came down out of the north and pressed across Canada and the northern part of the United States. A vast complex of similar ice sheets extended over other areas of the world. The climate and sea level changed dramatically. Plants and animals accommodated to the changes, moved south, or died.

The glacier eventually reached a southern limit. The melting of the edge was matched by the southern movement of the ice mass in response to the additional weight of ice being continually added in the north. Rocks, sands, and gravels scraped from the land by the ice were piled up at this southern limit. The piles, called *moraines*, grew as years passed. A continual flow of meltwater ran out from the ice in streams. These were milky from the rock flour they carried: rocks ground to dust by the weight of the ice. Sands and gravels were also washed out by the water and even rocks were rolled along for a short distance where the flow was swiftest. All this debris was spread out as *outwash plains in front of the moraines.*

Then the ice retreated for a short distance and again paused for hundreds or thousands of years. Another moraine was laid down and more outwash plains deposited. These moraines and plains were small in relation to the mass of ice responsible for them but look large in the present landscape and are called Long Island, Martha's Vineyard, Nantucket, and Cape Cod.

Suddenly, for no certain reason, the climate changed. Ice was no longer added to the center of the glacier and it no longer moved south. The glacier began to melt. Thinner places disappeared first and the sheet broke up, first at the southern edge, then more generally. Finally the Laurentide Glacier disappeared altogether.

The landscape of the glacier was strange and awesome. Far from its edges, the five thousand to ten thousand feet thick ice sheet was probably quite flat and covered deeply with snow as the Greenland Glacier is now. A thin layer of soil accumulated on top of the edge of the ice sheet as the dust and debris, which had been locked in the ice, was freed by melting. This soil was augmented by dust blown onto the ice sheet from the surrounding, uncovered countryside. Small plants, larger plants, and even spruce forests grew atop the accumulated soil. Streams of cold ice melt ran in rivulets between the trees. Occasionally a huge crack would open up in the surface soil, exposing the mass of clear ice below.

This landscape was a temporary affair and changed as melting occurred. The forests eventually fell as the base beneath them melted and were swept away in the ice melt.

Water was everywhere. It ran in streams and rivers on rocky beds over the surface of the ice. It issued from the ice where it had run in tunnels cut in the glacier. It came forth in fountains and artesian springs that burst out of cracks in the ice. The springs were fed by a system of internal rivers which coursed through the ice from northern elevations. The water carried with it a mixture of rock flour and sand: a very erosive, fluid sandpaper that cut through ice and rock alike.

Before the new soil was finally held in place by a plant cover, it blew everywhere on the fierce winds that raced down from the snowy ice uplands. The scene was desolate but was one that was gradually to change. At times dust covered everything: ice, sand, till, and plants. Finally it was washed down into the mud and became part of the soil. It became a good soil on which windblown seeds soon sprouted.

Rain fell in torrents. Dense fogs wet the new plants. Their roots were watered by frigid water from the melting ice. Nutrient rich rock flours fertilized the new seedlings. The plants grew abundantly and where they flourished atop the glacier, they insulated the ice below.

Unusually well-protected areas of ice remained unmelted long after the main mass of ice had disappeared. The climate steadily grew warmer and eventually the sheltered ice, too, melted. When it did the forests atop the ice fell, leaving great holes in the landscape. If they were deep enough, the holes became lakes. If they were not, they became kettle holes, rounded depressions in the ground which grew new forests at the new lower level.

Torrents of meltwater from the complex of glaciers around the world ran into the sea. The level of the sea rose. While the land was being uncovered in the north by melting ice, it was being covered again in the south by rising sea. Land which had carried the crushing weight of the glacier sprang up when relieved of its burden and so the land rose as well as the sea.

These dramatic changes occurred at a rapid rate during the early waning of the ice. The edge of the sea was colonized by plants. Marsh plants grew, only to be drowned. More marshes started again, only to be destroyed. In this era of cataclysmic change, there was no time for extensive marsh development.

There came a time, however, when the ice remained only in the distant north. The land by now had finished its rapid rebound. The advance of the sea slowed. Plants, as well as changes in climate and sea level, began to work their slow effect on the features of the earth's surface where the land met the sea.

The retreat of the Laurentide Glacier occurred about ten thousand years ago. At this time, at a point along the New England coast, there was a flooded river valley which had carried glacial meltwater and rainwater to the sea. It was drowned at its mouth by the rise of the sea and shut off from its ancient sources of water by tons of glacial debris. A stream ran down to it from the surrounding hills. Well-worn, low mountains protruded from the flooded valley and protected the inner part of a small cove from waves and winds.

A flock of shorebirds settled on the protected shore in their northward search for tundra on which to nest. On the previous day, they had rested on wet mud on a salt marsh miles to the south. When they settled to rest the following day, the mud which had dried on their feet flaked off. In the mud were the seeds of marsh plants. Perhaps some seeds germinated and survived the first time they were deposited on the barren shore, or perhaps there were many arrivals and reseedings before the first plants took hold successfully, but successful they eventually were.

Grass began to grow at the edge of the water where the tides covered the ground less than half of the time. *Spartina alterniflora,* a tall coarse grass, grew above mid-tide level while *Spartina patens,* a finely textured relative, grew above the *S. alterniflora* at high water level. Other plants shared small areas of the tidal region. Sea lavender bloomed among the *Spartinas.* A stubby little plant with water-swollen stems, *Salicornia,* grew on sandy banks along the water's edge.

Salt marshes lay to the south and the east around the shores of a large island. For, where George's Bank now provides good fishing ground, it then provided a nesting area for wandering birds, grazing for mammoths and caribou, and coves where *Spartina* formed salt marshes. The marshes to the south grew and remained. Those to the east were eventually drowned and destroyed by the sea which had given them life.

The particular bit of marsh where the birds had rested continued to grow. Sand washed down the river from recently uncovered land and was carried into the sheltered cove. The sand was then moved along the shore by the winds, waves, and currents. Some of it was deposited in the cove and some built up a protective bar across the cove entrance. Small streams brought light soil material, fine particles of silt and clay, to the sea, some of which settled about the stems and roots of flourishing *Spartina.*

Gradually, as more and more sediment was trapped, and the plant roots bound it into a firm peat, the marsh grew in level and size. It reached out into the water over the sand which had been added to the cove. It reached high water level and above, at which time *Spartina alterniflora* gave ground to *Spartina patens,* with its greater ability to live in high marsh. The *S. patens* area enlarged as the marsh grew in total extent.

As new environments developed, animals moved into the marsh. Soft-shell clam and quahog larvae drifted in with the tide and settled in the soft mud around the pioneering stalks of marsh grass before the mud became filled with roots.

With the clams came clam-eating animals: families of raccoons and families of mink. Annelids and snails colonized the marsh also by means of their floating larvae. Insects flew in to lay eggs, and birds flew in to feed on the insects.

Sea level continued to rise. Plant growth raised the level of the marsh to keep step with the changing sea level. *Spartina patens* marsh flourished atop an accumulated layer of peat, formed from the roots and leaves of previous growth. Broken up, but not completely decomposed, the peat developed just fast enough to keep up with the water's rise and the sinking of the marsh surface as underlying peat was compressed by the weight of new forming peat.

As the sea level rose, the marsh extended inland over the edges of what had been land. Freshwater grasses and shrubs were engulfed by flooding salt water. Marsh grasses moved in: Land plant remains were buried under the marsh.

Lying just inland from the salt marsh, there was a shallow kettle hole made by glacial melting. Grass and trees grew on the bottom of the hole, which had been above the water table when it formed. As the water table rose with the rising sea level, a small pond formed with sedges and cattail around its edge. The kettle hole became filled with debris and peat from freshwater plants that had died under the advance of the marsh. Eventually a swamp developed around the pond. The bottom of the pond also filled but not enough to permit the growth of plants. It remained open water.

Gradually the kettle hole progressed to cedar swamp. Large trees grew over most of its area, but there remained a grassy zone in the center surrounding the pond.

The sea level rose to the point where the cedar swamp and the salt marsh met along the little stream that drained the kettle hole. Fresh-water and a dam of cattail kept the seawater out. For a time, the swamp lived on, but its future was tenuous. The dense cedars shaded the ground beneath themselves so that the growth of the swamp slowed. But the sea level did not slow its rise. It continued to encroach on the land, adding a foot of height every hundred years.

One autumn there was an unusually severe storm. Seawater blew directly into the cove. The devastation of the storm was heightened by the effects of a very high tide. Even the heavy rains accompanying the storm were not enough to keep seawater out of the swamp. The soil became soaked with salt.

The following spring, none of the freshwater plants leafed out and the cedars were dead. With little to hold it back, the sea invaded the area regularly. *Spartina* enlarged its domain into the now salty soil and claimed the entire area of the old swamp.

Some of the dead cedars stood for years, serving as perches for osprey. Generations of the birds lived in nests of sticks in the top of a large old rotting tree until it blew down in a gale. The last visible evidence of the freshwater swamp became entirely buried in the salt marsh.

There remained, deep under the surface, a layer of dark peat composed of freshwater plants dotted with the stumps of the forest which once covered the region. The salt marsh peat layer on top be-came so deep that if the trees still stood, only the highest ones would be able to reach into the air through the thick blanket of *Spartina* re-mains. The last vestige of the kettle hole was the small pond in its center. It never filled but remained a "bottomless" hole in the marsh.

As the sea rose and the marsh rose with it, the cove gradually dis-appeared. Sand washed in by the tide was slowly colonized, first by *S. alterniflora* and then by *S. patens*.

Pools formed on the marsh where the grass was killed for a variety of reasons. The pools became individual, isolated worlds inhabited by insects and bacteria. Sheets of algae grew across the bottom. Fish swam into the pools during some high tides, were trapped, and lived for weeks or months before another high tide might liberate them.

Sometimes shallow pools were formed by extra high tides which drove water up to shallow depressions lying on the highest parts of the marsh next to the land. The pools might remain days or even weeks but life in the pools was less lasting. Water evaporated and salts were concentrated until they finally settled to the bottom. As only a few bacteria are suited to live in strong brine, most of the residents died.

Ducks and shorebirds flying north and south during their migrations were attracted to all of the pools. Thousands of birds stopped to rest on their long flights. Yellowlegs stalked in the shallows and ducks upended in the pools to eat widgeon grass growing there. Dainty, graceful solitary sandpipers trembled their feet in the shallow pools without roiling the water, stirring up insects from the bottom. Dowitchers fed around the pool edges. Often they continued to jab their long bills in the mud well after dark, when other shorebirds had long since settled for the night. Some of the ducks, which stopped in the spring, stayed all summer to raise young. They grew and fattened themselves on the production of the marsh before undertaking the southward fall migration.

As the marsh grew, it and the bay became more productive. It became possible for larger numbers of fish to live in the water and larger numbers of animals to be supported on the surface soils. As the numbers of animals increased, so did the number of species.

A pair of bald eagles moved in to nest in the tallest pine on a high spot near the edge of the marsh. The birds ate fish picked up along the shore, fish stolen from the ospreys, which were smaller but better hunters, injured and sick ducks on the ponds, rabbits, mice, and other small animals on the marsh.

Marsh hawks, called harriers, nested on a hillock projecting out of the marsh and could be seen sailing above the grass searching for white-footed mice running between the *S. patens* stems, and for sharp-tailed sparrows, also running mouselike through the grass. Short-eared owls hawked over the marsh, competing with the harriers for the same food. The owls and harriers could not have been supported on the earlier marsh as it had been too small to support the large, inefficient hunters.

A pair of black-crowned night herons nested in a tree on an island in a freshwater pond near the marsh. At night they fished the marsh creeks. The parent birds raised a successful clutch. The following year the young birds returned with their mates, accompanied by other couples picked up in their migration. More birds were attracted the following year. In a short time there was a noisy, smelly hubbub on the island every summer. Hundreds of heron chicks were fed thousands of fish by their parents, and grew to adulthood.

The fish population was not depleted, nor were the mice and small birds fed upon by the raptors, for the predators snatched those individuals easiest to catch, the weak and lame. With these disposed of, the fish and game populations became healthier than ever.

Not all was idyllic about the growth of the marsh. Occasional but devastating disasters overtook both plants and animals. An unusually severe winter, with strong gales, sent great masses of ice and water over the end of the sandpit separating the ocean from the marsh. The surface of the soil was torn off. With the stabilizing plant cover gone, that part of the marsh eroded severely in the early spring storms. The slow advance of sediment deposit and plant growth repaired the damage in two hundred years.

Some floods were brought on by high wind-driven waves during seasonal hurricanes. Tons of rainwater were dumped on the marsh, compounding the wave damage. Thousands of birds, mammals and insects were drowned. The population of animals was small for a time, but reinstated itself, as the life-giving plants were not killed. New individuals of the depleted species moved into the marsh and the scanty survivors increased with the advent of amiable weather.

During occasional cold foggy summers the grass grew poorly. Many animals perished from exposure. During hot dry seasons the marsh pools were desiccated or evaporated until the salt concentration killed the animals. Occasional fires started by lightning in nearby forests spread onto the surface of the marsh when the grass was dry in autumn. At such times many animals were killed, especially those which moved slowly and those which could not draw themselves down to safety under the blanket of wet, insulating mud.

In spite of these large and small disasters, the marsh continued to exist and grow. The rising sea permitted it to spread out over what had been land ten feet above sea level a thousand years before. The hillock which supported the eagles' pine became an island in the marsh but eventually disappeared entirely beneath the grass. Eagle descendants, many generations distant from the first pair, moved from tree to tree inland as their home trees died and blew down or were engulfed by marsh.

Proposals to the Parks Commissions of Boston, Buffalo and Chicago

Frederick Law Olmsted *1822–1903*

If you've ever spent much time in the environs of big American cities, chances are you've entered the world of Frederick Law Olmsted's design.

From New York's Central Park to the campus of the University of California at Berkeley, Olmsted made a lasting mark on the face of America. Yet, despite the expanse and influence of his work, he was frustrated again and again by bureaucratic deadlocks—on at least two occasions to the point of mental breakdown.

Following are Olmsted's visions for waterside parks in the Back Bay region of Boston, the south side of Buffalo bordering Lake Erie, and southern Chicago on Lake Michigan.

Suggestions for the Improvement of Muddy River, Boston

The tidal part of Muddy River above the basin now under construction has the usual character of a salt creek winding through a valley, the marshy surface of which, lying from fifteen to twenty feet below the general level of the adjoining uplands, is partially submerged at extreme high-water. The tide ordinarily flows to a point about a mile above the basin. Streets have been laid out upon the uplands upon no continuous system; those of each side independently, and regardless of what may be eventually required in the low lands; the leading motive being to make small bodies of land immediately available, at little cost, for suburban residences. The city is rapidly advancing in compact blocks towards the region, and public convenience will, before many years, require a more comprehensive treatment of it.

It usually happens when a town is building up on both sides of a small water-course and valley that the sanitary and other disadvantages of the low ground prevent it from being much occupied, except in a way damaging to the value of the adjoining properties. In process of time the stream and valley and the uses to which they are put come to be regarded as a nuisance; and radical measures, such as the construction of a great underground channel, and the filling up of the valley, are urged as the only adequate remedy. The cost of these, and the local disturbance they make, excite opposition to them; their complete beneficial operation is long delayed, and the character of the district becomes so strongly fixed before this period is reached that it can only be partially changed. Though necessary, therefore, to public health and to convenience of general transit through the district the result in the increased tax-bearing capacity of the locality is no compensation for the required outlay.

As an alternative to such a possible course the policy now suggested for Muddy River would look to the preservation of the present channel with certain modifications and improvements adapted to make it permanently attractive and wholesome, and an element of constantly increasing advantage to the neighborhood. Except where the valley is now narrowest, it would be reduced in width by artificial banks, so that the river with its shores would everywhere have a general character, resembling that which it now has near Longwood bridge, only that its water would be kept at a nearly uniform level, and guarded from defilement by intercepting sewers and otherwise. The Brookline margin would be the broadened base of the present railroad embankment, bearing a woody thicket. The opposite or Boston bank would have an elevation above the water of ten feet, rising where the natural bank is used to twenty feet. Upon this would be laid out a public way ninety feet wide in continuation of that now forming upon the Back Bay basin; divided like that into foot, carriage, and saddle courses, and designed to serve as a public promenade along the river bank, as well as a trunk line giving an element of continuity to the street system of the neighborhood.

It is proposed that this park-way should be continued along the small water-course above and through the valley to Jamaica Pond, which would add another mile to its length. There are three smaller ponds near the head of the valley, which would thus be skirted, and below them a large marsh, which, though formerly reached by the tide, is now a fresh-water swamp, and cannot long remain in its present condition without great peril to the health and life of the increasing population of the adjoining parts, both of Boston and Brookline. Physicians practising in the neighborhood believe it to have been already the source of serious epidemics.

The supply of water to it from local springs is supposed to be large enough to maintain a pond to be formed by a dam at the lower end, by which it would be changed from a foul and noisome to a pleasing and healthful circumstance. The property is of little value speculatively, and of none otherwise, and the improvement thus projected would be neither difficult nor costly. If the fresh-water supply should finally be thought insufficient for the purpose, it would be possible to extend the salt-water basin to cover the ground. The swamp-soil excavated would be of value for covering the slopes below, and the operation would not be costly.

The Projected Park and Parkways on the South Side of Buffalo

There remains to be laid out about 180 acres of the low, flat, more or less swampy land to be protected by embankment from being occasionally submerged by the lake. What we propose for this is that it shall, in the first place, be thrown into ridges and furrows, mounds and hollows, the material taken from the depressions forming the elevations, being heaped for the purpose upon intervals of flat land left between them. The ridges being often discontinued, so that the furrows will wind round the ends of them, and water being then let in to a suitable height, the result will be a body of water nearly a mile in length, and a third in breadth, within which the elevations will form islands, savannas, capes and peninsulas.

The required water is expected to be drawn from Cazenovia Creek by gravity, either through the canal which has been projected for the relief of the Thirteenth Ward from floods, or if that and all similar schemes should be abandoned, by two miles of tile pipe laid for the purpose. The water thus brought would flow first through the park, then into the still-water bathing pool, and thence between the piers into the lake. The islands of the park water are to be of varied form and extent, and it has been a principal part of our study to so contrive them, that when overgrown by suitably designed verdure and foliage, they will, with the waters upon their borders, form pleasing landscape compositions of a natural character.

The half-decayed vegetable matter which forms the surface of the ground, having been thrown up, exposed to frost and aerated, will make the principal part of a deep, rich mould on the surface of the islands. This mould kept moist by the adjoining water, and the water shallow and heated by the sun, the conditions will be favorable to types of vegetation, such as it is rare to see profusely displayed in nature except at much inconvenience to the observer and in close association with disagreeable elements, and which it is still rarer to see exhibited in a large and intricate way in works of gardening. By varying the conditions, so that the water will at points be comparatively shallow and at others deep, and the land at points low and at others high, the shores here abrupt, there gently inclined; giving them, sometimes the form of beaches, at others of banks, and the banks being at some places shaded by trees, at some overgrown by bushes, at some dressed with turf, at some hidden by rushes, flags, irises and other waterside plants, an extended series of interesting passages of scenery will result. At intervals there will be open long vistas over water under broad leafy canopies; there will be coves completely overarched with foliage, forming verdant grottoes; some of the islands will be large enough to have within them spacious forest glades; some will be low and densely wooded, their shores so shallow that boats can not land upon them, and their skirts so hedged with thickets as to be impenetrable. These will be nurseries for song birds, where their nestlings will have protection from natural enemies. The waters will everywhere abound with water-fowl, for the breeding of which other islands, unapproachable by visitors, will be set apart. They will be navigated largely by a special class of boats gaily painted and gilded, decorated by day with bright awnings and bunting, and at night with colored lights. Small electric lights will also at night mark out the shores, the electricity to be supplied from storage batteries charged by dynamos to be run by windmills, for the use of which the locality has special advantages.

Plan for Laying Out the South Park, Chicago

We proceed to consider what is required . . . in the Lower Division. It naturally divides into two fields of landscape, the exterior lake expanse with its necessarily simple, raw, storm-lashed foreground, and the interior lagoon scenery, intricate, sequestered, sylvan and rich in variety of color and play of light and shade, both having the common and continuous element of water. Still, considering this park as the principal recreation ground of the city and one in which more than any other a general attendance from all parts of the city should be expected, invited, and prepared for, the fact remains that the distance to it from the centre and more northern quarters is so long that the access to it by land will be often uninteresting and tedious. Were it to be very much more so, mere approach by land to the Park wholly impracticable, as from Venice to the Lido, the means of access by water and the connection of the Park by water with the heart of the commercial part of the city would be so admirable that under ordinarily favorable conditions of weather, there would be thousands of the very class of citizens whose convenience most needs to be considered, to whom the Park would practically begin at the mouth of the Chicago river. Where great numbers are to be carried short distances, there is no transportation so cheap or so agreeable as that by water, and the time should be expected when the toiling population of Chicago, relieved from work at an early hour on the last of the week, will be carried to the South Park by many tens of thousands at the cost of a few cents. Its advantages in this respect will correspond to those of the Haga Park of Stockholm, one of the most popular and delightful public grounds in the world.

Aside from the actual advantages of access which it thus offers, it is most desirable that whatever sources of interest there may be in the lake should be as closely as possible associated with those of the Park and be made to appear, as much as possible, part and parcel of the Park. The introduction of artificial water with natural outlines and no perceptible current, so near the great lake, is, as a matter of art, not a little hazardous, and to fully insure it against a paltry and childish aspect it is indispensable that the character of the lagoon as an arm of the lake should be distinctly manifest. For this reason the channel between the water of the lake and the water within the Park should be given importance in the design, so that at all times, even when few or no boats are passing, this privilege of the Park will be felt by land visitors as an important distinction.

The channel must be cut through the beach, the break in it being guarded against the drift of sand from the northward by a pier, which should be fully two hundred feet in length, in order to create a strong eddy at the mouth of the inlet. It must be presumed that in any case the channel will need occasional dredging.

Such a pier would be the most prominent object connecting the Park with the lake, and experience shows that where an offset into the water from a tame coast has been thus formed people are strongly drawn to gather upon and near it. So well established is this attraction that at many of the places of resort on the English and French coasts, long piers have been built simply for the gratification of visitors.

For these reasons the pier and inlet must be treated as most important members of the design; they should not be thrust into a corner, but located as near to the heart of the Park as possible, and as visitors will inevitably be drawn to the pier special provision should be planned for the comfortable coming together of a large number in connection with it. From the view of the lake which these would command, the transition should be made easy and natural to some other point, also adapted to the coming together of large numbers, which will have a like central position with reference to the lagoon.

Life on the Mississippi

Mark Twain (Samuel L. Clemens) *1835–1910*

That Samuel Clemens came of age as a riverboat pilot on the Mississippi—and eventually took his pen name from the experience— is perhaps the best-known biographical fact about any American author. The Civil War brought an end to Clemens's career as a pilot, and he didn't return to the river until 1882, by then world famous as the teller of America's story. Twain came back at a time of flooding that he estimated would "be celebrated in the river's history for several generations before a deluge of like magnitude shall be seen."

Like the river that inspired it, *Life on the Mississippi* is full of surprises.

In this passage, Twain turns anthologist to convey the emotions aroused by the immense, relentless flow. We revisit the book and meet Uncle Mumford on page 110.

We met two steamboats at New Madrid. Two steamboats in sight at once! An infrequent spectacle now in the lonesome Mississippi. The loneliness of this solemn, stupendous flood is impressive—and depressing. League after league, and still league after league, it pours its chocolate tide along, between its solid forest walls, its almost untenanted shores, with seldom a sail or a moving object of any kind to disturb the surface and break the monotony of the blank, watery solitude; and so the day goes, the night comes, and again the day—and still the same, night after night and day after day,—majestic, unchanging sameness of serenity, repose, tranquillity, lethargy, vacancy—symbol of eternity, realization of the heaven pictured by priest and prophet, and longed for by the good and thoughtless!

Immediately after the war of 1812 tourists began to come to America, from England; scattering ones at first, then a sort of procession of them—a procession which kept up its plodding, patient march through the land during many, many years. Each tourist took notes, and went home and published a book—a book which was usually calm, truthful, reasonable, kind; but which seemed just the reverse to our tender-footed progenitors. A glance at these tourist-books shows us that in certain of its aspects the Mississippi has undergone no change since those strangers visited it, but remains to-day about as it was then. The emotions produced in those foreign breasts by these aspects were not all formed on one pattern, of course; they *had* to be various, along at first, because the earlier tourists were obliged to originate their emotions, whereas in older countries one can always borrow emotions from one's predecessors. And, mind you, emotions are among the toughest things in the world to manufacture out of whole cloth; it is easier to manufacture seven facts than one emotion. Captain Basil Hall, R. N., writing fifty-five years ago, says:

Here I caught the first glimpse of the object I had so long wished to behold, and felt myself amply repaid at that moment for all the trouble I had experienced in coming so far; and stood looking at the river flowing past till it was too dark to distinguish anything. But it was not until I had visited the same spot a dozen times that I came to a right comprehension of the grandeur of the scene.

Following are Mrs. Trollope's emotions. She is writing a few months later in the same year, 1827, and is coming in at the mouth of the Mississippi:

The first indication of our approach to land was the appearance of this mighty river pouring forth its muddy mass of waters, and mingling with the deep blue of the Mexican Gulf. I never beheld a scene so utterly desolate as this entrance of the Mississippi. Had Dante seen it, he might have drawn images of another Bolgia from its horrors. One only object rears itself above the eddying waters; this is the mast of a vessel long since wrecked in attempting to cross the bar, and it still stands, a dismal witness of the destruction that has been, and a boding prophet of that which is to come.

Emotions of Hon. Charles Augustus Murray (near St. Louis), seven years later:

It is only when you ascend the mighty current for fifty or a hundred miles, and use the eye of imagination as well as that of nature, that you begin to understand all his might and majesty. You see him fertilizing a boundless valley, bearing along in his course the trophies of his thousand victories over the shattered forest—here carrying away large masses of soil with all their growth, and there forming islands destined at some future period to be the residence of man; and while indulging in this prospect,

it is then time for reflection to suggest that the current before you has
flowed through two or three thousand miles, and has yet to travel one
thousand three hundred more before reaching its ocean destination.

Receive, now, the emotions of Captain Marryat, R. N., author of the
sea tales, writing in 1837, three years after Mr. Murray:

Never, perhaps, in the records of nations, was there an instance of a
century of such unvarying and unmitigated crime as is to be collected from
the history of the turbulent and blood-stained Mississippi. The stream
itself appears as if appropriate for the deeds which have been committed.
It is not like most rivers, beautiful to the sight, bestowing fertility in this
course; not one that the eye loves to dwell upon as it sweeps along, nor can
you wander upon its bank, or trust yourself without danger to its stream.
It is a furious, rapid, desolating torrent, loaded with alluvial soil; and few
of those who are received into its waters ever rise again,* or can support
themselves long upon its surface without assistance from some friendly log.
It contains the coarsest and most uneatable of fish, such as catfish and such
genus, and, as you descend, its banks are occupied with the fetid alligator,
while the panther basks at its edge in the cane-brakes, almost impervious
to man. Pouring its impetuous waters through wild tracts covered with
trees of little value except for firewood, it sweeps down whole forests in
its course, which disappear in tumultuous confusion, whirled away by the
stream now loaded with the masses of soil which nourished their roots,
often blocking up and changing for a time the channel of the river, which,
as if in anger at its being opposed, inundates and devastates the whole
country round; and as soon as it forces its way through its former channel,
plants in every direction the uprooted monarchs of the forest (upon whose
branches the bird will never again perch, or the raccoon, the opossum,
or the squirrel climb) as traps to the adventurous navigators of its waters by

*There was a foolish superstition of some little prevalence in that day that the Mis-
sissippi would neither buoy up a swimmer nor permit a drowned person's body to rise
to the surface.

steam, who, borne down by these concealed dangers which pierce through the planks, very often have not time to steer for and gain the shore before they sink to the bottom. There are no pleasing associations connected with the great common sewer of the Western America, which pours out its mud into the Mexican Gulf, polluting the clear blue sea for many miles beyond its mouth. It is a river of desolation; and instead of reminding you, like other beautiful rivers, of an angel which has descended for the benefit of man, you imagine it a devil, whose energies have been only overcome by the wonderful power of steam.

It is pretty crude literature for a man accustomed to handling a pen; still, as a panorama of the emotions sent weltering through this noted visitor's breast by the aspect and traditions of the "great common sewer," it has a value. A value, though marred in the matter of statistics by inaccuracies; for the catfish is a plenty good enough fish for anybody, and there are no panthers that are "impervious to man."

Later still comes Alexander Mackay, of the Middle Temple, Barrister at Law, with a better digestion, and no catfish dinner aboard, and feels as follows:

The Mississippi! It was with indescribable emotions that I first felt myself afloat upon its waters. How often in my schoolboy dreams, and in my waking visions afterward, had my imagination pictured to itself the lordly stream, rolling with tumultuous current through the boundless region to which it has given its name, and gathering into itself, in its course to the ocean, the tributary waters of almost every latitude in the temperate zone! Here it was then in its reality, and I, at length, steaming against its tide. I looked upon it with that reverence with which every one must regard a great feature of external nature.

So much for the emotions. The tourists, one and all, remark upon the deep, brooding loneliness and desolation of the vast river. Captain Basil Hall, who saw it at flood-stage, says:

Sometimes we passed along distances of twenty or thirty miles without seeing a single habitation. An artist, in search of hints for a painting of the deluge, would here have found them in abundance.

The first shall be last, etc. Just two hundred years ago, the old original first and gallantest of all the foreign tourists, pioneer, head of the procession, ended his weary and tedious discovery voyage down the solemn stretches of the great river—La Salle, whose name will last as long as the river itself shall last. We quote from Mr. Parkman:

And now they neared their journey's end. On the 6th of April, the river divided itself into three broad channels. La Salle followed that of the west, and D'Autray that of the east; while Tonty took the middle passage. As he drifted down the turbid current, between the low and marshy shores, the brackish water changed to brine, and the breeze grew fresh with the salt breath of the sea. Then the broad bosom of the great Gulf opened on his sight, tossing its restless billows, limitless, voiceless, lonely as when born of chaos, without a sail, without a sign of life.

Then, on a spot of solid ground, La Salle reared a column "bearing the arms of France; the Frenchmen were mustered under arms; and while the New England Indians and their squaws looked on in wondering silence, they chanted the *Te Deum,* the *Exaudiat,* and the *Domine, salvum fac regem.*"

Then, while the musketry volleyed and rejoicing shouts burst forth, the victorious discoverer planted the column, and made proclamation in a loud voice, taking formal possession of the river and the vast countries watered by it, in the name of the King. The column bore this inscription:

LOUIS LE GRAND, ROY DE FRANCE ET DE NAVARRE, REGNE;
LE NEUVIÈME AVRIL, 1682.

New Orleans intended to fittingly celebrate, this present year, the bicentennial anniversary of this illustrious event; but when the time

came, all her energies and surplus money were required in other directions for the flood was upon the land then, making havoc and
devastation everywhere.

Clandeboye, Manitoba

Aldo Leopold *1887–1948*

Aldo Leopold was both a government biologist and an eloquent
conservationist. He has been credited with founding the profession of
game management, but is best remembered for *A Sand County Almanac,*
a book that "tells what my family sees and does at its week-end refuge from
too much modernity."

Even in the relatively pristine setting of Sand County, Wisconsin, over
half a century ago, Leopold saw impacts of civilization almost everywhere.
To experience a "marsh apart" he traveled to the vast, wetland-strewn
prairie of central Canada. The following excerpt originally appeared in
a collection of writings titled *Sketches Here and There.*

Education, I fear, is learning to see one thing by going blind to another.

One thing most of us have gone blind to is the quality of marshes.
I am reminded of this when, as a special favor, I take a visitor to Clandeboye, only to find that, to him, it is merely lonelier to look upon,
and stickier to navigate, than other boggy places.

This is strange, for any pelican, duckhawk, godwit, or western
grebe is aware that Clandeboye is a marsh apart. Why else do they
seek it out in preference to other marshes? Why else do they resent

my intrusion within its precincts not as mere trespass, but as some kind of cosmic impropriety?

I think the secret is this: Clandeboye is a marsh apart, not only in space, but in time. Only the uncritical consumers of hand-me-down history suppose that 1941 arrived simultaneously in all marshes. The birds know better. Let a squadron of southbound pelicans but feel a lift of prairie breeze over Clandeboye, and they sense at once that here is a landing in the geological past, a refuge from that most relentless of aggressors, the future. With queer antediluvian grunts they set wing, descending in majestic spirals to the welcoming wastes of a bygone age.

Other refugees are already there, each accepting in his own fashion his respite from the march of time. Forster's terns, like troops of happy children, scream over the mudflats as if the first cold melt from the retreating ice sheet were shivering the spines of their minnowy prey. A file of sandhill cranes bugles defiance of whatever it is that cranes distrust and fear. A flotilla of swans rides the bay in quiet dignity, bemoaning the evanescence of swanly things. From the tip of a storm-wracked cottonwood, where the marsh discharges into the big lake, a peregrine stoops playfully at passing fowl. He is gorged with duck meat; but it amuses him to terrorize the squealing teals. This, too, was his after-dinner sport in the days when Lake Agassiz covered the prairies.

It is easy to classify the attitudes of these wildlings, for each wears his heart on his sleeve. But there is one refugee in Clandeboye whose mind I cannot read, for he tolerates no truck with human intruders. Let other birds spill easy confidence to upstarts in overalls, but not the western grebe! Stalk carefully as I will to the bordering reeds, all I get to see is a flash of silver as he sinks, soundless, into the bay. And then, from behind the reedy curtain of the far shore, he tinkles a little bell, warning all his kind of something. Of what?

I've never been able to guess, for there is some barrier between this bird and all mankind. One of my guests dismissed the grebe by checking off his name in the bird list, and jotting down a syllabic paraphrase of the tinkling bell: '*crick-crick,*' or some such inanity. The man failed to sense that here was something more than a bird-call, that here was a *secret* message, calling not for rendition in counterfeit syllables, but for translation and understanding. Alas, I was, and still am, as helpless to translate it or to understand it as he.

As the spring advances, the bell grows persistent; at dawn and at dusk it tinkles from every open water. I infer that the young grebes are now launched in their watery career, and are receiving parental instruction in the grebe philosophy. But to *see* this schoolroom scene, that is not so easy.

One day I buried myself, prone, in the muck of a muskrat house. While my clothes absorbed local color, my eyes absorbed the lore of the marsh. A hen redhead cruised by with her convoy of ducklings, pink-billed fluffs of greenish-golden down. A Virginia rail nearly brushed my nose. The shadow of a pelican sailed over a pool in which a yellow-leg alighted with warbling whistle; it occurred to me that whereas I *write* a poem by dint of mighty cerebration, the yellow-leg *walks* a better one just by lifting his foot.

A mink slithered up the shore behind me, nose in air, trailing. Marsh wrens made trip after trip to a knot in the bulrushes, whence came the clamor of nestlings. I was starting to doze in the sun when there emerged from the open pool a wild red eye, glaring from the head of a bird. Finding all quiet, the silver body emerged: big as a goose, with the lines of a slim torpedo. Before I was aware of when or whence, a second grebe was there, and on her broad back rode two pearly-silver young, neatly enclosed in a corral of humped-up wings. All rounded a bend before I recovered my breath. And now I heard the bell, clear and derisive, behind the curtain of the reeds.

A sense of history should be the most precious gift of science and of the arts, but I suspect that the grebe, who has neither, knows more history than we do. His dim primordial brain knows nothing of who won the Battle of Hastings, but it seems to sense who won the battle of time. If the race of men were as old as the race of grebes, we might better grasp the import of his call. Think what traditions, prides, disdains, and wisdoms even a few self-conscious generations bring to us! What pride of continuity, then, impels this bird, who was a grebe eons before there was a man.

Be that as it may, the call of the grebe is, by some peculiar authority, the sound that dominates and unifies the marshland chorus. Perhaps, by some immemorial authority, he wields the baton for the whole biota. Who beats the measure for the lakeshore rollers as they build reef after reef for marsh after marsh, as age after age the waters recede to lower levels? Who holds sago and bulrush to their task of sucking sun and air, lest in winter the muskrats starve, and the canes engulf the marsh in lifeless jungle? Who counsels patience to brooding ducks by day, and incites bloodthirst in marauding minks by night? Who exhorts precision for the heron's spear, and speed for the falcon's fist? We assume, because all these creatures perform their diverse tasks without admonition audible to us, that they receive none, that their skills are inborn and their industry automatic, that weariness is unknown to the wild. Perhaps weariness is unknown only to grebes; perhaps it is the grebe who reminds them that if all are to survive, each must ceaselessly feed and fight, breed and die.

The marshlands that once sprawled over the prairie from the Illinois to the Athabasca are shrinking northward. Man cannot live by marsh alone, therefore he must needs live marshless. Progress cannot abide that farmland and marshland, wild and tame, exist in mutual toleration and harmony.

So with dredge and dyke, tile and torch, we sucked the cornbelt dry, and now the wheatbelt. Blue lake becomes green bog, green bog becomes caked mud, caked mud becomes a wheatfield.

Some day my marsh, dyked and pumped, will lie forgotten under the wheat, just as today and yesterday will lie forgotten under the years. Before the last mud-minnow makes his last wiggle in the last pool, the terns will scream goodbye to Clandeboye, the swans will circle skyward in snowy dignity, and the cranes will blow their trumpets in farewell.

Journal of a Prairie Year

Paul Gruchow

Agriculture has devoured much of the natural wetland area of North America. The prairie pothole habitat described in this excerpt has been particularly affected.

Paul Gruchow teaches writing at Saint Olaf College in Minnesota and has written extensively on the prairie and plains environments.

There were once tens of thousands of potholes across the prairies, but almost all of them were drained of their water over the years and the land was put to agricultural uses. They attracted breeding waterfowl by the millions. A pair of ducks could always find a suitable place in the grass near a temporary pond for a nest, and the pond could generally be counted on to serve as a refuge for the callow ducklings until they had their feathers and were capable of fending for themselves.

The shallow waters of the temporary ponds warmed quickly. Many forms of microscopic life flourished in this warmth, and the microscopic life, with the droppings of the ducks and the organic wastes that the rainwater washed into the pools, provided sustenance for the crustaceans which made the temporary ponds a way of life.

There were the little one-eyed *Cyclops*, whose females carried saddlebags of eggs. Some of them got from temporary pond to temporary pond on the currents of the winds. When a pool of water dried up, they encased themselves in cysts. The cysts either protected them until the next rainfall or rendered them transportable.

There were the fairy shrimp, which came in a variety of bright colors—blue-green, orange, red. They managed to exist everywhere, even in the most ridiculously temporary of aquatic environments, in road ditch puddles among other places. The fairy shrimp had many leaflike legs, and they glided about on their backs by gracefully waving their comely legs. The stirrings of those legs brought to them a flow of water which ran through their mouths and was strained there of its edibles: bits of algae; one-celled protozoa and flagellates; rotifers; bacteria; bits of organic matter; microscopic fungi, ghostly and parasitic because they lacked the chlorophyll necessary to synthesize sustenance for themselves. The fairy shrimp were masterfully equipped for the art of survival. Their reproduction favored females, which could lay a clutch of as many as 250 eggs as often as every two days. These eggs had to be partially developed before they could be fully laid. They came in two varieties. There was a thin-shelled kind suitable for the high breeding season—May through early summer. And there was a thick-shelled kind which protected the embryo through such hardships as ice and drought.

Tadpole shrimp resided in the temporary ponds in vast numbers. They survived from wet season to wet season as eggs and gave to the prairie a touch of the sea: they looked like the tiny horseshoe crabs that abound on saltwater beaches. The tadpole shrimp had a taste for many things. They subsided chiefly on microscopic organisms, but they also ate eggs as they were available. When a creature occupied a niche as chancy as the one the tadpole shrimp did, it was healthy not to be too finicky.

There were water fleas with pale yellow blood and big oval hearts and outsized compound eyes. They had long antennae which propelled them about. Almost all of the water fleas that first appeared in a pond in spring were females. Their lives were spent in a series of molts. There were several molts from hatching to adulthood, which commenced with the first brood of eggs. After that, an adult female might molt twenty-five more times, each time producing still another batch of as many as forty eggs. As spring wore on, a few males began to appear in the broods. It was not clear what brought them there. Perhaps it was a critical water temperature, perhaps overcrowding and its attendant shortage of food, perhaps a buildup of excrement—maybe all of these factors came into play. Whatever, the appearance of the males in significant numbers happened as the females were starting to produce fewer eggs. These the males fertilized. The brood chamber in which the fertilized eggs developed thickened and darkened. At the next molt, the chamber dropped away from the female into the bottom mud. It was highly resistant to drying and freezing. If there should be water again in the fall in the temporary ponds, the eggs would hatch, and the sequence would repeat itself. There would be an increase in populations until males were produced, and these would fertilize eggs that would fall away from the brood chamber and remain safe in the mud over winter, ready to hatch with the first rains of spring. If there were no fall rains, the eggs from the spring broods were equipped to last through the winter.

The same temporary waters that produced the teeming populations of one-celled animals and the rich variety of crustaceans that fed upon them, and which offered refuge for growing ducks, were also nursery chambers for the nymphal stages of many insects, of mayflies, of dragonflies, of damselflies, of mosquitoes and midges and gnats. When these insects had metamorphosed into adults, they took to the air or crawled out upon the land and became part of the chain of life beyond the waters.

There were the tadpoles of spadefoot toads in the temporary ponds. They were creatures with a genius for surviving drought. One cousin lived on the southwestern deserts in places where the rains were so scarce that there might be pools of water adequate for breeding only once every couple of years. The desert toads survived by burrowing deep into the ground before the onset of the summer heat. There they found both much cooler temperatures and some moisture that they could use, and they conserved such moisture as they had by growing a protective sheath of dead skin and by retaining their urine so as not to lose its water content. Because the spadefoot toads were dependent upon temporary pools for breeding, pools which might dry up at any time, they were able to reproduce in a hurry. A male led the way out of the underground chambers. When he reached the surface, he let out a call so commanding that all the other toads within some hundreds of yards responded. They marched en masse to the pool and mated there. Within forty-eight hours, the eggs had hatched, and in another sixteen days the first young adults were ready to leave for land. But the temporary ponds were drying up early this season, and life crowded in them. So the young tadpoles turned upon each other. When their numbers had been reduced by half, those that remained accelerated their development. The first of them were ready to begin their adult life as burrowers in the grasslands only twelve days after hatching.

The tiger salamanders had also gone in companies to the ponds in spring to mate and to deposit their eggs. The eggs had incubated for more than a month before the water temperature was right for hatching. They had spent another month and a half in the water as larvae before achieving adulthood. Then they, like so many other pond creatures, left the water and came up to chains of life on the land. For the salamanders, life on land was lived mainly at night and mainly underground.

The crustaceans, toads, salamanders, ducks drew sustenance from the smaller creatures which found life possible in the accumulated melts and rains of the prairie spring. These creatures would in turn feed on insects and play host to parasites and graze grasses that would become the sources of energy for bigger predators on the grasslands. And the largest predators and the great herbivores, the bison and the elk and the antelope, would in their turn become ill and die from the advanced forms of the parasites that had begun their lives in the tiny creatures of the temporary ponds. When the creatures at the top of the food chain had fallen, their remains would be broken down by the hosts of scavengers, and the carcasses and excrement that the scavengers produced would be washed away the next spring into the temporary ponds again, and the whole cycle would begin anew.

In the meantime, the ponds that were now almost dry had served to keep the rainwaters of spring at hand, not only to fuel the cycle of energy transfers, but also to feed the water table that flowed beneath the grasses. The underground reservoir kept the level of moisture in the subsoil high even while the topsoil was crumbling into dust. It was on that subsoil moisture that the deep-rooted prairie perennials survived drought.

But the prairie world is now crisscrossed by a labyrinth of tiles and drainage ditches. Its ponds don't hold water anymore. With the disappearing ponds have vanished many of the waterfowl, many of the insects, many of the predators. The great herbivores have long since disappeared. It is by now a pale ghost of the world that once existed in this place.

Exploration of the Colorado River of the West and Its Tributaries

John Wesley Powell *1834–1902*

Major John Wesley Powell was a one-armed veteran of Civil War artillery who led the first recorded expedition down the Colorado River—running the rapids of the Grand Canyon when the river was unmapped and undammed. Powell drew the map and wrote the book on the geology of the parched, yet water-sculpted lands of the Southwest. He became director of the U.S. Geological and Geographic Survey and, in his later years, first director of the U.S. Bureau of Ethnology.

In this passage, Powell recounts his impressions of the waters and the native people of the otherworldly high country where tributaries to the three great rivers of the West part ways.

Green River has its source in Fremont's Peak, high in the Wind River Mountains among glacial lakes and mountain cascades. This is the real source of the Colorado River, and it stands in strange contrast with the mouth of that stream where it pours into the Gulf of California. The general course of the river is from north to south and from great altitudes to the level of the sea. Thus it runs "from land of snow to land of sun." The Wind River Mountains constitute one of the most imposing ranges of the United States. Fremont's Peak, the culminating point, is 13,790 feet above the level of the sea. It stands in a wilderness of crags. Here at Fremont's Peak three great rivers have their sources: Wind River flows eastward into the Mississippi; Green River flows southward into the Colorado; and Gros Ventre River flows northwestward into the Columbia. From this dominating height many ranges can be seen on every hand. About the sources of the Platte and the Big Horn, that flow ultimately into the Gulf of Mexico, great ranges stand with their culminating peaks among the clouds; and the mountains that extend into Yellowstone Park, the land of geyser wonders, are seen. The Yellowstone Park is at the southern extremity of a great system of mountain ranges, the northern Rocky Mountains, sometimes called the Geyser Ranges. This geological province extends into British America, but its most wonderful scenery is in the upper Yellowstone basin, where geysers bombard the heavens with vapor distilled in subterranean depths. The springs which pour out their boiling waters are loaded with quartz, and the waters of the springs, flowing away over the rocks, slowly discharge their fluid magma, which crystallizes in beautiful forms and builds jeweled basins that hold pellucid waters.

To the north and west of Fremont's Peak are mountain ranges that give birth to rivers flowing into the great Columbia. Conspicuous among these from this point of view is the great Teton Range, with its towering façade of storm-carved rocks; then the Gros Ventre Mountains, the Snake River Range, the Wyoming Range, and, still beyond the latter, the Bear River Range, are seen. Far in the distant south, scarcely to be distinguished from the blue clouds on the horizon, stand the Uinta Mountains. On every hand are deep mountain gorges where snows accumulate to form glaciers. Below the glaciers throughout the entire Wind River Range great numbers of morainal lakes are found. These lakes are gems—deep sapphire waters fringed with emerald zones. From these lakes creeks and rivers flow, by cataracts and rapids, to form the Green. The mountain slopes below are covered with dense forests of pines and firs. The lakes are often fringed with beautiful aspens, and when the autumn winds come their golden leaves are carried over the landscape in clouds of resplendent sheen. The creeks descend from the mountains in wild rocky gorges, until they flow out into the valley. On the west side of the valley stand the Gros Ventre and the Wyoming mountains, low ranges of peaks, but picturesque in form and forest stretch. Leaving the mountain, the river meanders through the

Green River Plains, a cold elevated district much like that of northern Norway, except that the humidity of Norway is replaced by the aridity of Wyoming. South of the plains the Big Sandy joins the Green from the east. South of the Big Sandy a long zone of sanddunes stretches eastward. The western winds blowing up the valley drift these sands from hill to hill, so that the hills themselves are slowly journeying eastward on the wings of arid gales, and sand tempests may be encountered more terrible than storms of snow or hail. Here the northern boundary of the Plateau Province is found, for mesas and high table lands are found on either side of the river.

On the east side of the Green, mesas and plateaus have irregular escarpments with points extending into the valleys, and between these points canyons come down that head in the highlands. Everywhere the escarpments are fringed with outlying buttes. Many portions of the region are characterized by bad lands. These are hills carved out of sandstone, shales, and easily disintegrated rocks, which present many fantastic forms and are highly colored in a great variety of tint and tone, and everywhere they are naked of vegetation. Now and then low mountains crown the plateaus. Altogether it is a region of desolation. Through the midst of the country, from east to west, flows an intermittent stream known as Bitter Creek. In seasons of rain it carries floods; in seasons of drought it disappears in the sands, and its waters are alkaline and often poisonous. Stretches of bad-land desert are interrupted by other stretches of sage plain, and on the highlands gnarled and picturesque forests of juniper and piñon are found. On the west side of the river the mesas rise by grassy slopes to the westward into high plateaus that are forest-clad, first with juniper and piñon, and still higher with pines and firs. Some of the streams run in canyons and others have elevated valleys along their courses. On the south border of this mesa and plateau country are the Bridger Bad Lands, lying at the foot of the Uinta Mountains.

These bad lands are of gray, green, and brown shales that are carved in picturesque forms—domes, towers, pinnacles, and minarets, and bold cliffs with deep alcoves; and all are naked rock, the sediments of an ancient lake. These lake beds are filled with fossils,—the preserved bones of fishes, reptiles, and mammals, of strange and often gigantic forms, no longer found living on the globe. It is a desert to the agriculturist, a mine to the paleontologist, and a paradise to the artist.

The region thus described, from Fremont's Peak to the Uinta Mountains, has been the home of tribes of Indians of the Shoshonean family from time immemorial. It is a great hunting and fishing region, and the vigorous Shoshones still obtain a part of their livelihood from mesa and plain and river and lake. The flesh of the animals killed in fall and winter was dried in the arid winds for summer use; the trout abounding in the streams and lakes were caught at all seasons of the year; and the seeds and fruits of harvest time were gathered and preserved for winter use. When the seeds were gathered they were winnowed by tossing them in trays so that the winds might carry away the chaff. Then they were roasted in the same trays. Burning coals and seeds were mixed in the basket trays and kept in motion by a tossing process which fanned the coals until the seeds were done; then they were separated from the coals by dexterous manipulation. Afterwards the seeds were ground on mealingstones and molded into cakes, often huge loaves, that were stored away for use in time of need. Raspberries, chokecherries, and buffalo berries are abundant, and these fruits were gathered and mixed with the bread. Such fruit cakes were great dainties among these people.

In this Shoshone land the long winter night is dedicated to worship and festival. About their camp fires scattered in forest glades by brooks and lakes, they assemble to dance and sing in honor of their gods—wonderful mythic animals, for they hold as divine the ancient of bears, the eagle of the lost centuries, the rattlesnake of primeval times, and a host of other zoic deities.

The Uinta Range stands across the course of Green River, which finds its way through it by series of stupendous canyons. The range has an east-and-west trend. The Wasatch Mountains, a long north-and-south range, here divide the Plateau Province, on the west. The latter is the great interior basin whose waters run into salt lakes and sinks, there being no drainage to the sea. The Great Salt Lake is the most important of these interior bodies of water.

The Great Basin, which lies to the west of the Plateau Province, forms a part of the Basin Range Province. In past geological times it was the site of a vast system of lakes, but the climate has since changed and the water of most of these lakes has evaporated and the sediments of the old lake beds are now desert sands. The ancient lake shores are often represented by conspicuous terraces, each one marking a stage in the height of a dead lake. While these lakes existed the region was one of great volcanic activity and many eruptive mountains were formed. Some burst out beneath the waters; others were piled up on the dry land.

From the desert valleys below, the Wasatch Mountains rise abruptly and are crowned with craggy peaks. But on the east side of the mountains the descent to the plateau is comparatively slight. The Uinta Mountains are carved out of the great plateau which extends more than two hundred miles to the eastward of the summit of the Wasatch Range. Its mountain peaks are cameos, its upper valleys are meadows, its higher slopes are forest groves, and its streams run in deep, solemn, and majestic canyons. The snows never melt from its crowning heights, and an undying anthem is sung by its falling waters.

The Owiyukuts Plateau is situated at the northeastern end of the

Uinta Mountains. It is a great integral block of the Uinta system. A beautiful creek heads in this plateau, near its center, and descends northward into the bad lands of Vermilion Creek, to which stream it is tributary. "Once upon a time" this creek, after descending from the plateau, turned east and then southward and found its way by a beautiful canyon into Brown's Park, where it joined the Green; but a great bend of the Vermilion, near the foot of the plateau, was gradually enlarged—the stream cutting away its banks—until it encroached upon the little valley of the creek born on the Owiyukuts Plateau. This encroachment continued until at last Vermilion Creek stole the Owiyukuts Creek and carried its waters away by its own channel. Then the canyon channel through which Owiyukuts Creek had previously run, no longer having a stream to flow through its deep gorge, gathered the waters of brooks flowing along its course into little lakelets, which are connected by a running stream only through seasons of great rainfall. These lakelets in the gorge of the dead creek are now favorite resorts of Ute Indians.

South of the Uinta Mountains is the Uinta River, a stream with many mountain tributaries, some heading in the Uinta Mountains, other in the Wasatch Mountains on the west, and still others in the western Tavaputs Plateau.

The Uinta Valley is the ancient and present home of the Uinta Indians, a tribe speaking the Uinta language of the Shoshonean family. Their habits, customs, institutions, and mythology are essentially the same as those of the Ute Indians of the Grand River country, already described. In this valley there are also found many ruins of ancient pueblo-building peoples—of what stock is not known.

The Tavaputs Plateau is one of the stupendous features of this country. On the west it merges into the Wasatch Mountains; on the north it descends by wooded slopes into the Uinta Valley. Its summit is forest-clad and among the forests are many beautiful parks. On the south it ends in a great escarpment which descends into Castle Valley. This southern escarpment presents one of the most wonderful façades of the world. It is from 2,000 to 4,000 feet high. The descent is not made by one bold step, for it is cut by canyons and cliffs. It is a zone several miles in width which is a vast labyrinth of canyons, cliffs, buttes, pinnacles, minarets, and detached rocks of Cyclopean magnitude, the whole destitute of soil and vegetation, colored in many brilliant tones and tints, and carved in many weird forms,—a land of desolation, dedicated forever to the geologist and the artist, where civilization can find no resting-place.

Tales of the Fish Patrol

Jack London *1876–1916*

Quick to mature to formidable size, self-supporting at an early age by necessity, Jack London went to work as a deputy for the Fish Patrol on San Francisco Bay while still a teenager. In this autobiographical account, he tells of using the Bay itself to corral a gang of oyster poachers. Nature and adventure continued to be dominant themes throughout London's writing career and in his own life.

Wetlands provide some of the world's richest habitat for wildlife and consequently some of the most productive hunting grounds for wildlife poachers. For the story of a modern-day undercover game warden, turn to the excerpt from Marc Reisner's *Game Wars* on page 210.

At this point I may as well explain that we of the fish patrol were free lances in a way. While Neil Partington, who was a patrolman proper, received a regular salary, Charley and I, being merely deputies, received only what we earned—that is to say, a certain percentage of the fines imposed on convicted violators of the fish laws. Also, any rewards that chanced our way were ours. We offered to share with Partington whatever we should get from Mr. Taft, but the patrolman would not hear of it. He was only too happy, he said, to do a good turn for us, who had done so many for him.

We held a long council of war, and mapped out the following line of action. Our faces were unfamiliar on the Lower Bay, but as the *Reindeer* was well known as a fish-patrol sloop, the Greek boy, whose name was Nicholas, and I were to sail some innocent-looking craft down to Asparagus Island and join the oyster pirates' fleet. Here, according to Nicholas's description of the beds and the manner of raiding, it was possible for us to catch the pirates in the act of stealing oysters, and at the same time to get them in our power. Charley was to be on the shore, with Mr. Taft's watchmen and a posse of constables, to help us at the right time.

"I know just the boat," Neil said, at the conclusion of the discussion, "a crazy old sloop that's lying over at Tiburon. You and Nicholas can go over by the ferry, charter it for a song, and sail direct for the beds."

"Good luck be with you, boys," he said at parting, two days later. "Remember, they are dangerous men, so be careful."

Nicholas and I succeeded in chartering the sloop very cheaply; and between laughs, while getting up sail, we agreed that she was even crazier and older than she had been described. She was a big, flat-bottomed, square-sterned craft, sloop-rigged, with a sprung mast, slack rigging, dilapidated sails, and rotten running-gear, clumsy to handle and uncertain in bringing about, and she smelled vilely of coal tar, with which strange stuff she had been smeared from stem to stern and from cabin-roof to centreboard. And to cap it all,

Coal Tar Maggie was printed in great white letters the whole length of either side.

It was an uneventful though laughable run from Tiburon to Asparagus Island, where we arrived in the afternoon of the following day. The oyster pirates, a fleet of a dozen sloops, were lying at anchor on what was known as the "Deserted Beds." The *Coal Tar Maggie* came sloshing into their midst with a light breeze astern, and they crowded on deck to see us. Nicholas and I had caught the spirit of the crazy craft, and we handled her in most lubberly fashion.

"Wot is it?" some one called.

"Name it 'n' ye kin have it!" called another.

"I swan naow, ef it ain't the old Ark itself!" mimicked the Centipede from the deck of the *Ghost*.

"Hey! Ahoy there, clipper ship!" another wag shouted. "Wot's yer port?"

We took no notice of the joking, but acted, after the manner of greenhorns, as though the *Coal Tar Maggie* required our undivided attention. I rounded her well to windward of the *Ghost*, and Nicholas ran for'ard to drop the anchor. To all appearances it was a bungle, the way the chain tangled and kept the anchor from reaching the bottom. And to all appearances Nicholas and I were terribly excited as we strove to clear it. At any rate, we quite deceived the pirates, who took huge delight in our predicament.

But the chain remained tangled, and amid all kinds of mocking advice we drifted down upon and fouled the *Ghost*, whose bowsprit poked square through our main-sail and ripped a hole in it as big as a barn door. The Centipede and the Porpoise doubled up on the cabin in paroxysms of laughter, and left us to get clear as best we could. This, with much unseamanlike performance, we succeeded in doing, and likewise in clearing the anchor-chain, of which we let out about three hundred feet. With only ten feet of water under us, this would permit the *Coal Tar Maggie* to swing in a circle six hundred feet in diameter, in which circle she would be able to foul at least half the fleet.

The oyster pirates lay snugly together at short hawsers, the weather being fine, and they protested loudly at our ignorance in putting out such an unwarranted length of anchor-chain. And not only did they protest, for they made us heave it in again, all but thirty feet.

Having sufficiently impressed them with our general lubberliness, Nicholas and I went below to congratulate ourselves and to cook supper. Hardly had we finished the meal and washed the dishes, when a skiff ground against the *Coal Tar Maggie's* side, and heavy feet trampled on deck. Then the Centipede's brutal face appeared in the companionway, and he descended into the cabin, followed by the Porpoise. Before they could seat themselves on a bunk, another skiff came alongside, and another, and another, till the whole fleet was represented by the gathering in the cabin.

"Where'd you swipe the old tub?" asked a squat and hairy man, with cruel eyes and Mexican features.

"Didn't swipe it," Nicholas answered, meeting them on their own ground and encouraging the idea that we had stolen the *Coal Tar Maggie.* "And if we did, what of it?"

"Well, I don't admire your taste, that's all," sneered he of the Mexican features. "I'd rot on the beach first before I'd take a tub that couldn't get out of its own way."

"How were we to know till we tried her?" Nicholas asked, so innocently as to cause a laugh. "And how do you get the oysters?" he hurried on. "We want a load of them; that's what we came for, a load of oysters."

"What d'ye want 'em for?" demanded the Porpoise.

"Oh, to give away to our friends, of course," Nicholas retorted. "That's what you do with yours, I suppose."

This started another laugh, and as our visitors grew more genial we could see that they had not the slightest suspicion of our identity or purpose.

"Didn't I see you on the dock in Oakland the other day?" the Centipede asked suddenly of me.

"Yep," I answered boldly, taking the bull by the horns. "I was watching you fellows and figuring out whether we'd go oystering or not. It's a pretty good business, I calculate, and so we're going in for it. That is," I hastened to add, "if you fellows don't mind."

"I'll tell you one thing, which ain't two things," he replied, "and that is you'll have to hump yerself an' get a better boat. We won't stand to be disgraced by any such box as this. Understand?"

"Sure," I said. "Soon as we sell some oysters we'll outfit in style."

"And if you show yerself square an' the right sort," he went on, "why, you kin run with us. But if you don't" (here his voice became stern and menacing), "why, it'll be the sickest day of yer life. Understand?"

"Sure," I said.

After that and more warning and advice of similar nature, the conversation became general, and we learned that the beds were to be raided that very night. As they got into their boats, after an hour's stay, we were invited to join them in the raid with the assurance of "the more the merrier."

"Did you notice that short, Mexican-looking chap?" Nicholas asked, when they had departed to their various sloops. "He's Barchi, of the Sporting Life Gang, and the fellow that came with him is Skilling. They're both out now on five thousand dollars' bail."

I had heard of the Sporting Life Gang before, a crowd of hoodlums and criminals that terrorized the lower quarters of Oakland, and two-thirds of which were usually to be found in state's prison for crimes that ranged from perjury and ballot-box stuffing to murder.

"They are not regular oyster pirates," Nicholas continued.

"They've just come down for the lark and to make a few dollars. But we'll have to watch out for them."

We sat in the cockpit and discussed the details of our plan till eleven o'clock had passed, when we heard the rattle of an oar in a boat from the direction of the *Ghost*. We hauled up our own skiff, tossed in a few sacks, and rowed over. There we found all the skiffs assembling, it being the intention to raid the beds in a body.

To my surprise, I found barely a foot of water where we had dropped anchor in ten feet. It was the big June run-out of the full moon, and as the ebb had yet an hour and a half to run, I knew that our anchorage would be dry ground before slack water.

Mr. Taft's beds were three miles away, and for a long time we rowed silently in the wake of the other boats, once in a while grounding and our oar blades constantly striking bottom. At last we came upon soft mud covered with not more than two inches of water—not enough to float the boats. But the pirates at once were over the side, and by pushing and pulling on the flat-bottomed skiffs, we moved steadily along.

The full moon was partly obscured by high-flying clouds, but the pirates went their way with the familiarity born of long practice. After half a mile of the mud, we came upon a deep channel, up which we rowed, with dead oyster shoals looming high and dry on either side. At last we reached the picking grounds. Two men, on one of the shoals, hailed us and warned us off. But the Centipede, the Porpoise, Barchi, and Skilling took the lead, and followed by the rest of us, at least thirty men in half as many boats, rowed right up to the watchmen.

"You'd better slide outa this here," Barchi said threateningly, "or we'll fill you so full of holes you wouldn't float in molasses."

The watchmen wisely retreated before so overwhelming a force, and rowed their boat along the channel toward where the shore should be. Besides, it was in the plan for them to retreat.

We hauled the noses of the boats up on the shore side of a big shoal, and all hands, with sacks, spread out and begin picking. Every now and again the clouds thinned before the face of the moon, and we could see the big oysters quite distinctly. In almost no time sacks were filled and carried back to the boats, where fresh ones were obtained. Nicholas and I returned often and anxiously to the boats with our little loads, but always found some one of the pirates coming or going.

"Never mind," he said; "no hurry. As they pick farther and farther away, it will take too long to carry to the boats. Then they'll stand the full sacks on end and pick them up when the tide comes in and the skiffs will float to them."

Fully half an hour went by, and the tide had begun to flood, when this came to pass. Leaving the pirates at their work, we stole back to the boats. One by one, and noiselessly, we shoved them off and made them fast in an awkward flotilla. Just as we were shoving off the last skiff, our own, one of the men came upon us. It was Barchi. His quick eye took in the situation at a glance, and he sprang for us; but we went clear with a mighty shove, and he was left floundering in the water over his head. As soon as he got back to the shoal he raised his voice and gave the alarm.

We rowed with all our strength, but it was slow going with so many boats in tow. A pistol cracked from the shoal, a second, and a third; then a regular fusillade began. The bullets spat and spat all about us; but thick clouds had covered the moon, and in the dim darkness it was no more than random firing. It was only by chance that we could be hit.

"Wish we had a little steam launch," I panted.

"I'd just as soon the moon stayed hidden," Nicholas panted back.

It was slow work, but every stroke carried us farther away from the shoal and nearer the shore, till at last the shooting died down, and when the moon did come out we were too far away to be in danger.

Not long afterward we answered a shoreward hail, and two White-hall boats, each pulled by three pairs of oars, darted up to us. Char-ley's welcome face bent over to us, and he gripped us by the hands while he cried, "Oh, you joys! You joys! Both of you!"

When the flotilla had been landed, Nicholas and I and a watch-man rowed out in one of the Whitehalls, with Charley in the stern-sheets. Two other Whitehalls followed us, and as the moon now shone brightly, we easily made out the oyster pirates on their lonely shoal. As we drew closer, they fired a rattling volley from their re-volvers, and we promptly retreated beyond range.

"Lot of time," Charley said. "The flood is setting in fast, and by the time it's up to their necks there won't be any fight left in them."

So we lay on our oars and waited for the tide to do its work. This was the predicament of the pirates: because of the big run-out, the tide was now rushing back like a mill-race, and it was impossible for the strongest swimmer in the world to make against it the three miles to the sloops. Between the pirates and the shore were we, precluding escape in that direction. On the other hand, the water was rising rapidly over the shoals, and it was only a question of a few hours when it would be over their heads.

It was beautifully calm, and in the brilliant white moonlight we watched them through our night glasses and told Charley of the voy-age of the *Coal Tar Maggie*. One o'clock came, and two o'clock, and the pirates were clustering on the highest shoal, waist-deep in water.

"Now this illustrates the value of imagination," Charley was say-ing. "Taft has been trying for years to get them, but he went at it with bull strength and failed. Now we used our heads . . ."

Just then I heard a scarcely audible gurgle of water, and holding up my hand for silence, I turned and pointed to a ripple slowly widening out in a growing circle. It was not more than fifty feet from us. We kept perfectly quiet and waited. After a minute the water broke six feet away, and a black head and white shoulder showed in the moonlight. With a snort of surprise and of suddenly expelled breath, the head and shoulder went down.

We pulled ahead several strokes and drifted with the current. Four pairs of eyes searched the surface of the water, but never another ripple showed, and never another glimpse did we catch of the black head and white shoulder.

"It's the Porpoise," Nicholas said. "It would take broad daylight for us to catch him."

At a quarter to three the pirates gave their first sign of weakening. We heard cries for help, in the unmistakable voice of the Centipede, and this time, on rowing closer, we were not fired upon. The Centipede was in a truly perilous plight. Only the heads and shoulders of his fellow-marauders showed above the water as they braced themselves against the current, while his feet were off the bottom and they were supporting him.

"Now, lads," Charley said briskly, "we have got you, and you can't get away. If you cut up rough, we'll have to leave you alone and the water will finish you. But if you're good, we'll take you aboard, one man at a time, and you'll all be saved. What do you say?"

"Ay," they chorused hoarsely between their chattering teeth.

"Then one man at a time, and the short men first."

The Centipede was the first to be pulled aboard, and he came willingly, though he objected when the constable put the handcuffs on him. Barchi was next hauled in, quite meek and resigned from his soaking. When we had ten in our boat we drew back, and the second Whitehall was loaded. The third Whitehall received nine prisoners only—a catch of twenty-nine in all.

"You didn't get the Porpoise," the Centipede said exultantly, as though his escape materially diminished our success.

Charley laughed. "But we saw him just the same, a-snorting for shore like a puffing pig."

It was a mild and shivering band of pirates that we marched up the beach to the oyster house. In answer to Charley's knock, the door was flung open, and a pleasant wave of warm air rushed out upon us.

"You can dry your clothes here, lads, and get some hot coffee," Charley announced, as they filed in.

And there, sitting ruefully by the fire, with a steaming mug in his hand, was the Porpoise. With one accord Nicholas and I looked at Charley. He laughed gleefully.

"That comes of imagination," he said. "When you see a thing, you've got to see it all around, or what's the good of seeing it at all? I saw the beach, so I left a couple of constables behind to keep an eye on it. That's all."

Between Pacific Tides

Edward F. Ricketts and Jack Calvin

An engagingly literary sort of natural history, *Between Pacific Tides* might show the influence of an author who doesn't appear on the title page. John Steinbeck met Ricketts in 1930 and was a frequent companion and co-worker in his Pacific Biological Laboratory on Cannery Row in Monterey, California. Ricketts collected and distributed West Coast biological specimens to research institutions and schools. Ricketts was the model for several characters in novels by Steinbeck, and they collaborated on the book *Sea of Cortez: A Leisurely Journal of Travel and Research*. They maintained a close friendship until Ricketts's death in 1948.

Mud Flats

The problems of respiration and food-getting in mud flats and the lack of attachment sites make for a rather specialized fauna. The skin breathing of starfish and urchins makes them unsuited to this environment, and, with the exception of an occasional *Pisaster brevispinus,* none occur. There are only one sponge and one hydroid, and there are no chitons or bryozoa, but the many worms, clams, and snails make up for the scarcity of other animals.

Even in the south the animals extend farther up into the intertidal [zone] on the mud flats proper than they do on the sand flats anywhere on the coast. Some of them, like the fiddler crab, seem to be changing into land dwellers—a tendency that reaches an extreme in Japan, where one of the land crabs has worked up to a point almost two thousand feet above sea level.

ZONES 1 AND 2. *Uppermost beach and high-tide horizon from highest tide mark to the mean of the lower of the two highs.*

§284. The little fiddler crabs, *Uca,* . . . are characterized, in the males, by the possession of one relatively enormous claw which is normally carried close to the body. It is a formidable-looking weapon, but seems never to be used except in combat with other males of the same species and as a secondary aid to digging. In battle the two contestants lock claws, each apparently endeavoring to tear the other's claw from its body. Sometimes, according to one capable observer, a crab loses its hold on the substratum and is "thrown back over his opponent for a distance of a foot or more"—a performance that suggests a jujitsu wrestling match. At breeding time, and particularly when a female is near by, the males make a peculiar gesture, extending the big claw to its full length and then whipping it suddenly back toward the body. One might conclude, with some logic, that the big claw is a distinctly sexual attribute comparable to the horns of a stag.

The Japanese call the fiddler crab *siho maneki,* which is translated as "beckoning for the return of the tide." It is too picturesque a name to quibble over, but one might reasonably ask why Mahomet does not go to the mountain, for the presumably free-willed fiddler digs its burrow as far away from the tide as it can get without abandoning the sea entirely. There it feeds, like so many other animals occurring on this type of shore, on whatever minute plants and animals are contained in the substratum. Instead of passing quantities of inert matter through its body, however, the fiddler crab selects daintily such morsels as appeal to it. The selecting process begins with the little claws (the female using both claws and the male his one small one) and is completed at the mouth, the rejected mud collecting below the mouth in little balls which either drop off of their own weight or are removed by the crab.

Dembowski, working with the sand fiddler of the East coast, made careful observations of the animal's behavior and came to the interesting conclusion that its behavior is no more stereotyped than that of a man. He found that in their natural habitat the fiddlers construct oblique burrows up to three feet long that never branch and usually end in a horizontal chamber. In sand-filled glass jars in the laboratory they actually sought the light, digging their burrows along the sides of the jars. Apparently it was an advantage to be able to see what they were doing, and although such a condition had never existed in nature they made use of the opportunity when it did occur. They dig by packing the wet sand between legs and carapace and pressing it into pellets which they then carefully remove from the burrow. The smallest leg prevents loose grains from falling back while the pellet is being carried. Sometimes hours are spent in the very careful work of making the end chamber, the depth of which Dembowski thinks is determined by how far down the fiddler must go to reach sand that is very moist but not wet. In pure sand water would filter into the burrow at high tide, but the fiddler crab always takes care to locate in substratum that has so high a mud content as to be practically impervious to water. Furthermore it lines its burrow—a process that probably adds to its airtightness—and plugs the entrance before each high tide. Thus at high tide or during heavy rains the animal lives in an airtight compartment.

Under experimentally unchanging conditions the crabs showed no sign of periodicity such as might be expected in an animal that stoppers up its burrow against each high tide. Evidently the door-closing process is due not to memory of the tidal rhythm but to the stimulus of an actually rising tide which would moisten the air chamber before the surface of the ground was covered. If a little water was poured into the jars the crabs became active as soon as the moisture reached them, carrying pellets to build a door. If the water was poured in rapidly the crabs rushed to the entrance and pulled pellets in with great haste, not pausing to construct a door. If the jar was then filled up carefully, so as not to damage the burrows, the crabs would stay in their air chambers and not stir for a week. Dumping water in, however, filled the burrows and caved them in, burying the animals. Their response this time was to dig out and wait on the surface of the sandy mud for the "tide" to ebb.

Each "high" high tide destroys part of the burrow, and the animal must dig itself out by somewhat reversing its former operations. It "causes the chamber to rise slowly in an oblique direction, still keeping its volume unaltered, as the sand is always carried from the roof of it to the bottom," again by means of pellets. The procedure varies widely with the "individuality" of the animal. Dembowski insists that this and other reactions are plastic, very little being automatic. Thus the fiddler crab has to adjust not merely a pellet of sand but "always *this single pellet* with all its individual particularities." The animal's nervous system (including its nearest approach to a brain) is too simple to account for such a variety of reactions. To further quote the investigator: "We are compelled to admit a plasticity of the nervous centers; they must possess a certain creative power that enables them to become adapted to entirely new situations. The number of possible nervous connections is limited, but the number of possible reactions is infinite. This discrepancy may be avoided only by admitting that each nervous center may perform an infinity of functions."

Ken Ward in the Jungle

Zane Grey 1872–1939

For better or worse, more than one generation of American youth has been influenced by dentist-turned-action-novelist Zane Grey. This passage is from a story set in Mexico.

The first thing about this glade that Ken noted particularly, after the difficulties presented by the steep steps, was the multitude of snakes sunning themselves along the line of further progress.

"Boys, it'll be great wading down there, hey?" he queried.

Pepe grumbled for the first time on the trip. Ken gathered from the native's looks and speech that he did not like snakes.

"Watch me peg 'em!" yelled Hal, and he began to throw stones with remarkable accuracy. "Hike, you brown sons-of-guns!"

George, not to be outdone, made a dive for his .22 and began to pop as if he had no love for snakes. Ken had doubts about this species. The snakes were short, thick, dull brown in color, and the way they slipped into the stream proved they were water-snakes. Ken had never read of a brown water-moccasin, so he doubted that these belonged to that poisonous family. Anyway, snakes were the least of his troubles.

"Boys, you're doing fine," he said. "There are about a thousand snakes there, and you've hit about six."

He walked down through the glade into the forest, and was overjoyed to hear once more the heavy roar of rapids. He went on. The timber grew thinner, and light penetrated the jungle. Presently he saw the gleam of water through the trees. Then he hurried back.

"All right, boys," he shouted. "Here's the river."

The boys were so immensely relieved that packing the outfit round the waterfalls was work they set about with alacrity. Ken, who had on his boots, broke a trail through the ferns and deep moss. Pepe, being barefoot, wasted time looking for snakes. George teased him. But Pepe was deadly serious. And the way he stepped and looked made Ken thoughtful. He had made his last trip with supplies, and was about to start back to solve the problem of getting the boat down, when a hoarse yell resounded through the sleeping jungle. Parrots screeched, and other birds set up a cackling.

Ken bounded up the slope.

"Santa Maria!" cried Pepe.

Ken followed the direction indicated by Pepe's staring eyes and trembling finger. Hanging from a limb of a tree was a huge blacksnake. It was as thick as Ken's leg. The branch upon which it poised its neck so gracefully was ten feet high, and the tail curled into the ferns on the ground.

"Boys, it's one of the big fellows," cried Ken.

"Didn't I tell you!" yelled George, running down for his gun.

Hal seemed rooted to the spot. Pepe began to jabber. Ken watched the snake, and felt instinctively from its sinister looks that it was dangerous. George came running back with his .32 and waved it in the air as he shot. He was so frightened that he forgot to aim. Ken took the rifle from him.

"You can't hit him with this. Run after your shotgun. Quick!"

But the sixteen-gage was clogged with a shell that would not eject. Ken's guns were in their cases.

"Holy smoke!" cried George. "He's coming down."

The black-snake moved his body and began to slide toward the tree-trunk.

Ken shot twice at the head of the snake. It was a slow-swaying mark hard to hit. The reptile stopped and poised wonderfully on the limb. He was not coiled about it, but lay over it with about four feet of neck waving, swaying to and fro. He watched the boys, and his tongue, like a thin, black streak, darted out viciously.

Ken could not hit the head, so he sent a bullet through the thick part of the body. Swift as a gleam the snake darted from the limb.

"Santa Maria!" yelled Pepe, and he ran off.

"Look out, boys," shouted Ken. He picked up Pepe's *machete* and took to his heels. George and Hal scrambled before him. They ran a hundred yards or more, and Ken halted in an open rocky spot. He was angry, and a little ashamed that he had run. The snake did not pursue, and probably was as badly frightened as the boys had been. Pepe stopped some distance away, and Hal and George came cautiously back.

"I don't see anything of him," said Ken. "I'm going back."

He walked slowly, keeping a sharp outlook, and, returning to the glade, found blood-stains under the tree. The snake had disappeared without leaving a trail.

"If I'd had my shotgun ready!" exclaimed Ken, in disgust. And he made a note that in the future he would be prepared to shoot.

The Shorebirds of North America

Peter Matthiessen

The following excerpt serves as a transition to the next series of readings, which deal with the switch of America's attitude on wetlands from a belief that they ought to be obliterated to a consensus that we'd better do something to save what remains of them. Migratory birds are significant for a couple of reasons. Historically, the crash of their populations early in this century was the first warning taken seriously. More recently, the federal government has largely based its claims of jurisdiction over wetlands on migratory waterfowl as agents of interstate commerce.

Peter Matthiessen's literary accomplishments include writings on natural history, sociopolitical commentary, travel, and fiction. He has also been a commercial fisherman, captain of a deep-sea charter vessel, and Zen Buddhist. An excerpt from a fictional work in progress begins on page 194.

By May the great migration routes have opened out, scattering shorebirds all across the north. The hardy black turnstone, migrating across the water from California, is one of the first shorebirds to appear on the coast of west Alaska, and the ruddy turnstone, knot, and sanderling fly much farther still, nesting as close to the North Pole as farthest Ellesmere Island, near latitude 83. These species build their nests all around the Arctic circumference, and so close to the North Pole that a sanderling in Russia and another in Canada may nest no more than a thousand miles apart over the top of the world. Other shorebirds are not far to the southward, including the Baird's sandpiper, which also nests entirely within the Arctic Circle, under the midnight sun.

It would seem logical that a species hardy enough to winter in North America would nest correspondingly farther north than relatives that come from South America, but except for the dunlin and a few others, the exact reverse is true. Even the purple sandpiper, uncommon in winter south of New Jersey, flies no deeper into the Arctic than do several species that winter in South America. Many species which winter in the United States migrate northward little if at all, and others move but a limited distance into southern Canada.

In other words, a strong migratory urge impels the bird to great lengths in *both* directions; this phenomenon, called leap-frog migration, in which northerly breeders also winter farther south than more sedentary relatives of the same or related species, is very pronounced among the shorebirds.

The species breeding south of Canada are very much in the minority. Most of the world's sandpipers breed in the far north, which has led to the supposition that the Scolopacidae, at least, originated in the Northern Hemisphere; shorebirds make up two-thirds of the few nesting species that are not common to the Arctic bird fauna of both Asia and America. Twenty-three North American shorebird species nest customarily beyond the Arctic Circle; thirteen more nest north of the Canadian border; and another thirteen breed in Canada as well as the United States, leaving but seven species of shorebirds—jaçana; thick-knee; American oystercatcher; snowy, mountain, and Wilson's plovers; and black-necked stilt—that confine their breeding on this continent to the United States. In Audubon's time, the American oystercatcher bred in Labrador, and one day it may do so again.

None of this southern group, curiously, is among the familiar wind birds of the United States; it is the woodcock and the common snipe, which are still included among the game birds, that are the best-known shorebirds in America. The snipe is also known through euphemisms: "snipe hunt" and "gutter snipe" are familiar terms, and the word "sniper" was doubtless used first to describe a man skilled enough with a gun to hit such erratic fliers. (Even in the old days, the snipe was a favorite among sportsmen; it was not only abundant and widespread but due to its hardihood was an available target the greater part of the year, being common throughout the winter in the southern states. Careful records kept from 1867 to 1887 by James J. Pringle, a southern gentleman of Louisiana, indicate a personal bag of 69,087 snipe, plus several thousand other birds "killed incidentally." Since many gunners consider the snipe the most difficult of all gamebirds to bring down, these figures bear stern witness to Mr. Pringle's prowess as well as to snipe prosperity: Pringle notes one splendid day when over the space of six hours the snipe fell to his gun at better than one a minute. To achieve his records, Mr. Pringle employed two beaters, a marker, and one or two retrievers, though "I shot with only one gun at a time; had no loader, but loaded my gun myself.")

The snipe is a quite common bird even today, but the average person, lacking a taste for marshy ground and "snipe bogs," does not often see one. The shorebirds actually *seen* most often are probably the killdeer and the spotted sandpiper, not only because they are common, but because, in more seasons than not, they may be found almost everywhere throughout the land. Unlike the woodcock, which eats earthworms almost exclusively, or the jaçana, with its specialized lily-pad habitat, both killdeer and spotted sandpiper can and will make do with a wide variety of foods, climates, local conditions, and companions. This tolerance is based on a capacity for dispersal over a wide range of habitats that is the key to general distribution.

The killdeer, alone among North American ring plovers, has a shrill and strident cry, *kill-dee, kill-dee,* that has earned it both its common name and the species name *vociferous.* Its voice, which may be heard in day or night, is a familiar one to the majority of rural inhabitants of the Americas, since the killdeer nests in a variety of localities from southern Canada to northern Chile: this range is matched only by the American oystercatcher which, nesting on both coasts of the United States, south into Chile and the Argentine, has the longest latitudinal breeding range of any shorebird in the Americas.

The killdeer's flexibility accounts for its irregular migration pattern; it migrates, that is, as conditions warrant, and where life suits it all year around, it does not migrate at all. From the northern part of its range, it flies southward far enough to escape the snow, returning in spring almost as early as the red-winged blackbird. It is willing to nest on roof tops or next to the railroad tracks of man, and is partial to cleared and cultivated ground; in communities where it is common, "it is difficult to get beyond reach of its notes."

Similarly, the spotted sandpiper has a vast breeding range, extending from northwest Alaska to Texas and North Carolina, and will make its home with equal aplomb at sea level or at 14,000 feet. This jaunty bird sets forth into the world straight from the egg, and if pursued, even at the tender age of several hours, will step smartly to the water and swim away. The adult swims as readily as a phalarope, and dives readily, as the phalarope cannot; in shallow water, if it pleases, "it can go to the bottom and run a short distance with head held low and tail raised like a Dipper," before its buoyancy restores it to the surface. (True underwater locomotion is uncommon among shorebirds, but almost all of them will dive and "swim" if wounded or pursued; a marbled godwit has been seen to dive to escape a peregrine falcon, and snipe and other species will cling to the bottom with their bills, like wounded ducks. The jaçana, ever an exception, clings to the bottom with its feet.)

The dipper, like the spotted sandpiper, also feeds along water margins *and also teeters;* so do the water thrushes and the wagtails. (The wagtails frequent dry places as well.) The similarity of habit and habitat in species so unrelated is a striking example of parallel evolution, and surely the purpose of the teeter is common to all: the most interesting hypothesis yet put forward is that the teetering or "tipping" causes the hunting or hiding bird to "blend into the lapping wavelets and the play of light and shadow they create on shore."

Among the many attainments of the spotted sandpiper is its ability to fly straight up out of the water, or for that matter, fly straight *into* it if pursued while aloft, using its wings to continue its flight beneath the surface. It seems inevitable that such a dynamic and successful bird should have an air-bubble adaptation which not only keeps its feathers dry but gives it an attractive sparkle as it promenades over the bottom.

Part Two

IMPACTS AND COMPENSATIONS

The Swamp Lands Act

As it was passed in 1849, the federal Swamp Lands Act applied only to the inundated lands of Louisiana, but the policy was extended to the rest of the states the following year. The upshot of it was to sell lands "subject to overflow and unfit for cultivation" for the price of "reclaiming" them. Throughout American history most reclamation—about 80 percent—has been aimed at making land suitable for agriculture.

CHAP. LXXXVII.—*An Act to aid the State of Louisiana in draining the Swamp Lands therein.*

Be it enacted by the Senate and House of Representatives of the United States of America in Congress assembled, That to aid the State of Louisiana in constructing the necessary levees and drains to reclaim the swamp and overflowed lands therein, the whole of those swamp and overflowed lands, which may be or are found unfit for cultivation, shall be, and the same are hereby, granted to that State.

SEC. 2. *And be it further enacted,* That as soon as the Secretary of the Treasury shall be advised, by the Governor of Louisiana, that that State has made the necessary preparation to defray the expenses thereof, he shall cause a personal examination to be made, under the direction of the surveyor-general thereof, by experienced and faithful deputies, of all the swamp lands therein which are subject to overflow and unfit for cultivation; and a list of the same to be made out, and certified by the deputies and surveyor-general, to the Secretary of the Treasury, who shall approve the same, so far as they are not claimed or held by individuals; and on that approval, the fee simple to said lands shall vest in the said State of Louisiana, subject to the disposal of the legislature thereof: *Provided, however,* That the proceeds of said lands shall be applied exclusively, as far as necessary, to the construction of the levees and drains aforesaid.

SEC. 3. *And be it further enacted,* That in making out a list of these swamp lands, subject to overflow and unfit for cultivation, all legal subdivisions, the greater part of which is of that character, shall be included in said list; but when the greater part of a subdivision is not of that character, the whole of it shall be excluded therefrom: *Provided, however,* That the provisions of this act shall not apply to any lands fronting on rivers, creeks, bayous, watercourses, &c., which have been surveyed into lots or tracts under the acts of third March, eighteen hundred and eleven, and twenty-fourth May, eighteen hundred and twenty-four: *And provided, further,* That the United States shall in no manner be held liable for any expense incurred in selecting these lands and making out the lists thereof, or for making any surveys that may be required to carry out the provisions of this act.

APPROVED, March 2, 1849.

Uncle Mumford Unloads

Mark Twain

Mark Twain rarely found himself at a loss for words, but apparently there was at least one subject that deserved a sort of invective he didn't feel up to: the efforts of the River Commission, forerunner of today's Army Corps of Engineers, to tame the Mississippi. So he called on Uncle Mumford to take over. When Mumford's tirade had run its course, however, Twain himself expressed his own ambivalence about "Mississippi Improvement."

This is the second passage from *Life on the Mississippi* in this book; the first begins on page 65.

All day we swung along down the river, and had the stream almost wholly to ourselves. Formerly, at such a stage of the water, we should have passed acres of lumber rafts, and dozens of big coal barges; also occasional little trading-scows, peddling along from farm to farm, with the peddler's family on board; possibly a random scow, bearing a humble Hamlet and Co. on an itinerant dramatic trip. But these were all absent. Far along in the day we saw one steamboat; just one, and no more. She was lying at rest in the shade, within the wooded mouth of the Obion River. The spyglass revealed the fact that she was named for me—or *he* was named for me, whichever you prefer. As this was the first time I had ever encountered this species of honor, it seems excusable to mention it, and at the same time call the attention of the authorities to the tardiness of my recognition of it.

Noted a big change in the river at Island 21. It was a very large island, and used to lie out toward midstream; but it is joined fast to the main shore now, and has retired from business as an island.

As we approached famous and formidable Plum Point darkness fell, but that was nothing to shudder about—in these modern times. For now the national Government has turned the Mississippi into a sort of two-thousand-mile torchlight procession. In the head of every crossing, and in the foot of every crossing, the Government has set up a clear-burning lamp. You are never entirely in the dark, now; there is always a beacon in sight, either before you, or behind you, or abreast. One might almost say that lamps have been squandered there. Dozens of crossings are lighted which were not shoal when they were created, and have never been shoal since; crossings so plain, too, and also so straight, that a steamboat can take herself through them without any help, after she has been through once. Lamps in such places are of course not wasted; it is much more convenient and comfortable for a pilot to hold on them than on a spread of formless blackness that won't stay still; and money is saved to the boat, at the same time, for she can of course make more miles with her rudder amidships than she can with it squared across her stern and holding her back.

But this thing has knocked the romance out of piloting, to a large extent. It and some other things together have knocked all the romance out of it. For instance, the peril from snags is not now what it once was. The Government's snag-boats go patrolling up and down, in these matter-of-fact days, pulling the river's teeth; they have rooted out all the old clusters which made many localities so formidable; and they allow no new ones to collect. Formerly, if your boat got away from you, on a black night, and broke for the woods, it was an anxious time with you; so was it, also, when you were groping your way through solidified darkness in a narrow chute, but all that is changed now—you flash out your electric light, transform night into day in the twinkling of an eye, and your perils and anxieties are at an end. Horace Bixby and George Ritchie have charted the crossings and laid out the courses by compass; they have invented a lamp to go with the chart, and have patented the whole. With these helps, one may run in the fog now, with considerable security, and with a confidence unknown in the old days.

With these abundant beacons, and the banishment of snags, plenty of daylight in a box and ready to be turned on whenever needed, and a chart compass to fight the fog with, piloting, at a good stage of water, is now nearly as safe and simple as driving stage, and is hardly more than three times as romantic.

And now, in these new days of infinite change, the Anchor Line have raised the captain above the pilot by giving him the bigger wages of the two. This was going far, but they have not stopped there. They have decreed that the pilot shall remain at his post, and stand his watch clear through, whether the boat be under way or tied up to the shore. We, that were once the aristocrats of the river, can't go to bed now, as we used to do, and sleep while a hundred tons of freight are lugged aboard; no, we must sit in the pilot-house; and keep awake, too. Verily we are being treated like a parcel of mates and engineers. The Government has taken away the romance of our calling; the Company has taken away its state and dignity.

Plum Point looked as it had always looked by night, with the exception that now there were beacons to mark the crossings, and also a lot of other lights on the Point and along its shore; these latter glinting from the fleet of the United States River Commission, and from a village which the officials have built on the land for offices and for the employés of the service. The military engineers of the Commission have taken upon their shoulders the job of making the Mississippi over again—a job transcended in size by only the original job of creating it. They are building wing-dams here and there, to deflect the current; and dikes to confine it in narrower bounds; and other dikes to make it stay there; and for unnumbered miles along the Mississippi they are felling the timber-front for fifty yards back, with the purpose of shaving the bank down to lower-water mark with the slant of a house-roof, and ballasting it with stones; and in many places they have protected the wasting shores with rows of piles. One who knows the Mississippi will promptly aver—not aloud but to himself—that ten thousand River Commissions, with the mines of the world at their back, cannot tame that lawless stream, cannot curb it or confine it, cannot say to it, "Go here," or "Go there," and make it obey; cannot save a shore which it has sentenced; cannot bar its path with an obstruction which it will not tear down, dance over, and laugh at. But a discreet man will not put these things into spoken words; for the West Point engineers have not their superiors anywhere; they know all that can be known of their abstruse science; and so since they conceive that they can fetter and handcuff that river and boss him, it is but wisdom for the unscientific man to keep still, lie low, and wait till they do it. Captain Eads, with his jetties, has done a work at the mouth of the Mississippi which seemed clearly impossible; so we do not feel full confidence now to prophesy against like impossibilities. Otherwise one would pipe out and say the Commission might as well bully the comets in their courses and undertake to make them behave, as try to bully the Mississippi into right and reasonable conduct.

I consulted Uncle Mumford concerning this and cognate matters; and I give here the result, stenographically reported, and therefore to relied on as being full and correct; except that I have here and there left out remarks which were addressed to the men, such as "*Where* in blazes are you going with that barrel now?" and which seemed to me to break the flow of the written statement, without compensating by adding to its information or its clearness. Not that I have ventured to strike out all such interjections; I have removed only those which were obviously irrelevant; wherever one occurred which I felt any question about, I have judged it safest to let it remain.

UNCLE MUMFORD'S IMPRESSIONS

Uncle Mumford said:

"As long as I have been mate of a steamboat—thirty years—I have watched this river and studied it. Maybe I could have learned more about it at West Point, but if I believe it I wish I may be WHAT *are you sucking your fingers there for?—Collar that kag of nails!* Four years at West Point, and plenty of books and schooling, will learn a man a good deal, I reckon, but it won't learn him the river. You turn one of those little European rivers over this Commission, with its hard bottom and clear water, and it would just be a holiday job for them to wall it, and pile it, and dike it, and tame it down, and boss it around, and make it go wherever they wanted it to, and stay where they put it, and do just as they said, every time. But this ain't that kind of a river. They have started in here with a big confidence, and the best intentions in the world; but they are going to get left. What does Ecclesiastes vii.13 say? Says enough to knock *their* little game galley-west, don't it? Now you look at their methods once. There at Devil's Island, in the Upper River, they wanted the water to go one way, the water wanted to go another. So they put up a stone wall. But what does the river care for a stone wall? When it got ready, it just bulged through it. Maybe they can build another that will stay; that is, up there—but not down here they can't. Down here in the Lower River, they drive some pegs to turn the water away from the shore and stop it from slicing off the bank; very well, don't it go straight over and cut somebody else's bank? Certainly. Are they going to peg *all* the banks? Why, they could buy ground and build a new Mississippi cheaper. They are pegging Bulletin Tow-head now. It won't do any good. If the river has got a mortgage on that island, it will foreclose, sure; pegs or no pegs. Away down yonder, they have driven two rows of piles straight through the middle of a dry bar half a mile long, which is forty foot out of the water when the river is low. What do you reckon that is for? If I know, I wish I may land in HUMP *yourself, you son of an undertaker!—out with that coal-oil, now, lively,* LIVELY! And just look at what they are trying to do down there at Milliken's Bend. There's been a cut-off in that section, and Vicksburg is left out in the cold. It's a country town now. The river strikes in below it; and a boat can't go up to the town except in high water. Well, they are going to build wing-dams in the bend opposite the foot of 103, and throw the water over and cut off the foot of the island and plow down into an old ditch where the river used to be in ancient times; and they think they can persuade the water around that way, and get it to strike in above

Vicksburg, as it used to do, and fetch the town back into the world again. That is, they are going to take this whole Mississippi, and twist it around and make it run several miles *up stream*. Well, you've got to admire men that deal in ideas of that size and can tote them around without crutches; but you haven't got to believe they can *do* such miracles, have you? And yet you ain't absolutely obliged to believe they can't. I reckon the safe way, where a man can afford it, is to *copper* the operation, and at the same time buy enough property in Vicksburg to square you up in case they win. Government is doing a deal for the Mississippi, now—spending loads of money on her. When there used to be four thousand steamboats and ten thousand acres of coal-barges, and rafts, and trading-scows, there wasn't a lantern from St. Paul to New Orleans, and the snags were thicker than bristles on a hog's back; and now, when there's three dozen steamboats and nary barge or raft, Government has snatched out all the snags, and lit up the shores like Broadway, and a boat's as safe on the river as she'd be in heaven. And I reckon that by the time there ain't any boats left at all, the Commission will have the old thing all reorganized, and dredged out, and fenced in, and tidied up, to a degree that will make navigation just simply perfect, and absolutely safe and profitable; and all the days will be Sundays, and all the mates will be Sunday-school suWHAT-*in-the-nation-you-fooling-around-there-for, you sons of unrighteousness, heirs of perdition! Going to be a* YEAR *getting that hogshead ashore?*"

During our trip to New Orleans and back, we had many conversations with river men, planters, journalists, and officers of the River Commission—with conflicting and confusing results. To wit:

1. Some believed in the Commission's scheme to arbitrarily and permanently confine (and thus deepen) the channel, preserve threatened shores, etc.
2. Some believed that the Commission's money ought to be

spent only on building and repairing the great system of levees.

3. Some believed that the higher you build your levee, the higher the river's bottom will rise; and that consequently the levee system is a mistake.

4. Some believed in the scheme to relieve the river, in flood-time, by turning its surplus waters off into Lake Borgne, etc.

5. Some believed that the scheme of northern lake-reservoirs to replenish the Mississippi in low-water seasons.

Whenever you find a man down there who believes in one of these theories you may turn to the next man and frame your talk upon the hypothesis that he does *not* believe in that theory; and after you have had experience, you do not take this course doubtfully or hesitatingly, but with the confidence of a dying murderer—converted one, I mean. For you will have come to know, with a deep and restful certainty, that you are not going to meet two people sick of the same theory, one right after the other. No, there will always be one or two with the other diseases along between. And as you proceed, you will find out one or two other things. You will find out that there is no distemper of the lot but is contagious; and you cannot go where it is without catching it. You may vaccinate yourself with deterrent facts as much as you please—it will do no good; it will seem to "take," but it doesn't; the moment you rub against any one of those theorists, make up your mind that it is time to hang out your yellow flag.

Yes, you are his sure victim: yet his work is not all to your hurt—only part of it; for he is like your family physician, who comes and cures the mumps, and leaves the scarlet fever behind. If your man is a Lake-Borgne-relief theorist, for instance, he will exhale a cloud of deadly facts and statistics which will lay you out with that disease, sure; but at the same time he will cure you of any other of the five theories that may have previously got into your system.

I have had all the five; and had them "bad"; but ask me not, in mournful numbers, which one racked me hardest, or which one numbered the biggest sick list, for I do not know. In truth, no one can answer the latter question. Mississippi Improvement is a mighty topic, down yonder. Every man on the river banks, south of Cairo, talks about it every day, during such moments as he is able to spare from talking about the war; and each of the several chief theories has its host of zealous partisans; but, as I have said, it is not possible to determine which cause numbers the most recruits.

All were agreed upon one point, however: if Congress would make a sufficient appropriation, a colossal benefit would result. Very well; since then the appropriation has been made—possibly a sufficient one, certainly not too large a one. Let us hope that the prophecy will be amply fulfilled. . . .

Sometimes half a dozen figures will reveal, as with a lightning-flash, the importance of a subject which ten thousand labored words, with the same purpose in view, had left at last but dim and uncertain. Here is a case of the sort—paragraph from the *Cincinnati Commercial*:

The towboat *Jos. B. Williams* is on her way to New Orleans with a tow of thirty-two barges, containing six hundred thousand bushels (seventy-six pounds to the bushel) of coal exclusive of her fuel, being the largest tow ever taken to New Orleans or anywhere else in the world. Her freight bill, at three cents a bushel, amounts to $18,000. It would take eighteen hundred cars, of three hundred and thirty-three bushels to the car, to transport this amount of coal. At $10 per ton, or $100 per car, which would be a fair price for the distance by rail, the freight bill would amount to $180,000, or $162,000 more by rail than by river. The tow will be taken from Pittsburg to New Orleans in fourteen or fifteen days. It would take one hundred trains of eighteen cars to the train to transport this one tow of six hundred thousand bushels of coal, and even if it made the usual speed of fast freight lines, it would take one whole summer to put it through by rail.

When a river in good condition can enable one to save $162,000, and a whole summer's time, on a single cargo, the wisdom of taking measures to keep the river in good condition is made plain to even the uncommercial mind.

Our Great Reclamation Problem

Edward F. Adams

Nowhere has the manipulation of water been more intensely contested than in California. Today the concern is over apportionment to wildlife, ever-sprawling cities, and the most productive agriculture in the world. In 1904, however, getting excess water out of the way was viewed as the problem, and a speaker at San Francisco's Commonwealth Club reported that state policies for implementing the federal Swamp Lands Act were a hopeless muddle. One consequence was certain, however; ownership of reclaimed land was trending toward a wealthy few.

It is noteworthy that the gold-mining operations that brought boom times to California exacerbated the reclamation problem. In the Sierra, slopes were blasted away with water cannons to release the gold, and the slurry flowed into the rivers and sloughs of the Central Valley and on into the immense network of channels meandering through the backwaters of San Francisco Bay. As the silt settled out, it obliterated some channels and forced the flow elsewhere, rapidly changing the face of the landscape and frustrating attempts to establish riparian rights.

The Swamp and Overflowed Lands of the Sacramento and Lower San Joaquin.

At the meeting of the Club held on May 11th, 1904, the following paper was read by Edward F. Adams and referred to the Section of Commercial Interests:

I have heard of the managing editor of an important daily journal who regarded it as an essential prerequisite to the production of a good editorial that the writer should know nothing whatever about his subject, because he would then write without any prejudices. Having looked at over ninety of the statutes which the Legislature has passed in relation to the reclamation of swamp and overflowed lands—and I do not doubt that a good many got away—and fifty-four sections of the Political Code dealing with the subject, and read a good many of both; visited some of the "reclaimed" islands and basin lands in summer, and gazed over the waters flowing over them in the winter; read all the official and other reports dealing with the subject which I could get hold of, and carefully examined the accompanying maps; and last and worst, looked over the digests of all the decisions of our Supreme Court—and read many of them—which have been made in the course of the innumerable lawsuits which have grown out of our attempts at reclamation—there are eighty-seven cases cited, if I have counted straight, in the latest edition of the Political Code—I am of the opinion that I should satisfy the requirements of that managing editor. In the present condition of the reclamation service I am convinced that the more one studies it the less he will know about it, for he will be lost in a morass of infinite detail. . . .

HISTORY OF RECLAMATION LEGISLATION TO 1868.

With the foregoing statement of the problem to be dealt with, and the magnitude of the interests involved, and the legal and equitable obligations resting upon the State and upon the land owners, we may proceed to examine the manner in which the State has discharged its trust. The Legislature has enacted a large number of Statutes dealing with the subject. A summary of the essential features of those which have determined for the time being the varying policies of the State follows, with a brief statement of the administrative work under them.

I. Act approved May 1st, 1851. (Page 409, Statutes [of] 1851.)

Granted 640 acres of Swamp land on Merritt Island to John F. Booth and David Galloway, provided they should reclaim the land, bring it under cultivation and report results to Legislature. Unless this was accomplished within three years, the Act to be void.

I find no record of anything done under this Act, and presume further search would disclose only a more or less interesting story of misfortune.

II. Act approved April 28th, 1855. (Page 189, Statutes of 1855.)

Allowed Swamp lands to be taken up for $1.00 per acre, with no agreement to reclaim, or upon credit of five years with obligation to reclaim one-half within five years or forfeit claim. No provision for any reclamation fund; tide lands and lands within certain distances of specified cities excepted from operation of Act. Limit to be sold to one person, 320 acres.

III. Act approved April 21, 1858. (Page 198, Statutes of 1858.)

Swamp lands allowed to be taken up at $1.00 per acre, cash, with no agreement to reclaim, and title to be patent equivalent to a quitclaim deed. Limit to one person, 320 acres. Proceeds to be paid into a State Reclamation Fund. No salt marsh to be taken up for six months except by owners of adjoining "arable" land, except in Counties of Napa, Solano, Yolo, Contra Costa and San Joaquin. Lands near certain cities excepted from operation of Act. Act of 1855 repealed.

In this Act there is by the creation of a "Reclamation Fund" Statutory evidence that the Legislature recognized that the State had an obligation to reclaim the land.

IV. Act approved April 18th, 1859. (Page 340, Statutes of 1859.)

Amended Act of 1858 by increasing the limit permitted to be taken by one person from 320 to 640 acres. Price $1.00 per acre, or 20 per cent. cash, balance on five years. Limitations to one-half mile of frontage on any navigable stream or bay. Land to be taxable after purchase. Proceeds to go to State Reclamation Funds. No agreement to reclaim required.

This Act was in force until 1861, and like the Acts of 1855 and 1858 imposed no obligation on purchasers to reclaim. The patents issued were the equivalent to a quit-claim deed of the State. This would apparently leave them, however, subject to the obligation to reclaim, the State simply transferring its responsibility, so far as it could do so, to the purchasers. Either these laws were not attractive, or the State was not ready for reclamation work, as but a small amount of land was sold, and that, presumably, where reclamation was easy. I have not deemed it worth while to ascertain the amount of land sold under these Acts in the district under consideration.

V. Act approved May 13th, 1861. (Page 355, Statutes of 1861.)

J. C. Pemberton, William J. Horton, B. B. Redding, T. T. Bouldin and A. M. Winn appointed [as] Board of Reclamation Commissioners to hold office for two years and until their successors were elected by the Legislature in joint session. Upon a petition of owners of one-third the acreage of any tract of swamp or overflowed lands "capable of reclamation in one body" Reclamation Commissioners to cause their Engineer to survey and make plans and estimates, and if probable cost appear not to exceed $1.00 per acre, plus any sums which may have been subscribed and paid in, to advertise for bids and let contracts. Any existing works found available to be accepted and paid for. Authority granted to enter upon lands without consent of owners. No district organization provided, but contiguous basins of land to be reclaimed are spoken of in the Act as in subsequent Acts as "Districts". . . .

THE LAW OF 1868.

VIII. Act approved March 28th, 1868. (Page 507, Statutes of 1868.)

This is the Act creating regular reclamation Districts, and in the main is still in force. It repealed all previous Acts for the disposal of swamp lands or in any respect conflicting with this Act. It is a general Act for the disposal of all Swamp lands.

This Act continued the price of the Swamp lands at $1.00 per acre, 20 per cent. cash, balance one year after call by Legislature, with no limit to the amount to be taken by one person. It permitted County Treasurers to retain proceeds of Swamp lands sold within the County for "County Swamp Land Fund" subject to disposal by Boards of Supervisors. Bonds or warrants of reclamation Districts were made receivable for lands within the District. Frontage on navigable water was restricted to one-quarter mile, and 90 days were allowed for owners of arable lands to file preferential claims on swamp or overflowed lands adjoining. Reclamation Districts could be organized on petition of one-half or more of the owners of any body of reclaimable land, said Districts to be created by Boards of Supervisors upon proof of regularity of proceedings. Each District was to elect three Trustees, and By-Laws were to be signed by owners of at least one-half the land within the District. Trustees were to certify cost of proposed improvements to Supervisors, who must appoint Commissioners to assess benefits and damages. Land owners who have paid up were to be credited with 80 cents per acre payable from the State or County reclamation fund. Owners who are unanimous in so desiring might proceed to reclaim without intervention of Trustees and might receive their 80 cents per acre from the reclamation fund. When a District has been formed, all new purchasers of land from the State are members of the District and subject to its By-Laws. Owners whose land is capable of "independent" reclamation may have their land set off at any time before complete reclamation, providing the District is not in debt. Swamp lands within one mile of San Quentin Prison or within five miles of Oakland or San Francisco are excepted from the operation of the Act.

This Act placed the entire management of reclamation work in the hands of the District Trustees and required the Boards of Supervisors to levy upon the District such assessments as the Trustees might certify to be necessary for reclamation work. While repealing all previous laws, it re-enacted their essential provisions so far as they were applicable to a condition of local control. In the main this remains the law today. Of course, there have been many amendments and previous to the adoption of the present Constitution there were a multitude of special laws applying to particular Districts. The present condition of the law may be seen by reference to Sections 3440 to 3493½, Political Code. While the State has expended a good deal of money in reclamation, and for some years, as will be seen, maintained a State Engineer, and now maintains a Commissioner of Public Works, both of whom have concerned themselves with reclamation works, no attempt has been made to exercise any effective control over the Districts, which are to-day as independent of each other, and of the State, as ever. The State money has been expended by State Officials, but it has been supplementary to the work of the Districts.

In this connection it is important to note that no "vested rights" as against the State have accrued to any Reclamation District. The Supreme Court has held that the State has not granted any swamp land to Counties, but has merely made Counties and County Officials agencies of the State for purposes of reclamation, and the State may alter or amend the laws relating to the subject at pleasure. (Kings County vs. County of Tulare, 119 Cal., Page 509.)

So long as the law permitted only 320 acres to be purchased by one person, very little land was taken up in the river district, and that, presumably, on the higher lands. Some more was taken when a purchase of 640 acres was permitted, but it was not until all limits were removed by the Act of 1861, and what was thought to be a workable plan of reclamation was provided by the Act of 1868, that the lands really began to go. It was evidently impossible for owners of half a section in the river district to do any effective "reclaiming," and equally impossible for a large number of small owners to agree upon any plan or to provide the money. Since the State would not undertake the work, it must be done, if at all, by men of large means, co-operating with each other. While this law has been much abused, as opening the way to "land monopoly," it was the only way by which there was any possibility of reclaiming the lands by private enterprise.

The Inside Story of Ducks Unlimited

Harold Titus

While most people still believed that the only good swamp was a reclaimed swamp, an oddly named fraternity of duck hunters realized the urgency of preserving wetland habitat and quickly fashioned itself into a transnational influence. Ducks Unlimited was founded in the 1930s, when the immediate concern was the prolonged drought in the vast prairie region of the United States and Canada that coincided with the Great Depression. This article ran in *Field and Stream* magazine in 1942. Today Ducks Unlimited manages over five million acres of wetlands in Canada and also has a presence in Mexico.

In recent years, every American duck hunter who didn't want to risk having John Law jerk him out of his blind and lug him into court has paid his Federal Government one dollar in addition to all other licenses and levies. This dollar went to defray the costs of restoring and administering waterfowl breeding, feeding and resting areas in the United States which had been impaired by drought, drainage or abuse.

Few begrudged the assessment. The duck-restoration program has met with lusty support, and most gunners take a proprietary pride in the string of projects that today produce ducks where, in the desperately dry 'thirties, few if any ducks were to be found.

But since 1938 some 20,000 duck hunters—besides paying their American dollar to their American Government for American duck restoration—have been sending well over $100,000 annually across the Canadian border for the purpose of doing exactly the same thing on the vast reaches of prairie provinces. For it is there that the greatest concentration of nesting ducks on the continent has prevailed. . . .

Look back to 1928. That is when rainfall commenced to slacken in western Canada, where ducks by the million had nested since man can remember. Subsoil moisture, however, was sufficient to hold the water-table up until 1930. Then it started to drop, and went down like an express elevator.

Ducks, winging northward in April, found pleasant prairies in Manitoba, Saskatchewan and Alberta. That is, they looked pleasant. Winter run-off had freshened grass roots, water had collected in depressions and glinted blue, and the land was greening under the brilliant sun.

Ducks couldn't look beneath the surface. They couldn't see those parched strata just inches under the top, sucking up that transient moisture. So they picked a likely-looking place—perhaps a place where generations of their ancestors had nested—and started doing business.

So did the sun start doing business. The average mean summer temperature of these provinces has gone up 4½ degrees in the last fifty years, which hastens evaporation. Between the pull from below and the draw from above the meager water supplies disappeared.

Before the water disappeared, however, eggs had started to hatch. Downy ducklings paddled in skimpy puddles, feeding on the abundant animal organisms that nature provides for their kind in such places. And before feathers had replaced the down, the puddles had shrunk to pools in cattle tracks; and before the young could fly, those cow tracks had blown away, and that meant disaster.

Across the prairie started the broods, putting one webbed footlet in front of the other in a brave trek for that element which ducks must have or perish. The food they had to have wasn't available on the way. Small bones and muscles weakened. Cactus spines penetrated tender throats, bellies and feet, and took hold to stay. In the end a distracted hen lay down and died beside the last of her offspring.

Not a pretty picture, lads! It's one that goes deeper than your interest in a supply of something to shoot at. It's one that excited a great many persons besides duck hunters. It's one that was a natural for the starting of an organization like Ducks Unlimited.

There was Canada, principal breeding ground for North America's ducks, but without men or money to tackle the job of nesting-ground restoration. And here was the United States, where the great bulk of that Canadian duck crop is harvested. Here were enough hunters, with dimes to spare, to finance a large-scale drive in an effort to rectify what nature had done to those Northern prairie sloughs and lakes. Bringing the two together meant action, and that's what was done.

"Sure, there were other things than drought to be considered," says Tom Main, Canadian manager for Ducks Unlimited. "There was drainage and the fire problem and predators and disease. But first of all came the problem of water. Ducks could put up with a lot of the other bad influences, but they just had to have water!"

Tom Main, by the way, is no biologist or ornithologist. He is an engineer, on leave from a great Canadian railway system where he has practiced his profession through most of his active life. His branch of engineering has to do with water, and his experience has always been almost exclusively with prairie water. He's as much at home in a slough as a duck!

"But it wasn't just *any* water we had to have," says Tom. "It was strategic water. It had to be water that ducks had used—the right kind of water in the right place. This meant that it had to be so situated that ducks could nest within waddling distance, and of sufficient depth to last against the forces of evaporation until the ducks hatched in range of it and could get up and get out under their own wing power and look for more."

How many ducks perished because strategic water wasn't available during the big drought—which, by the way, is still current on the prairies, though not so severe as it was a decade ago—will never be known. How many ducks have been saved by Ducks Unlimited is another question that may never be answered beyond challenge.

But Tom Main, being an engineer, got busy on some mathematical equations with one hand while with the other he sketched out dams and revetments and what-not. Some biologists raise a skeptical eyebrow when Tom gets into his duck mathematics, and, of course, there's a chance that in time he may want to alter his conceptions of what has and may happen. At the moment, he'll defend his computations for any and all; and if you're in a mood to challenge his facts or logic just go prepared, brother; just go prepared!

In 1940, says Tom, the Ducks Unlimited census showed that 40,000,000 ducks returned to the Canadian West from their wintering grounds. Keep that in mind, 40,000,000: with a sex ratio of six drakes to four females, which leaves just forty nesting pairs out of every hundred. Figures show that perhaps 20 per cent of the ducks are infertile. Granting this, you have only thirty-two nesting pairs for that same hundred.

Observation has convinced Ducks Unlimited that the average clutch for all species is 8.5 eggs, which would give a potential crop of 272 ducklings for every hundred adults that came back north. Blow those figures up to the 40,000,000 breeders that we started talking about, and it indicates 109,000,000 young ducks, which would make a good raft on any man's favorite ground!

Before young ducks can raft, however, pre-migration losses must be reckoned. In 1940, Ducks Unlimited estimated that 73.5 per cent perished on the breeding areas. In figures, that's around 80,000,000 birds. Those totals take your breath, and they are the ones that make some game administrators reach for their pencils and tell Tom to hold on a minute.

Tom Main declares that drought destroys 22,000,000 ducks in Canada each year. Twenty-two *million!* That's two and a half times what American gunners bag normally. It's the big item, but only the starter. Crows and magpies, Ducks Unlimited contends, account for upward of 16,000,000 each season. These figures were arrived at by studying sample areas and using the multiplication table, and are certainly the highest on record.

Jackfish—northern pike, pickerel or whatever they are called in your locality—take another 9,000,000 or thereabouts. Minor predators are believed by Main's staff to do away with 8,000,000. Then there's fire licking away in marshes and muskeg, and it's blamed for a loss of 13,000,000, while flooding, land abuse and other minor factors get another dozen million.

So, for 1940, Ducks Unlimited reckoned a net crop of 29,000,000 young, and that, added to the 40,000,000 censused in the spring, gave an expected August population of 69,000,000 for the whole area. Another census, in that month, turned up a total of 71,000,000.

"The percentages of increase and loss," Main reports, "are based upon the facts as indicated by present information. As further data are available we shall, of course, amend our duck mathematics as indicated."

No doubt, debate over the validity of these data will go on for a long time. Perhaps Ducks Unlimited stuck its neck out by being so specific. It won't matter a great deal to the average hunter. Slice the estimated losses in two, and he would still be in a sweat. In that debate may the best man win, and as it starts let's have a look at a brace of nesting areas that went sour and came back when Ducks Unlimited started to work.

In late July, 1938, Tom Main visited Many Island Lake, near Medicine Hat. Normally it held 8,000 acres of water. It was down to 30. That's right—30! Tom estimated that 100,000 ducks were trying to use that puddle and making no go of it. They were dying by the thousands in that one area alone.

Rescue work was started—a fine, humane gesture, but of small practical value even with the best of luck. Less than 800 ducks were transferred to good water, and the rest went up in smoke. Literally. Carcasses were gathered and burned! Two months later DU had a dam built there which would back up 2,300 acres of permanent water from the spring run-off, and Many Island is a duck factory again. Tom needs no projected curves of expected gains or losses to make a job like that look desirable.

Then there's Netley Marsh, at the south end of Lake Winnipeg. It comprises 50,000 acres of public land, and the estimate is that half a million ducks, mostly redheads, nest there annually. But Netley Marsh grew hay for which there was a demand. Hay rights had been leased by the municipality for many years. And every spring the lessees burned it off slick to insure a weed-clean crop. That is, they did every spring until 1939. By May, you see, a goodly proportion of those redheads had nested, and fire meant that many were lost and all had to start laying again. Of course, a duck's time isn't worth a whale of a lot, but the joker was that haying always started about July 10. So with fire on one end of the season and hay harvest on the other, the ducks were in a fix to follow the cosmic urge and predators got the principal benefit of their efforts.

Ducks Unlimited went to work. It persuaded farmers to burn in April, before the ducks started nest building, and to burn under control. Out of its own funds it put in the fire breaks to make this possible. Later, with all concerned around a table—conservationists, farmers, municipal authorities—no cutting before July 25 was agreed on, giving the redheads another two weeks of grace. It costs Ducks Unlimited $400 a year to supervise that area, and such an amount, contrasted with the number of ducks using the marsh, is enough to convince the average dude that it's a sound investment.

One of the first obstacles which the outfit encountered on this side of the border was the objection to buying land in Canada with American dollars. Well, practically no land has been bought. Ducks Unlimited owns exactly 380 Canadian acres and boasts that, up to the fall of 1941, 960,940 acres of nesting areas, once stricken, have been rejuvenated.

The answer to this is easy: Canadian authorities, both provincial and Dominion, are cooperating like gears in a transmission. In the beginning it didn't seem that such a happy state of affairs could be brought to pass, which is another trouble that Ducks Unlimited had in its first years.

"Why," some Canadians asked, "should we let these folks from the States buy up our land and stop our shooting? They'll get 'em in migration, and we won't even have a smell!"

A natural suspicion, that, but it faded out when the neighbors learned that these reclaimed projects weren't sanctuaries at all unless they were established on acres that had already been so designated.

"We don't need sanctuaries up here," Tom Main explains. "Our ducks are on the wing before the season opens. Some hang around to get shot, sure; but our human population is thin. We don't have many duck hunters as you know them down below, and the annual kill is negligible. It's really no problem at all. A third of our improvement sites have no restrictions against gunning whatever."

With ordinary folks feeling better, then, authorities came along. As soon as Ducks Unlimited puts a new dam in any of the provinces, all the area it will serve—which means all the nesting ground within duckling travel—is forthwith covered by an order in council setting it aside in perpetuity for the propagation of wildlife. No individual or group has to own it then. It's safe. Forever.

To be sure, there are new dams and restored waters in localities where the guns simply can't go. Big Grass Marsh in Manitoba is an example. Here are 50,000 acres that had been grazed and cut since 1916, the rights being leased by the province. It was already a game preserve, so dedicated to safeguard range stock from careless guns. In 1938, Ducks Unlimited leased it for twenty years and banned wandering cattle and destructive cutting-bars, but the designation of game preserve remained. So guns are still prohibited.

But in discussing this job you can't keep off the item of water very long. Where a series of pot-holes or sloughs fills up each spring, attracts ducks and then dries out, the technique is not to attempt to keep them all filled. A piece of key water is selected by engineers and only enough dams built to make permanent water accessible to all broods in the vicinity. If nests are built on sloughs which will fade out in summer, the ducklings will still get along if they can make it to another which holds up. That's the yardstick. Can ducklings make it from nests to water? If not, the try is made to establish enough water nearer the nests.

So when Tom Main's men tell you they have this many improved acres, they do not mean flooded acres. They mean that sufficient water is available to take care of all the ducks that might nest on that area. The units vary all the way from a few hundred acres up to Gordon Lake project in Alberta, which has an area of 322,000 acres. . . .

Well, that's a part of the story. Seventy-five projects—thirty-five of them entailing dam construction which means an outlay of from $300 to $9,000 per unit—and nearly a million acres made into happier homes for ducks. This is a brave venture indeed. Much remains to be done, of course; the job has hardly been started. But Ducks Unlimited, with the handicaps of its beginnings overcome, appears to be a going concern that's here to stay.

The Clean Water Act

With passage of the 1972 Federal Water Pollution Control Act, better known as the Clean Water Act, the United States established a comprehensive program of regulations and permits to improve water quality. Some critics of subsequent enforcement of the law have contended that wetlands protection was not part of the original intent—for example, the act's reference to "navigable waters" was only later interpreted as "waters of the U.S."—but federal policies on wetlands have been based on the act's Section 404.

The legislation essentially gives responsibility for administering water quality policy to the Environmental Protection Agency (EPA), while turning over certain enforcement responsibilities to the Army Corps of Engineers (Corps). However, the agencies have overlapping, sometimes conflicting, jurisdictions. The act also provides the potential for states to take over regulatory responsibilities, which some have done.

Following are the most significant paragraphs of Section 404. References to the "Secretary" indicate the Secretary of the Army. "Administrator" refers to the EPA.

The next reading, "Guide to Wetlands Regulation," gives more detail on the development of specific wetlands policies. Updated information on federal policies and referrals to state and local contacts can be obtained by calling the EPA's wetlands hotline, 1-800-832-7828.

§1344. [FWPCA §404]

Permits for dredged or fill material

a. *Discharge into navigable waters at specified disposal sites*

The Secretary may issue permits, after notice and opportunity for public hearings for the discharge of dredged or fill material into the navigable waters at specified disposal sites. Not later than the fifteenth day after the date an applicant submits all the information required to complete an application for a permit under this subsection, the Secretary shall publish the notice required by this subsection.

b. *Specification for disposal sites*

Subject to subsection (c) of this section, each such disposal site shall be specified for each such permit by the Secretary (1) through the application of guidelines developed by the Administrator, in conjunction with the Secretary, which guidelines shall be based upon criteria comparable to the criteria applicable to the territorial seas, the contiguous zone, and the ocean under section 1343(c) of this title, and (2) in any case where such guidelines under clause (1) alone would prohibit the specification of a site, through the application additionally of the economic impact of the site on navigation and anchorage.

c. *Denial or restriction of use of defined areas as disposal sites*

The Administrator is authorized to prohibit the specification (including the withdrawal of specification) of any defined area as a disposal site, and he is authorized to deny or restrict the use of any defined area for specification (including the withdrawal of specification) as a disposal site, whenever he determines, after notice and opportunity for public hearings, that the discharge of such materials into such area will have an unacceptable adverse effect on municipal water supplies, shellfish beds and fishery areas (including spawning and breeding areas), wildlife, or recreational areas. Before making such determination, the Administrator shall consult with the Secretary. The Administrator shall set forth in writing and make public his findings and his reasons for making any determination under this subsection.

d. *"Secretary" defined*

The term "Secretary" as used in this section means the Secretary of the Army, acting through the Chief of Engineers.

e. *General permits on State, regional, or nationwide basis*

1. In carrying out his functions relating to the discharge of dredged or fill material under this section, the Secretary may, after notice and opportunity for public hearing, issue general permits on a State, regional, or nationwide basis for any category of activities involving discharges of dredged or fill mate-

rial if the Secretary determines that the activities in such category are similar in nature, will cause only minimal adverse environmental effects when performed separately, and will have only minimal cumulative adverse effect on the environment. Any general permit issued under this subsection shall (A) be based on the guidelines described in subsection (b)(1) of this section, and (B) set forth the requirements and standards which shall apply to any activity authorized by such general permit.

2. No general permit issued under this subsection shall be for a period of more than five years after the date of its issuance and such general permit may be revoked or modified by the Secretary if, after opportunity for public hearing, the Secretary determines that the activities authorized by such general permit have an adverse impact on the environment or such activities are more appropriately authorized by individual permits.

f. *Non-prohibited discharge of dredged or fill material*

1. Except as provided in paragraph (2) of this subsection, the discharge of dredged or fill material—

   A. from normal farming, silviculture, and ranching activities such as plowing, seeding, cultivating, minor drainage, harvesting for the production of food, fiber, and forest products, or upland soil and water conservation practices;

   B. for the purpose of maintenance, including emergency reconstruction of recently damaged parts, of currently serviceable structures such as dikes, dams, levees, groins, riprap, breakwaters, causeways, and bridge abutments or approaches, and transportation structures;

   C. for the purpose of construction or maintenance of farm or stock ponds or irrigation ditches, or the maintenance of drainage ditches;

D. for the purpose of construction of temporary sedimentation basins on a construction site which does not include placement of fill material into the navigable waters;

E. for the purpose of construction or maintenance of farm roads or forest roads, or temporary roads for moving mining equipment, where such roads are constructed and maintained, in accordance with best management practices, to assure that flow and circulation patterns and chemical and biological characteristics of the navigable waters are not impaired, that the reach of the navigable waters is not reduced, and that any adverse effect on the aquatic environment will be otherwise minimized;

F. resulting from any activity with respect to which a State has an approved program under section 1288(b)(4) of this title which meets the requirements of subparagraphs (B) and (C) of such section,

is not prohibited by or otherwise subject to regulation under this section or section 1311(a) or 1342 of this title (except for effluent standards or prohibitions under section 1317 of this title).

2. Any discharge of dredged or fill material into the navigable waters incidental to any activity having as its purpose bringing an area of the navigable waters into a use to which it was not previously subject, where the flow or circulation of navigable waters may be impaired or the reach of such waters be reduced, shall be required to have a permit under this section.

g. *State administration*

1. The Governor of any State desiring to administer its own individual and general permit program for the discharge of dredged or fill material into the navigable waters (other than those waters which are presently used, or are susceptible to

use in their natural condition or by reasonable improvement as a means to transport interstate or foreign commerce shoreward to their ordinary high water mark, including all waters which are subject to the ebb and flow of the tide shoreward to their mean high water mark, or mean higher high water mark on the west coast, including wetlands adjacent thereto) within its jurisdiction may submit to the Administrator a full and complete description of the program it proposes to establish and administer under State law or under an interstate compact. In addition, such State shall submit a statement from the attorney general (or the attorney for those State agencies which have independent legal counsel), or from the chief legal officer in the case of an interstate agency, that the laws of such State, or the interstate compact, as the case may be, provide adequate authority to carry out the described program.

Guide to Wetlands Regulation

David Ivester

Wetlands regulation has its basis in Section 404 of the Clean Water Act, although the act does not directly address wetlands. In this article, a land-use lawyer discusses the evolution of more specific wetlands policies which have developed via myriad channels and which are subject to ongoing modification. In the years since 1992, when an extended version of the article first appeared in the *Land Use Forum* of the Bar-California, the Corps has taken a more active role in regulating excavation and drainage of wetland areas. In addition, the National Resources Conservation Service, formerly the Soil Conservation

Service (SCS), a branch of the U.S. Department of Agriculture, has become the lead agency concerned with wetland delineations on agricultural lands.

The following abbreviations are used in this article: "USC" stands for United States Code; "Ops US Atty Gen" for Opinions of the U.S. Attorney General; "CFR" for Code of Federal Regulations; "Fed Reg" for Federal Register; "US" for United States Reports; "Pub L" for Public Law; "Stat" for U.S. Statutes at Large; and "HR" for House of Representatives bill.

Wetlands, long thought watery wastelands to be either avoided or drained for productive use, have recently come to be recognized as important, dwindling natural resources. Wetlands are now valued for their intrinsic qualities as natural areas, for their recreational and educational uses, and for their ecological services, *e.g.*, ground water recharge, floodpeak reduction, water quality improvement, wildlife habitat, food chain support, and shoreline stabilization. Although this change of attitude is perceptible in the popular press and public hearing rooms, so far it has prompted neither Congress nor the California Legislature to adopt comprehensive protective legislation.

In the backwaters of governmental agencies, however, the new attitude has produced a bewildering array of federal, state, and local regulatory schemes to control the use of wetlands. Sometimes the regulations are adopted with little public scrutiny. Often they overlap and conflict.

Much of the law governing wetlands is not readily available; some can be found in statutes, cases, and agency regulations, but much is buried in various agency documents—manuals, memoranda of agreement, regulatory guidance letters, and administrative decisions on individual permits or enforcement problems. The following is therefore provided as a primer on the primary federal agencies and regulatory programs dealing with wetlands.

Role of Federal Agencies

U.S. Army Corps of Engineers The U.S. Army Corps of Engineers (Corps) administers the most pervasive wetland regulatory program in the United States. The sources of its authority— the Clean Water Act and the Rivers and Harbors Act—are discussed below. A landowner may encounter the Corps' regulatory program in either of two ways: (1) the permit process, when the landowner seeks the Corps' approval of a project, or (2) the enforcement process, in which the Corps seeks to stop the landowner from conducting an allegedly unauthorized activity.

The day-to-day operations of the Corps are handled by 36 district offices around the country, each commanded by a district engineer, typically a colonel or lieutenant colonel who serves two or three years in that position. Each district engineer reports to one of nine division commanders, usually a brigadier general. At the top of the hierarchy is the Chief of Engineers in Washington, D.C.

CLEAN WATER ACT

Under §404 of the Clean Water Act, the Corps regulates the discharge of "dredged or fill material" into "navigable waters." 33 USC § 1344. For purposes of the Act, the term "navigable waters" is defined to mean "waters of the United States." 33 USC §1362(7). The Environmental Protection Agency (EPA) is primarily responsible for administering the Clean Water Act. See 43 Ops US Atty Gen 15 (1979). Under §402 of the Act (33 USC §1342), the EPA administers a permit program for pollutant discharges, known as the National Pollutant Discharge Elimination System. Section 404 carves an exception out of the EPA's authority and gives to the Corps the authority to permit discharges of two particular types of "pollutants": "dredged" and "fill materials." 33 USC §§1342, 1344; 33 CFR §§322.5, 323.6.

Why should landowners (and their lawyers) concern themselves with a program to regulate fill in rivers, lakes, and other water-bodies, whether navigable or otherwise? The simple reason is that the Corps, largely with the acquiescence of the federal courts, has broadly defined "waters of the United States" to include not only rivers, lakes, and other readily recognizable waterbodies, but also "wetlands." 33 CFR §328.3; see *e.g., U.S. v Riverside Bayview Homes, Inc.* (1985) 474 US 121. Caught in the political and legal crossfire between those who see wetlands as natural resources and those who view them as private property, the Corps over the past 15 years has stretched the meaning of "wetlands" beyond the original notion of swamps, marshes, and bogs to encompass much drier areas, including some hardwood forests, fields, and cultivated farmland, that may be saturated with rainwater for as little as a few weeks during the course of a year. Moreover, the Corps has classified as "streams" not only readily recognizable perennial streams, but also intermittent water channels, some of which may be little more than a foot or two wide and may experience water flows for little more than a few days each year. Every low-lying field and every wrinkle in a hillside, therefore, is potentially subject to regulation by the Corps. Furthermore, even though the Corps must usually confine itself to regulating discharges of dredged or fill material, it has viewed that mandate broadly enough to include moving the surface soil around by deep plowing or removing vegetation with mechanized equipment (such as bulldozers with blades). Regulatory Guidance Letter Nos. 86–1 (Feb. 11, 1986) and 90–5 (July 18, 1990). The validity of the Corps' view on these points is an open legal question. (The Corps issues regulatory guidance letters to interpret or clarify regulatory program policies. Even though these letters typically expire on December 31 of the second year following issuance, the Corps often continues to follow them.)

The Clean Water Act is not, however, a comprehensive wetlands protection statute. It is essentially a water quality statute that has been used, with some success, to accomplish a purpose for which it was not specifically designed. The Act basically seeks to protect the quality of the nation's waters by prohibiting the discharge of pollutants.

The Act affords less than comprehensive protection of wetlands in at least two respects. First, it does not cover all wetlands. It reaches only three types: (1) interstate wetlands, *i.e.*, those straddling state borders, (2) those that are "adjacent" to a waterbody, and (3) those other so-called isolated wetlands that, if used, degraded, or destroyed, would substantially affect interstate commerce. 33 CFR §328.3(a)(2), (3), and (7). According to the EPA and the Corps, the latter includes any wetland that is or would be used as habitat by migratory birds or endangered species. 51 Fed Reg 41217 (Nov. 13, 1986). The validity of the agencies' claim of jurisdiction over isolated wetlands, as well as their use of migratory birds and endangered species to make such claims, remain open legal questions.

Second, the Act regulates only the type of activity—discharges of pollutants, particularly dredged and fill materials. Many other activities, wholly beyond the scope of the Act, may freely be undertaken notwithstanding their adverse effects on wetlands as long as they are not associated with any discharge of dredged or fill material. These acts generally include removing vegetation (without using mechanized equipment), draining, plowing, excavating, shading, burning, and flooding. The Congressional Office of Technology Assessment has estimated that of the freshwater wetlands converted to nonwetland areas from the mid-1950s to the mid-1970s, only about 6 percent resulted from fill for urban uses; the vast majority were lawfully converted by other activities, notably farming (80 percent). U.S. Congress, Office of Technology Assessment, *Wetlands: Their Use and Regulation,* p 7 (Mar. 1984).

RIVERS AND HARBORS ACT

Under §10 of the Rivers and Harbors Act, the geographic reach of the Corps' regulatory program extends only to "navigable waters" as traditionally defined by the courts—generally, those waters that are subject to the ebb and flow of the tide, and/or those that are presently used, or have been used in the past, or may be susceptible for use, to transport interstate or foreign commerce. 33 USC §403; 33 CFR §§329.1–329.16. This definition encompasses only those wetlands below the ordinary high water mark in nontidal waterbodies and below the mean high water line in tidal waterbodies. 33 CFR §§329.11, 329.12; *Leslie Salt Co. v. Froehlke* (9th Cir 1978) 578 F2d 742.

While the Rivers and Harbors Act covers a smaller area than the Clean Water Act, the scope of activities regulated under the Rivers and Harbors Act extends beyond discharges of dredged or fill material and generally includes the creation of any obstruction or any "work" that involves excavating, filling, or in any manner altering or modifying the course, location, condition or capacity of a navigable water. 33 USC §403; 33 CFR §§321.1–322.5.

SCOPE OF CORPS' JURISDICTION: WHAT IS A "WETLAND"?

The Corps defines wetlands as "those areas that are inundated or saturated by surface or groundwater at a frequency and duration sufficient to support, and that under normal circumstances do support, a prevalence of vegetation typically adapted for life in saturated soil conditions. Wetlands generally include swamps, marshes, bogs, and similar areas." 33 CFR §328.3(b). Although this regulatory definition has remained the same since 1977, its application in the field has changed continuously, with the result that gradually more areas, and drier areas, have been labelled "wetlands."

To locate wetlands on the ground, the Corps employs what is called a three-parameter approach, examining (1) the vegetation, (2) the hydrology, and (3) the soils of the site. As a general rule, only if wetland indicators are found for each of these three parameters will the Corps classify an area as a wetland. Exceptions to the rule abound, however. The Corps basically looks for areas that presently are wet enough under "normal circumstances" to support a prevalence of wetland vegetation. "Normal circumstances" does not mean only natural or historical circumstances; the impact of human lawful activities, *e.g.*, farming, also is taken into account. Thus, people may create wetlands (and consequently create Corps jurisdiction), as in the case of a flood control channel that normally supports wetland vegetation, or remove wetlands (and consequently remove Corps jurisdiction), as in the case of a wetland that is drained and kept dry in order to farm upland crops. See Regulatory Guidance Letter Nos. 90–7 (Sept. 26, 1990), 86–9 (Aug. 27, 1986), and 82–2 90–7 (Feb. 11, 1982). The Corps does not take kindly, however, to drainage of wetlands by pumping for the specific purpose of evading its jurisdiction, and may in such instances continue to assert jurisdiction notwithstanding the drainage. Corps, Memorandum re Evading 404 Jurisdiction by Pumping Water from Wetlands (Apr. 10, 1990).

Because a full description of the Corps' controversial and continually evolving methodology for making wetland determinations would glaze the eyes of all but those with an appetite for technical detail, little more will be said about it here other than to recite recent events and note that the delineation methodology remains unresolved. In 1989, the Corps, EPA, U.S. Fish and Wildlife Service, and Soil Conservation Service issued a Federal Manual for Identifying and Delineating Jurisdictional Wetlands, which again expanded the areas subject to regulation by the Corps. The manual touched off a political firestorm, and bills to trim back the Corps' jurisdiction were introduced in Congress. *See* HR 404 (1991); HR 1330 (1991). In response to criticism by farmers, the Corps issued additional guidance in September 1990 effectively withdrawing its jurisdiction from certain drained farmlands. Regulatory Guidance Letter No. 90–7 (Sept. 26, 1990). In August 1991, the EPA and the Corps, under direction from the White House, proposed a revised manual that would effectively reduce the Corps' jurisdiction. See 56 Fed Reg 40446 (Aug. 14, 1991). Lobbying by those on both sides of the controversy have yet to produce a decision by the agencies.

In the meantime, Congress passed, and the President signed, an appropriation bill forbidding the Corps from expending any funds delineating wetlands using the 1989 manual or any subsequent manual not adopted as a regulation as prescribed by the Administrative Procedure Act. Pub L 102–104, 105 Stat 518 (1991). As a result, the Corps now uses its draft 1987 manual, which is slightly less expansive than the 1989 manual but not as restrictive as the 1991 proposed manual.

From the Corps' standpoint, the procedure for making a jurisdictional determination is fairly straightforward. A landowner need only send the Corps a letter requesting a jurisdictional determination and provide an adequate description of the land and the proposed project, if any, and a suitable map. The Corps will then conduct an investigation, usually including a site inspection, and then respond with a letter and map describing any jurisdictional claims the Corps asserts.

From the landowner's standpoint, prudence usually demands that some homework be performed before requesting that the Corps make a determination. Depending on the characteristics of the land, it may be useful to conduct studies of the vegetation, hydrology, and soils of the site and present those studies to the Corps with an analysis of the limits of the Corps' jurisdiction. In this fashion, needless factual disputes and expansive jurisdictional claims can sometimes be minimized, as can the time required to get a determination. In fact, the Corps encourages landowners to provide preliminary wetland jurisdictional determinations prepared by private experts in order to reduce its workload. Regulatory Guidance Letter No. 88-3 (Apr. 4, 1988).

The district engineer makes the jurisdictional determination, and his or her decision is final. The Corps' regulations do not provide for an administrative appeal to the division engineer or the Chief of Engineers. Nonetheless, these superior officers have, on rare occasions, responded to informal appeals by exercising their command authority to reverse a district engineer's determination. Apart from that, review of a district engineer's jurisdictional determination can be obtained only by resort to the federal courts.

"NATIONWIDE" PERMITS AND EXEMPTIONS

Before applying to the Corps for a fill permit, the landowner should check whether the project is already authorized under a "nationwide permit" or whether the project is exempt from regulation.

There are 36 "nationwide permits" covering a variety of activities involving only minimal environmental impacts such as backfill for utility lines, minor road crossings, and maintenance and repair of existing facilities. 33 CFR Part 330, 56 Fed Reg 59110 (Nov. 22, 1991). Other general permits may authorize activities in a certain state or region. These permits authorize landowners to undertake covered activities with no paperwork or delay or, in some instances, with an abbreviated notice process. See 33 CFR §330.1, 56 Fed Reg 59135 (Nov. 22, 1991).

Perhaps the most significant nationwide permit is No. 26, the so-called "isolated waters" or "headwaters" permit. This permit generally authorizes fill activities that result in the filling, flooding, or drainage of less then ten acres of (1) isolated waters and wetlands, or

(2) waters and adjacent wetlands within the "headwaters" of nontidal streams, *i.e.*, where the average annual flow is less than five cubic feet per second (33 CFR §330.2(d)). If more than one acre of jurisdictional area is affected, notice must be given to the Corps, and the Corps has 30 days to decide whether to allow the project or require the landowner to seek an individual permit. 33 CFR Part 330, App A, 56 Fed Reg 59143 (Nov. 22, 1991).

Some projects are exempt from regulation under §404. Perhaps the most important exemption is for normal farming, silviculture, and ranching activities such as plowing, seeding, cultivating, minor drainage, harvesting, and soil and water conservation practices. 33 USC §1344(f)(1)(A); 33 CFR §323.4(a)(1). The Corps and the courts have ruled that this exemption applies only to activities that are part of an established ongoing operation and not to activities that convert a wetland for the first time to farming and forestry uses. Corps Memorandum for the Field, Clean Water Act Section 404 Regulatory Program and Agricultural Activities (May 3, 1990).

These exemptions are limited, however, by a so-called recapture provision making them inapplicable if the purpose of the activity is to bring an area of waters or wetlands into a use to which it was not previously subject, where the flow or circulation of waters may be impaired or the reach of such waters reduced.

If a proposed discharge of dredged or fill material into jurisdictional waters or wetlands is neither exempt nor authorized under a nationwide permit, then an "individual permit" is required.

INDIVIDUAL PERMITS

Once the Corps' jurisdictional area has been established (and assuming the landowner does not design the project to avoid it), the landowner can apply to the Corps for a fill permit. The application typically includes (1) detailed information and maps describing the project, (2) an alternatives analysis, and (3) a mitigation plan. See 33 CFR §325.1. Depending on the nature of the project and the site, preparation of a permit application may be simple or complex, sometimes requiring the assistance of experts in one or more fields, *e.g.*, biologists, planners, engineers, lawyers.

Procedurally, the Corps permit process may be divided into a series of steps:

- The applicant submits an application, which contains documents and drawings describing the proposed project, analyzing project alternatives, addressing environmental impacts, and proposing mitigation for any wetland losses.
- The Corps prepares a summary of the project proposal, which it issues as a public notice to various federal, state and local agencies, as well as special interest groups and interested individuals.
- A 30-day public comment period follows the public notice, during which anyone may submit comments to the Corps. The Corps may, of its own volition or at the request of others, extend the comment period for another 30 days and also hold a public hearing.
- After the close of the public comment period, or any public hearing, the Corps sends the comments to the applicant and typically allows about 45 days for the applicant to resolve objections and respond to any comments. An applicant who needs more time may request that the Corps temporarily suspend processing of the application.
- Once the applicant has had an opportunity to respond to the comments, the Corps evaluates the project proposal and all the comments and reaches a decision to deny or grant (and, if so, with what conditions) a permit.

The time required to complete the Corps permit process varies significantly from project to project. Relatively minor, uncontroversial development projects may typically be processed in three to eight months. Sizeable or controversial projects may require one or two years, sometimes longer.

During the permit process, the Corps typically reviews the environmental effects of the proposed project by preparing a relatively brief written environmental assessment. The Corps may decide, however, particularly with respect to a large project, that an environmental impact statement [EIS] must be prepared under the National Environmental Policy Act (NEPA) (42 USC §§4321–4347). Preparation of an EIS typically adds 9 to 18 months to the permit process.

Substantively, the Corps permit process presents two major hurdles. First, guidelines issued by the EPA generally prohibit the Corps from issuing a permit if there is a practicable alternative to the proposed discharge that would have less adverse impact on the aquatic ecosystem, as long as the alternative does not have other significant adverse environmental consequences.

As implemented by the EPA and the Corps, the practicable alternatives test is a tough nut to crack. Basically, the applicant must demonstrate why the proposed project cannot be located at a different site, whether owned by the applicant or not, or why the project cannot be reconfigured on site to avoid the wetlands.

The second hurdle is that the applicant must also show that the project is in the "public interest." 33 CFR §320.4(a). In making this determination, the Corps will consider any number of factors, *e.g.*, economics (need for jobs, housing), property ownership, food production, aesthetics, and the general welfare of the people. Looming large among the pertinent factors, however, are general environmental concerns and particularly wildlife habitat and water quality.

The "public interest," as articulated by the Corps, typically translates into a requirement that the applicant mitigate any wetland losses resulting from the project.

Under current policies, generally an applicant must first demonstrate that he or she has avoided and minimized the project's impact on wetlands to the extent possible, and then must create new wetlands (from existing uplands) that are at least equal in both size and quality to the wetlands unavoidably lost as part of the project. Moreover, the newly created wetlands must be on the project site or as near to it as possible.

As a practical matter, the Corps permit process serves as a framework for negotiating with various interested agencies. Generally, such negotiations should be conducted before, during, and after the public comment period. Solicitation of favorable comments from local, state, and federal legislators and officials, trade organizations, interest groups, and individuals can be helpful.

If the Corps decides to grant a permit over the objection of certain federal agencies, it must provide those agencies with advance notice of its intended decision and give them an opportunity to explain their concerns again to the Corps. Should the Corps still decide to issue a permit, the agencies may "elevate" the permit decision to someone high in the Corps hierarchy. Memorandum of Agreement Between the Department of the Interior and the Department of the Army (Nov. 8, 1985); Memorandum of Agreement Between the Environmental Protection Agency and the Department of the Army (Nov. 12, 1985); Memorandum of Agreement Between the Department of Commerce and the Department of the Army (Mar. 25, 1986); Regulatory Guidance Letter No. 86–5 (May 23, 1986).

In contrast, should the Corps decide to deny a permit, there is no established administrative appeal for the landowner. Notwithstanding the absence of any established procedure, a landowner may, of course, seek the assistance and guidance of higher Corps decision makers. As a last resort, relief may be sought in court.

ENFORCEMENT PROGRAM

The Corps, on discovering unauthorized fill activity within its jurisdiction, generally issues a cease and desist order or a letter of violation directing the landowner to stop the filling and either restore the area to its former condition or apply for an after-the-fact permit.

A landowner receiving a Corps cease and desist order or a letter of violation may, depending on the circumstances, negotiate with the Corps regarding restoration of the site or the validity and extent of the Corps' jurisdictional claim, or apply for an after-the-fact permit (which involves most of the considerations discussed above).

If the alleged violation is not resolved administratively, the Corps may bring a civil or criminal enforcement action in federal court seeking a restoration order, monetary penalties, and even imprisonment. 33 USC §§406, 1319, 1344(s); 33 CFR §326.5. In recent years, severe penalties have been assessed, including a civil penalty of $1.3 million for filling 5.2 acres of wetlands in Guam to develop a resort, a three-year jail sentence for ignoring several Corps warnings and a court order to stop filling 14 acres of wetlands in Pennsylvania, and a $2 million fine for negligently filling 87 acres of wetlands in Maryland.

Environmental Protection Agency Under the Clean Water Act, the EPA shares authority with the Corps over the regulation of fill in "waters of the United States." The long-standing tug of war between these two agencies has added to the confusion and inefficiency associated with the Corps' regulatory program.

Although never as active as the Corps, the EPA has lately devoted more resources to wetlands protection, particularly in enforcement actions. The Corps and the EPA have nonetheless agreed that the Corps, because it has more field resources, will generally serve as the lead enforcement agency for permit violations as well as unpermitted discharges unless the case involves repeat violators or flagrant violations, the EPA requests a class of cases or a particular case, or the Corps recommends that an EPA administrative penalty process be initiated.

A landowner applying for a Corps permit will likely encounter the EPA in its role as a "commenting" agency. The Corps naturally gives considerable weight to the EPA's comments. It is the EPA that issued the guidelines that the Corps must follow when deciding whether to issue a permit. And if the Corps decides to grant a permit over the objection of the EPA, the EPA can "elevate" the permit decision, so it is made by someone higher in the Corps hierarchy. If the Corps still grants a permit, notwithstanding the EPA's objection, the EPA may resort to a rarely used administrative process to prohibit the use of the project site as a "disposal site" and thereby effectively veto the Corps' permit decision.

U.S. Fish and Wildlife Service The U.S. Fish and Wildlife Service (FWS) generally does not regulate waterbodies and wetlands. Rather, the FWS reviews permit applications to the Corps and other agencies and offers comments and recommendations on whether those permits should be granted. Under the Fish and Wildlife Coordination Act (16 USC §§661–666c), the Corps must consult with the FWS and give "full consideration" to its views on fish and wildlife matters.

If endangered or threatened species are found on a site, the FWS's already considerable influence swells. This situation occurs fairly often because many listed plant and animal species depend on wetlands for food and habitat. The Endangered Species Act (ESA) (16 USC §§1531–1544) prohibits the Corps and other federal agencies from taking any action (*e.g.,* granting a permit) that would jeopardize the continued existence of endangered or threatened species or modify their critical habitat. The ESA also specifies that, whenever such species might be affected, the agencies must consult with the FWS. During the consultation process, the FWS renders a biological opinion on whether the continued existence of a listed species is likely to be jeopardized by the proposed project. The Corps, however, makes the final decision on jeopardy, and the Corps can (but rarely does) issue a permit notwithstanding a jeopardy opinion by the FWS. *Sierra Club v. Froehlke* (8th Cir 1976) 534 F2d 1289.

Like the EPA, the FWS may elevate a permit decision if the Corps indicates it intends to grant a permit over the FWS's objection. Unlike the EPA, however, the FWS may not veto a Corps permit.

In administering its own nonregulatory programs, the FWS employs its own definition of wetlands—a definition even broader than that of the Corps—and this sometimes complicates matters. Basically, the FWS classifies as wetland any area that exhibits wetland indicators in any one of the three parameters (vegetation, soils, and hydrology) required by the Corps. U.S. Fish & Wildlife Service, Classification of Wetlands and Deepwater Habitats of the United States, p 3 (Dec. 1979).

The FWS influences Corps wetland delineations in another fashion as well. The Corps uses a National List of Plant Species that Occur in Wetlands, published by the FWS, to determine which plants are wetland indicators. Whether an area supports a prevalence of wetland plants, and thus qualifies as a wetland, may depend on how certain plant species are classified in this list. In recent years, controversial reclassifications of a few species have transformed some uplands to wetlands.

The FWS also continues to work with the Corps and the EPA on a joint mitigation banking policy. The FWS's own views, however, have already been published. U.S. Fish and Wildlife Service Biological Report 88(41), *Mitigation Banking* (July 1988).

Finally, the FWS also manages more than 90 million acres within the National Wildlife Refuge System, about one third of which are wetlands. In California, national wildlife refuges encompass wetlands at Humboldt Bay, San Pablo Bay, San Francisco Bay, Seal Beach, Central Valley, Klamath Lakes Basin, and the Colorado River. Additional wetlands along designated rivers are protected under the Wild and Scenic Rivers Act (16 USC §§1271–1287).

National Marine Fisheries Service Like the FWS, the National Marine Fisheries Service (NMFS) does not regulate wetlands, but rather reviews permit applications and provides comments and recommendations to the permitting agency. The Corps must give "full consideration" to the views of NMFS on fish and wildlife matters. Also, the NMFS, rather than the FWS, is responsible for protecting certain endangered and threatened species, generally marine animals, under the ESA and other federal statutes.

Soil Conservation Service The Soil Conservation Service (SCS) administers the "swampbuster" provisions of the 1985 Food Security Act (16 USC §§3801–3862). Under that act, anyone who converts a wetland to upland after December 23, 1985, in order to grow crops, generally is ineligible for various federal farm subsidies and benefits. The statute defines wetlands in terms similar, but not identical, to those in the Corps' regulatory definition. A determination by the SCS about the existence and extent of specific wetlands may, in some circumstances, be adopted by the Corps as a determination of the area governed by its regulatory program. Regulatory Guidance Letter No. 90–7 (Sept. 26, 1990).

The SCS also administers a Water Bank Program in conjunction with various federal and state agencies. The program is generally designed to preserve, restore, and improve migratory water-fowl habitat. Under the program, landowners may enter into ten-year agreements and receive annual payments for conserving wetland areas. See 16 USC §§1301–1311.

Corps of Engineers Wetlands Delineation Manual (1987)

The *Corps of Engineers Wetlands Delineation Manual* is the closest thing to a bible on what constitutes a wetland. It details the criteria by which the Corps and the EPA determine whether particular habitats fall under their jurisdiction. In practice, a developer or other entity that wants to change the hydrology of a disputed site typically hires a consultant with expertise in fulfilling the assessment techniques.

Wetlands delineation, however, is not a simple matter of "cookbook" analysis. Every site is more or less unique, and matters are further complicated in that the primary advisory agency to the Corps, the U.S. Fish and Wildlife Service, operates on a broader definition of "wetlands" (outlined in the next reading). Moreover, the agency with primary responsibility for delineating wetlands on agricultural lands, the Soil Conservation Service, has its own manual. All of these agencies, however, take the same characteristics into account: hydrology, soils, and vegetation.

Premise for use of the manual

18. Three key provisions of the CE/EPA definition of wetlands (see paragraph 26a) include:

a. Inundated or saturated soil conditions resulting from permanent or periodic inundation by ground water or surface water.

b. A prevalence of vegetation typically adapted for life in saturated soil conditions (hydrophytic vegetation).

c. The presence of "normal circumstances."

19. Explicit in the definition is the consideration of three environmental parameters: hydrology, soil, and vegetation. Positive wetland indicators of all three parameters are normally present in wetlands. Although vegetation is often the most readily observed parameter, sole reliance on vegetation or either of the other parameters as the determinant of wetlands can sometimes be misleading. Many plant species can grow successfully in both wetlands and nonwetlands, and hydrophytic vegetation and hydric soils may persist for decades following alteration of hydrology that will render an area a nonwetland. The presence of hydric soils and wetland hydrology indicators in addition to vegetation indicators will provide a logical, easily defensible, and technical basis for the presence of wetlands. The combined use of indicators for all three parameters will enhance the technical accuracy, consistency, and credibility of wetland determinations. Therefore, all three parameters were used in developing the technical guidelines for wetlands and all approaches for applying the technical guideline embody the multiparameter concept.

Approaches

20. The approach used for wetland delineations will vary, based primarily on the complexity of the area in question. Two basic approaches described in the manual are (a) routine and (b) comprehensive.

21. Routine approach. The routine approach normally will be used in the vast majority of determinations. The routine approach requires minimal level of effort, using primarily qual-

itative procedures. This approach can be further subdivided into three levels of required effort, depending on the complexity of the area and the amount and quality of preliminary data available. The following levels of effort may be used for routine determinations:

a. Level 1 – Onsite inspection unnecessary. (PART IV, Section D, Subsection 1).

b. Level 2 – Onsite inspection necessary. (PART IV, Section D, Subsection 2).

c. Level 3 – Combination of Levels 1 and 2. (PART IV, Section D, Subsection 3).

22. Comprehensive approach. The comprehensive approach requires application of quantitative procedures for making wetland determinations. It should seldom be necessary, and its use should be restricted to situations in which the wetland is very complex and/or is the subject of likely or pending litigation. Application of the comprehensive approach (PART IV, Section E) requires a greater level of expertise than application of the routine approach, and only experienced field personnel with sufficient training should use this approach.

Flexibility

23. Procedures described for both routine and comprehensive wetland determinations have been tested and found to be reliable. However, site-specific conditions may require modification of field procedures. For example, slope configuration in a complex area may necessitate modification of the baseline and transect positions. Since specific characteristics (e.g. plant density) of a given plant community may necessitate the use of alternate methods for determining the dominant species, the user has the flexibility to employ sampling procedures other than those described. However, the basic

approach for making wetland determinations should not be altered (i.e. the determination should be based on the dominant plant species, soil characteristics, <u>and</u> hydrologic characteristics of the area in question). The user should document reasons for using a different characterization procedure than described in the manual. *CAUTION: Application of methods described in the manual or the modified sampling procedures requires that the user be familiar with wetlands of the area and use his training, experience, and good judgment in making wetland determinations.*

Classification of Wetlands and Deepwater Habitats of the United States

U.S. Fish and Wildlife Service

The U.S. Fish and Wildlife Service (FWS) is a branch of the U.S. Department of the Interior and a primary advisory agency to the Army Corps of Engineers in reviewing potential wetland impacts. Of the several concerned federal agencies, the FWS is the most vigorous environmental watchdog, and this is reflected in a relatively broad definition of what constitutes a wetland. Whereas the Corps' delineation manual (excerpted in the previous reading) specifies that "the determination should be based on the dominant plant species, soil characteristics, <u>and</u> hydrologic characteristics of the area in question," the FWS allows that "one or more" of these attributes is adequate for a positive identification. Hence, the FWS tends to find wetlands where the Corps doesn't.

Beyond the FWS definition of "wetlands," the following excerpt outlines criteria for differentiating between wetlands and deepwater habitats.

Wetlands and Deepwater Habitats

Concepts and Definitions Marshes, swamps, and bogs have been well-known terms for centuries, but only relatively recently have attempts been made to group these landscape units under the single term "wetlands." This general term has grown out of a need to understand and describe the characteristics and values of all types of land, and to wisely and effectively manage wetland ecosystems. There is no single, correct, indisputable, ecologically sound definition for wetlands, primarily because of the diversity of wetlands and because the demarcation between dry and wet environments lies along a continuum. Because reasons or needs for defining wetlands also vary, a great proliferation of definitions has arisen. The primary objective of this classification is to impose boundaries on natural ecosystems for the purposes of inventory, evaluation, and management.

WETLANDS

In general terms, wetlands are lands where saturation with water is the dominant factor determining the nature of soil development and the types of plant and animal communities living in the soil and on its surface. The single feature that most wetlands share is soil or substrate that is at least periodically saturated with or covered by water. The water creates severe physiological problems for all plants and animals except those that are adapted for life in water or in saturated soil.

WETLANDS *are lands transitional between terrestrial and aquatic systems where the water table is usually at or near the surface or the land is covered by shallow water. For purposes of this classification wetlands must have one or more of the following three attributes: (1) at least periodically, the land supports predominantly hydrophytes; (2) the substrate is predominantly undrained hydric soil; and (3) the substrate is nonsoil and is saturated with water or covered by shallow water at some time during the growing season of each year.*

The term wetland includes a variety of areas that fall into one of five categories: (1) areas with hydrophytes and hydric soils, such as those commonly known as marshes, swamps, and bogs; (2) areas without hydrophytes but with hydric soils—for example, flats where drastic fluctuation in water level, wave action, turbidity, or high concentration of salts may prevent the growth of hydrophytes; (3) areas with hydrophytes but nonhydric soils, such as margins of impoundments or excavations where hydrophytes have become established but hydric soils have not yet developed; (4) areas without soils but with hydrophytes such as the seaweed-covered portion of rocky shores; and (5) wetlands without soil and without hydrophytes, such as gravel beaches or rocky shores without vegetation.

Drained hydric soils that are now incapable of supporting hydrophytes because of a change in water regime are not considered wetlands by our definition. These drained hydric soils furnish a valuable record of historic wetlands, as well as an indication of areas that may be suitable for restoration.

Wetlands as defined here include lands that are identified under other categories in some land-use classifications. For example, wetlands and farmlands are not necessarily exclusive. Many areas that we define as wetlands are farmed during dry periods, but if they are not tilled or planted to crops, a practice that destroys the natural vegetation, they will support hydrophytes.

DEEPWATER HABITATS

DEEPWATER HABITATS are permanently flooded lands lying below the deepwater boundary of wetlands. Deepwater habitats include environments where surface water is permanent and often deep, so that water, rather than air, is the principal medium within which the dominant organisms live, whether or not they are attached to the substrate. As in wetlands, the dominant plants are hydrophytes; however, the substrates are considered nonsoil because the water is too deep to support emergent vegetation.

Wetlands and Deepwater Habitats are defined separately because traditionally the term wetland has not included deep permanent water; however, both must be considered in an ecological approach to classification. We define five major systems: Marine, Estuarine, Riverine, Lacustrine, and Palustrine. The first four of these include both wetland and deepwater habitats but the Palustrine includes only wetland habitats.

Limits The upland limit of wetland is designated as (1) the boundary between land with predominantly hydrophytic cover and land with predominantly mesophytic or xerophytic cover; (2) the boundary between soil that is predominantly hydric and soil that is predominantly nonhydric; or (3) in the case of wetlands without vegetation or soil, the boundary between land that is flooded or saturated at some time each year and land that is not.

The boundary between wetland and deepwater habitat in the Marine and Estuarine systems coincides with the elevation of the extreme low water of spring tide; permanently flooded areas are considered deepwater habitats in these systems. The boundary between wetland and deepwater habitat in the Riverine, Lacustrine, and Palustrine systems lies at a depth of 2 m (6.6 feet) below low water; however, if emergents, shrubs, or trees grow beyond this depth at any time, their deepwater edge is the boundary.

The 2-m lower limit for inland wetlands was selected because it represents the maximum depth to which emergent plants normally grow. . . . Emergents are not true aquatic plants, but are "amphibious," growing in both permanently flooded and wet, nonflooded soils.

Surfing Wetlands on the Internet

The Internet, the global merging of telecommunications and computers, has grown tremendously in recent years, particularly in the scientific community. A popular feature of the Internet is the thematically focused discussion group, or "list," which permits users worldwide to participate in dialogues in almost-real time.

The following exchange occurred on the ECOLOG-L list in October of 1993. If reflects the subjective, conversational quality of Internet exchanges, as well as the typically casual attitude toward spelling and grammar. It also reflects the uncertainty of a profession and a society that still has no clear definition of "wetlands."

In giving permission to reproduce their comments here, certain of the authors wished to make it clear that the expressed opinions are not necessarily indicative of the opinions or policies of the agencies or institutions for which they work.

Date Thu, 7 Oct 1993 20:20:11-0400
From ken klemow ⟨kklemow@WILKES1.WILKES.EDU⟩
Subject Who defines wetlands?
To Multiple recipients of list ECOLOG-L ⟨ECOLOG-L@
UMDD.UMD.EDU⟩

Dear Colleagues,
   In the September 1993 issue of the National Wetlands Newsletter, Jay A. Leitch, of North Dakota State University writes ". . . a common misconception among wetland proponents (is) that wetlands are defined by scientists. Wetlands, in fact, are defined by society with the technical assistance of scientists. If society's definition of wetlands includes saturation for 30 consecutive days, then that is what a wetland is. Thus, changing the definition does not eliminate protection for wetlands, it simply changes the definition."
   I invite comments on Leitch's assertions.

Ken Klemow
Wilkes University
kklemow@wilkes1.wilkes,edu

Date Thu, 7 Oct 1993 21:59:49 EDT
From Mike Conroy ⟨MCONROY@UGA.CC.UGA.EDU⟩
Subject Re: Who defines wetlands?
To Multiple recipients of list ECOLOG-L ⟨ECOLOG-L@
UMDD.UMD.EDU⟩

Scientists seem to agree __qualitatively__ what a wetland is, and this __has + been represented in statutory definitions. The 3 essential elements are 1) presence (at least periodically) of hydrophytes; or 2) hydric soils; or 3) saturated soils during the growing season. THe rub has come in the insistence on narrow definitions, usually by anti-regulatory proponents, for example the insistence that all 3 criteria strictly hold, or that even temporal deviation from (arbitrary) length of saturation criteria (eg during drought) render a wetland a statutory non-entity. If "society" (ie, politicians up for re-election) start defining wetlands, they may as well define species (as in, endangered or threatened) and ecosystems, and ecologists should consider new careers.

It would certainly be more intellectually honest if "society", having received whatever definitions a consensus of scientists conveys on the topic, then makes the choice that certain amounts or types of wetlands (or species, ecosystems, or whatever) are or are not worth conserving, rather than taking solace in defining conflicts away via double-speak.

Date   Fri, 8 Oct 1993 15:24:50 EST.
From   Eric Ribbens 〈RIBBENS%UCONNVM.bitnet@ YALEVM.YCC.YALE.EDU〉
Subject   Re: Who defines wetlands?
To   Multiple recipients of list ECOLOG-L 〈ECOLOG-L@ UMDD.UMD.EDU〉

Ah, semantics! A word can be freighted with multiple meanings. I think that "wetlands" is one of those words with at least three meanings: a legal one, a scientific one, and a common-usage one. Each definition contains overlapping elements, unique elements, and is shaped by a different but potentially linked group. In an ideal world, the legal meaning would definitely be shaped by society, with the assistance/advice of scientists. But this would not require the alteration of the other meanings. Interestingly, for precise delineations of boundaries to word-meanings, we frequently revert to numbers!

ERIC RIBBENS
DEPT. OF ECOLOGY AND
EVOLUTIONARY BIOLOGY
UNIVERSITY OF CONNECTICUT
STORRS, CT 06269
(203) 486-4157
BITNET: RIBBENS@UCONNVM

```
       *
      ***
     *****
       |
```

"A LITTLE LEARNING IS A DANGEROUS THING, BUT A LOT OF IGNORANCE IS JUST AS BAD." —BOB EDWARDS

Date Fri, 8 Oct 1993 16:48:45 -0400
From Yugong Daniel Gao
⟨yugong@UTXVM.CC.UTEXAS.EDU⟩
Subject Re: Who defines wetlands?
To Multiple recipients of list ECOLOG-L ⟨ECOLOG-L@ UMDD.UMD.EDU⟩

Hi, there. Do you know the word "post-modernism"? From a post-modernist's point of view, every individual or group of people can have their own definitions of the term "wetland". There is no right definition there. Though sounds terribly ambiguous, this is usually the real situation in the real world for wetland or any other natural resources conservation. You just have to accept these many different definitions different groups of people are giving, and usually attached with them their attitude towards them.

Interesting? have fun and don't take it too seriously.

Date Fri, 8 Oct 1993 17:20:39 GMT
From rick sojda ⟨sojda@CS.COLOSTATE.EDU⟩
Subject WETLANDS - DEFINITION
To Multiple recipients of list ECOLOG-L⟨ECOLOG-L@
UMDD.UMD.EDU⟩

I'm sorry for having lost the original post about whether science or politics should define wetlands, but here are my thoughts . . .

Although not totally straightforward, a sound definition of wetlands is not difficult to develop. Certainly not all wetlands are wet all the time. And, there's the rub for society. Most people have a mental picture of a wetland as a the classic, cattail hemimarsh in the degenerating stage. Or possibly a cypress swamp. I would argue, : let scientists define what wetlands are, realizing there are many types. Then, scociety/politics has to decide which of those types will be protected. Hopefully, concerned scientists and the concerned public can muster enough political support to save them all!!! But, I am dreaming . . .

Rick Sojda

Date Sat, 9 Oct 1993 10:09:35 -0700
From david sucher ⟨dsucher@CYBERSPACE.COM⟩
Subject Re: who defines wetlands?
To Multiple recipients of list ECOLOG-L ⟨ECOLOG-L@
UMDD.UMD.EDU⟩

On Fri, 8 Oct 1993, Yugong Daniel Gao wrote:

Hi, there. Do you know the word "post-modernism?" From a post-modernist's point of view, every individual or group of people can have their own definitions of the term "wetland". There is no right definition there. Though sound terribly ambiguous, this is usually the real situation in the real world for wetland or any other natural resources conservation. You just have to accept these many different definitions different groups of people are giving, and usually attached with them their attitudes towards them.

Commentary:

We have a jokester amongst us! Above is a witty and clever attempt to create a furious discussion. I haven't gone through all my mail yet so heated response may very well be down below . . . BUT . . . I will take the bait, even knowing that the agent provacateur surely can't be serious.

***

No matter what one's political point of view, the definition of WETLAND is not simply a matter of opinion reflecting a person's values. If wetlands indeed have any long-term utility for the human species by helping keep the planet as a a healthy place to live and need to be 'preserved,' then some definition of WETLAND is a crucial one.

One may argue what the definition of wetland should be and how it should be applied, but it is an important definition and not simply a matter of today's or tomorrow's trend. The health of the world or the pocketbook of an individual may very well be at stake in our definition of WETLANDS; if we do not preserve wetlands, we may damn our children; if we preserve without or beyond any rationale need, we wipeout the economic assets and cause great harm to the lives of a relatively few people . . .

Whatever the case, the definition of wetland is very important and we should approach the question as openly and "scientifically" as possible: it is not a matter for casual conversation at a cafe.

***

Whew!!! Glad that initial comment was simply meant to provoke discussion!

Cheers!

David

Wetland Creation and Restoration

Jon A. Kusler and Mary E. Kentula

In granting permits for projects that will result in destruction of wetland habitat, the Corps typically requires mitigation that includes restoration or creation of an equal or (often) greater area of wetland at or near the project site. Hence, some compensatory installations involve a sort of reverse reclamation of areas that were drained or filled, while others involve attempts to establish wetland habitat where there is no historical precedent.

This excerpt is from an analysis of wetland restoration and creation originally published in 1990. In 1995 we asked Jon Kusler if the conclusions about how well such projects work were still valid. He said they were, but added that certain points ought to be emphasized:

- Success often depends on long-term caretaking, including manipulation of water levels, which is lacking in most projects.
- Wetlands are extremely sensitive to changes in watershed and sedimentation; attempts to create wetlands in unstable environments "are just window dressing." In areas of heavy sedimentation they might disappear in as little as a year.
- In many cases, money spent on planting wetland species is wasted. The planted species often don't survive, and "you tend to get species the hydrologic regime wants to give you."
- Although it is often possible to create adequate habitat for certain types of organisms, including fish and birds, biodiversity is typically lacking in created wetlands. Certain bottom-dwelling organisms, for example, depend on wetland substrates that have accumulated over thousands of years.

Jon A. Kusler is both a lawyer and a Ph.D. in water- and land-use planning who has served in various capacities in government and academe. Mary E. Kentula works with the EPA's Wetland Research Program.

Success of Restoration and Creation

1. *Restoration or creation of a wetland that "totally duplicates" a naturally occurring wetland is impossible; however, some systems may be approximated and individual wetland functions may be restored or created.*

   Total duplication of natural wetlands is impossible due to the complexity and variation in natural as well as created or restored systems and the subtle relationships of hydrology, soils, vegetation, animal life, and nutrients which may have developed over thousands of years in natural systems. Nevertheless, experience to date suggests that some types of wetlands can be approximated and certain wetland functions can be restored, created, or enhanced in particular contexts. It is often possible to restore or create a wetland with vegetation resembling that of a naturally occurring wetland. This does not mean, however, that it will have habitat or other values equaling those of a natural wetland nor that such a wetland will be a persistent, i.e., long term, feature in the landscape, as are many natural wetlands.

2. *Partial project failures are common.*

   For certain types of wetlands, total failures have been common (e.g., seagrasses, certain forested wetlands). Although the reasons for partial or total failures differ, common problems include:
   · lack of basic scientific knowledge;
   · lack of staff expertise in design, and lack of project supervision during implementation phases;
   · improper site conditions (e.g., water supply, hydroperiod, water depth, water velocity, salinity, wave action, substrate, nutrient concentration, light availability, sedimentation rate, improper grades (slopes);
   · invasion by exotic species;
   · grazing by geese, muskrats, other animals;

- destruction of vegetation or the substrate by floods, erosion, fires, other catastrophic events;
- failure of projects to be carried out as planned;
- failure to protect projects from on-site and off-site impacts such as sediments, toxics, off-road vehicles, groundwater pumping, etc.; and
- failure to adequately maintain water levels.

3. *Success varies with the type of wetland and target functions including the requirements of target species.*

A relatively high degree of success has been achieved with revegetation of coastal, estuarine, and freshwater marshes because elevations are less critical than for forested or shrub wetlands, native seed stocks are often present, and natural revegetation often occurs. Marsh vegetation also quickly reaches maturity in comparison with shrub or forest vegetation. However, some types of marshes, such as those dominated by *Spartina patens,* have been difficult to restore or recreate due to sensitive elevation requirements.

Much less success has been achieved to date with seagrasses and forested wetlands. The reasons for lack of success for seagrasses are not altogether clear, although use of a site where seagrasses have previously grown seems to improve the chances for establishing the plants. Lack of success for forested wetlands is due, at least in part, to their sensitive long term hydrologic requirements. Such systems also reach maturity slowly.

Although certain types of wetland vegetation may be restored or created, there have been few studies concerning the use of restored or created wetlands by particular animal species. Restoration or creation of habitat for ecologically sensitive animal or plant species is particularly difficult.

4. *The ability to restore or create particular wetland functions varies by function.*

The ability to restore or create particular wetland functions is influenced by (1) the amount of basic scientific knowledge available concerning the wetland function; (2) the ease and cost of restoring or creating certain characteristics (e.g., topography may be created with relative ease, while creation of infiltration capacity is difficult); and (3) varying probabilities that structural characteristics will give rise to specific functions. For example (note this is meant to be illustrative only):

- Flood storage and flood conveyance functions can be quantitatively assessed and restored or created with some certainty by applying the results of hydrologic studies. Togography is the critical parameter and this is probably the easiest parameter to restore or recreate.
- Waterfowl production functions may be assessed or created with fair confidence in some contexts, due to the large amount of experience, scientific knowledge, and information on marsh design, and marshes are, relatively speaking, easily restored or recreated.
- Wetland aesthetics may or may not be difficult to restore or create, depending on the wetland type and the site conditions. Visual characteristics are, in general, much easier to restore than subtle ecological functions.
- Some fisheries functions may be assessed and restored or created. However, the ability to restore or create fisheries habitat will depend on the species and the site conditions.
- Some food chain functions may be assessed, restored, or created. Other more subtle functions are difficult due to the lack of basic scientific knowledge and experience.
- Certain pollution control functions (e.g., sediment trapping)

may be relatively easy to assess and create. However, others (e.g., immobilization of toxic metals) may be difficult to create, particularly in the long term because of uncertainties concerning the long term fate of pollutants in wetlands and their impact on the wetland system.

· Groundwater recharge and discharge functions are difficult to assess and create. One confounding factor is that soil permeability may change in a creation or restoration context (e.g., a sandy substrate may quickly become impermeable due to deposition of organics).

· Heritage or archaeological functions (e.g., a shell midden located in a marsh) are impossible to restore or create since they depend upon history for their value.

5. *Long term success may be quite different from short term success.*
Revegetation of a restored or created wetland over a short period of time (e.g., one year) is no guarantee that the area will continue to function over time. Unanticipated fluctuations in hydrology are a particularly serious problem for efforts to restore or create wetland types (e.g., forested wetlands) with very sensitive elevation or hydroperiod requirements. Droughts or floods may destroy or change the targeted species composition of projects.

Hydrologic fluctuations also occur in natural wetlands. But hydrologic minima and maxima as well as "normal" conditions exist within tolerable ranges at particular locations, otherwise the natural wetland types would not exist. Natural wetlands have been tried and tested by natural processes and are, in many instances, "survivors."

Long term damage to or destruction of restored or created systems may be due to many other factors in addition to unanticipated hydrologic changes. Common threats include pollution, erosion and wave damage, off-road vehicle traffic, and grazing. Excessive sediment is a serious problem for many restored or created wetlands located in urban areas with high rates of erosion and sedimentation. Unlike many natural wetlands, restored or created wetlands also often lack erosional equilibrium (in a geomorphologic sense) with their watersheds.

6. *Long term success depends upon the ability to assess, recreate, and manipulate hydrology.*

The success of a project depends to a considerable extent upon the ease with which the hydrology can be determined and established, the availability of appropriate seeds and plant stocks, the rate of growth of key species, the water level manipulation potential built into the project, and other factors. To date, the least success has been achieved for wetlands for which it is very difficult to restore or create the proper hydrology. In general, the ease with which a project can be constructed and the probability of its success are:

· Greatest overall for estuarine marshes due to (1) the relative ease of determining proper hydrology; (2) the experience and literature base available on restoration and creation; (3) the relatively small number of wetland plant species that must be dealt with; (4) the general availability of seeds and plant stocks; and (5) the ease of establishing many of the plant species. However, it is difficult or impossible to restore or create certain estuarine wetland types due to narrow tidal range or salinity tolerances, e.g., high marshes dominated by *Spartina patens* on the East Coast. The same is true of estuarine wetlands in regions or areas with unique local conditions, e.g., the hypersaline soils common in southern California salt marshes.

· Second greatest for coastal marshes for the same reasons as those given for estuarine wetlands. However, high wave energies and tidal ranges of the open coast reduce the probability of success.

· Third greatest for freshwater marshes along lakes, rivers, and streams. The surface water elevations can often be determined from stream or lake gauging records. There is a fair amount of literature and experience in restoring and managing these systems. However, vegetation types are often more complex than those of coastal and estuarine systems. Problems with exotic species are common. Determination and restoration or creation of hydrology (including flood levels) and hydrology/sediment relationships are more difficult. This is frequently compounded by altered hydrology and sedimentation patterns due to dams and water extractions.

· Fourth greatest for isolated marshes supplied predominantly by surface water. There is limited experience and literature on restoring or creating such wetlands except for waterfowl production where water levels are manipulated on a continuing basis. Determination and restoration of hydrology is very difficult unless mechanisms are available for actively managing the water supply. Depending on the wetland type, plant assemblages can also be complex.

· Fifth greatest for forested wetlands along lakes, rivers, and streams. Determination and restoration or creation of hydrology is very difficult due to narrow ranges of tolerance. Water regimes may be evaluated with the use of records for adjacent waters, but such records are often not sensitive enough. There is also limited literature or experience in restoring such systems. Vegetation is diverse; both the understory and canopy communities may need to be established. Moreover, it may take many years for a mature forest to develop.

· Sixth greatest for isolated freshwater wetlands (ranging from marshes to forested wetlands) supplied predominantly with ground water. Determining and creating the hydrology is very difficult. There is limited experience and literature except on some prairie pothole wetlands.

7. *Success often depends upon the long term ability to manage, protect, and manipulate wetlands and adjacent buffer areas.*
Restored or created wetlands are often in need of "mid-course corrections" and management over time. Original design specifications may be insufficient to achieve project goals. Created or restored wetlands are also particularly susceptible to invasion by exotic species, sedimentation, pollution, and other impacts due to their location in urban settings and the inherent instability of many of their systems. Careful monitoring of systems after their original establishment and the ability to make mid-course corrections and, in some instances, to actively manage the systems, are often critical to long-term success.

Efforts to create or enhance waterfowl habitat by wildlife agencies and private organizations through the use of dikes, small dams, and other water control structures have been quite successful due, in large measure, to the ability to control and alter the hydrologic regime over time. Water levels may be changed if original water elevations prove incorrect for planned revegetation. Drawdown and flooding may be used to control exotics and vegetation successional sequences.

However, most wetland restoration or creation efforts proposed by private and public developers do not involve water control measures. In addition, few developers are willing to accept long-term responsibility for managing systems. Water level manipulation capability and long-term management capability are also insufficient, in themselves, without long-term assurances that the system will be managed to achieve particular wetland functional goals. For example, water level manipulation and long-term management capability exist for most flood control, stormwater, and water supply reservoirs. But wetlands along the margins of these reservoirs are often destroyed by fluctuations in water levels dictated by the primary management goals.

Restored or created wetlands should be designed as self-sustaining or self-managing systems unless a project sponsor (such as a wildlife agency or duck club) clearly has the incentive and capability for long-term management to optimize wetland values.

The management needs of restored or created wetlands are not limited to water level manipulation. Common management needs for both wetlands subject to water level manipulation and those not subject to such manipulation include:

· Replanting, regrading, and other mid-course corrections.
· Establishment of buffers to protect wetlands from sediment, excessive nutrients, pesticides, foot traffic, or other impacts from adjacent lands.
· Establishment (in some instances) of fences and barriers to restrict foot traffic, off-road vehicles, and grazing animals in wetlands.
· Adoption of point and non-point source pollution controls for streams, drainage ditches, and runoff flowing into wetlands.
· Control of exotics by burning, mechanical removal, herbicides, or other measures.
· Periodic dredging of certain portions of wetlands subject to high rates of sedimentation (e.g., stormwater facilities).

8. *Success depends upon expertise to project design and upon careful project supervision.*

Hydrologic and biological as well as botanical and engineering expertise are needed in the design of many projects. In addition, the involvement of experts with prior experience in wetland restoration or creation is highly desirable. This is particularly true where a wetland with multiple functions is to be created from an upland site. Less expertise may be needed where restoration is to occur, the original hydrology is intact, and nearby natural seed stocks exist.

Careful project supervision is also needed to insure implementation of project design. It is not enough to design a project and turn it over to traditional construction personnel. For example, bulldozer operators often need guidance with regard to critical elevation requirements, drainage, and the spreading of stockpiled soil. Plantings must be shaded from the sun and kept moist until they are placed in the ground.

9. *"Cook book" approaches for wetland restoration or creation will likely be only partially successful.*
Too little is known from a scientific perspective about wetland restoration to provide rigid, "cook book" guidance. The interdependence of a large number of site-specific factors also warrants against too rigid an approach. For example, in a salt marsh, maxima and minima in hydrologic conditions for particular plant species may depend not only on elevation but on salinity, wave action, light, nutrients, and other factors. Often the best model is a nearby wetland of similar type.

Although "cook book" prescribing, rigid design criteria are not desirable, guidance documents suggesting ranges of conditions conducive to success are possible. Requirements for wetland creation that incorporate such general criteria, combined with incentives and flexibility to allow for experimentation offer an increased probability of success as well as a contribution to the information base.

Banking on Wetlands

David Salvesen

Mitigation banking involves restoring or creating wetlands in one area to compensate for destruction of wetland habitat elsewhere. A single mitigation bank might serve as compensation for two or more unrelated development projects.

Environmentalists have voiced mixed feelings on mitigation banking. It can increase the likelihood that mitigation will succeed, because bank sites can be more carefully selected than individual mitigation sites; consolidating mitigation for small wetland losses can result in installations more ecologically viable than several isolated sites; and banking can provide mitigation in advance of wetland impacts. Yet it involves off-site mitigation; a net loss of small wetlands might result in loss of habitat values unique to such areas; and it could increase the rate of loss of natural wetland areas by making mitigation too easy to buy into.

The following largely positive view of the concept originally appeared in *Urban Land,* the journal of the Urban Land Institute. David Salvesen is an environmental consultant and freelance writer.

Walter Stephens, a crayfish farmer in Tifton, Georgia, has a vision. His future, he believes, lies not in raising the diminutive crustaceans which have earned him a respectable living for over a decade, but in raising wetlands: bottomland hardwood swamps, to be precise. Stephens believes he can grow and sell wetlands for profit. And he is prepared to bank his farm on it. . . .

The Many Faces of Mitigation Banking

Mitigation banking, which resembles a futures market more than a bank, generally works something like this: a degraded wetland is purchased and restored by one party, such as a government agency or an investor, and is designated as a bank. The values of the restored wetland are somehow quantified and the wetland assigned "credits" that a developer can withdraw, at a price, to compensate for unavoidable wetland fills elsewhere. Viewed broadly, mitigation banking encompasses a variety of mechanisms to offset or compensate for future losses of wetlands or wildlife habitat, including the following:

- *Single Owner/User Banks.* The most common form of mitigation banks, these usually are established by a large company or a public agency whose future development plans call for filling numerous small wetlands over several years. The company or agency may create a large wetland, from which it can later withdraw "credits" as compensation for wetland fills, rather than create a small wetland at each site on a case-by-case basis. Such banks are commonly established by port authorities, such as the Batiquitos Lagoon Mitigation Bank created by the Port of Los Angeles.
- *Entrepreneurial Banks.* These banks are similar in principle to single-owner banks, except that the bank is established by a landowner and/or investor and the credits can be purchased by anyone. Very few exist.
- *Joint Projects.* Common in California, these typically involve a consortium of developers that agrees to fund a mitigation project to compensate for specific, future losses of wetlands or endangered species habitat. For example, to mitigate for the adverse impacts of development in the habitat of the endangered Stephens kangaroo rat, developers in Riverside County, California, have contributed about $2,000 per acre to purchase and preserve habitat for the rodents.

Why Mitigation Banks?

Mitigation banking enjoys strong support among developers, land-owners, economists, and the Corps. Several bills introduced in Congress [have] included provisions for establishing mitigation banking. Numerous states—Oregon, Minnesota, and New Jersey, to name a few—have specifically authorized establishment of miti-gation banks. And former President Bush's August 1991 Wetlands Policy Statement encouraged the development of market-oriented mitigation banks. Mitigation banking is gradually gaining accep-tance in the EPA and among some environmental groups as well.

Mitigation banking's attractions are many. It can:

- consolidate the creation of numerous small, isolated wetlands into one large hydrologically and ecologically favorable site that may be easier to monitor and manage;
- streamline the permit process by making readily available a supply of credits to those who need and qualify for them;
- transfer the responsibility and hassle of creating wetlands from developers' hands to parties that likely will have a greater interest in the wetlands' long-term success; and
- provide incentives for the private sector to restore degraded wetlands.

Carefully designed wetlands created or restored for mitigation banks may perform better than those created on a case-by-case basis on individual development sites. According to John Studt, head of the regulatory branch of the Corps, "From a strictly ecological standpoint, we believe mitigation banking is superior to case-by-case mitigation."

Nonetheless, not everyone is enthralled with the concept. Oppo-nents of mitigation banking fear that banks will be susceptible to abuse: developers will have little incentive to reduce wetland losses if they can simply buy credits from a bank. Moreover, mitigation banks may fail to compensate for site-specific values of a destroyed wetland.

A Market in the Making

. . . Uncertainty is the highest hurdle faced by prospective bank owners. Mitigation banking is a creature of government; the market exists solely because of government regulations. Government plays a strong role in creating and sustaining the market, and in determining profitability. Until these and other issues, outlined below, can be worked out, the private sector will remain hesitant to invest in mitigation banks.

- *Assurances.* Investors will remain skittish about mitigation banking until the Corps and the EPA establish clear procedures and guidelines for creating and operating mitigation banks. Likewise, regulators need assurances that banks will perform as promised and that a bank's wetlands will be preserved in perpetuity. Currently, most permits are issued with little more than a promise that the work will be carried out. Presumably, mitigation banks will be held to a higher standard. The Corps could require that banks provide a performance bond to guarantee that a created wetland lives up to promises made.
- *Criteria for Success.* By what criteria should a created or restored wetland be judged successful? Plant cover? Number of birds? Whether the wetland is self sustaining? The Corps generally applies simple performance standards: for example, 80 percent of the site must be covered with grasses after three years. Typically,

after a few years, the permittee may walk away from the project with no further obligations. The standards for wetlands created in a mitigation bank are expected to be more stringent than for wetlands created on site. Who, if anyone, will be held liable when a created or restored wetland fails?

· *Timing.* Under current regulations, development in wetlands may proceed before or while a replacement wetland is created. When can a bank begin selling credits: as a wetland is being constructed, when the work is completed, or when the created wetland is considered successful? How can regulators account for the temporal loss in wetland values: the time between when a wetland is destroyed and when its functions and values are fully replaced (which could take more than 15 years)?

· *Location.* Under what circumstances will a permit applicant be able to purchase credits from a mitigation bank, rather than create a wetland on site? Regulators prefer that created wetlands be located in the same watershed as the destroyed wetland, which means that the entities that establish banks somehow must anticipate where future wetland losses will occur.

· *Long-Term Maintenance.* Many created or restored wetlands require periodic maintenance or remedial work: supplementary planting, weed control, sediment removal, and/or regrading of slopes. How long will mitigation banks have to be maintained? Who will pay for long-term maintenance? Many bank owners plan on donating their wetlands to a nonprofit organization or government agency once all the credits are sold. Should banks be required to establish a fund for long-term monitoring and maintenance?

· *Conversion of Wetland Values.* Determining what method should be used to measure the value of a wetland remains a sticky issue. What values are added when a degraded wetland is restored?

And, most importantly, how can these values be converted to some form of currency or credits? Some of the factors to be considered when calculating the number of credits created include the value of the wetland destroyed; its location and the location of the bank; whether the functions of the created wetland and the lost wetland are the same; temporal losses; and the likelihood of the created wetland's success.

· *Exchange Ratios.* If a created wetland is equal in value and function to a filled wetland, the exchange ratio should be 1:1, that is, one acre of a created wetland could be exchanged for one acre of filled wetland. In the absence of information on the specific functions and values of wetlands, say guidelines from the EPA's Region 9, a minimum ratio of 1:1 should be used. But to hedge against the risk of failure, or to account for the difference in values between a filled and a created wetland, the Corps sometimes requires higher ratios: 2:1 or even 3:1. The exchange ratio alone could determine whether a bank is profitable or not.

· *Wetland Type.* Driven by economics, bank owners likely will opt for wetlands that are easy and cheap to build and maintain. Simpler to create, marshes will be more common than more difficult bottomland hardwood swamps and bogs. Could a new freshwater marsh compensate for the loss of bottomland hardwood swamp? If so, what is the proper exchange ratio? Is a bog more valuable than a marsh, a mangrove swamp more valuable than bottomland hardwood swamp? Perhaps the exchange ratios should reflect the relative difficulty of creating different types of wetlands, with high ratios required for replacing bogs and low ratios (with a 1:1 minimum) for replacing marshes.

· *Sequencing.* Should the mitigation sequence apply if banks are available? If a wetland in a mitigation bank has been established successfully and is considered fully functional, can a developer skip the first two steps in the sequence of mitigation (avoid and minimize damage to existing wetlands) and simply write a check for the wetland credits?

What Lies Ahead?

Both regulators and the regulated community seem dissatisfied with the current regulatory program. Developers claim that the 404 permit program is unpredictable, time-consuming, and expensive, while regulators bemoan the loss of wetlands and the poor track record of restored or created wetlands. For these reasons, mitigation banking will likely become more popular. It offers the predictability and convenience that developers seek, and it could provide a reasonable solution to the problem of mitigating small, isolated wetlands, particularly if used in conjunction with areawide planning mechanisms, in which wetlands are identified in advance of permit applications as either suitable or unsuitable for fill. Government agencies and nonprofit groups could identify and set priorities for degraded wetlands as sites for mitigation banks.

A growing and largely untapped market exists for mitigation banks. According to Reed Holderman, manager of the Resource Enhancement Program with the California Coastal Conservancy, "If we could build a mitigation bank, we'd sell it out in one year." The Conservancy was involved with the creation of a mitigation bank in Huntington Beach, California. "We got ten calls a week for the Huntington mitigation bank, mostly for small fills of one-half acre or less," recalled Holderman. Given such demand, free market economics dictates that entrepreneurs will come forward to provide what developers will buy. But this is a purely government-derived demand. And while developers relish the idea of simply writing checks to meet their mitigation requirements, they will have to wait until the details of banking schemes become more sorted out. Without clear guidelines, mitigation banking is far too risky for most investors. Observes Dennis King, "Until investors are given greater assurance, they're better off going to Vegas."

Wetlands Valuation

Leonard Shabman

A step beyond mitigation banking (discussed in the preceding selection) might be what Leonard Shabman terms a "market-based approach," which would include a sort of development tax and a scheme for classifying wetlands by ecological value. Shabman is a professor in the Department of Agriculture and Applied Economics at Virginia Tech. This article originally appeared in the *National Wetlands Newsletter* of the Environmental Law Institute.

Where are we today in wetlands management? We now agree that some wetlands functions are worthy of protection and even enhancement from the current levels. We have moved on a variety of policies to turn this agreement into results. And, the results have been encouraging. We have succeeded in sharply reducing agricultural losses, partly as a result of regulation, but mostly due to a sharp shift in the economic feasibility of land clearing and drainage for agriculture. This was in part a result of changes in tax and agricultural policy made in the mid-1980s. In effect, we have turned the agricultural market loose and the market has said that wetlands are not worth draining.

The focus of the wetlands policy debate at this time is on programs such as §404 and state programs that regulate land development by filling for urban uses—commercial, industrial, and residential purposes and public infrastructure—where that land continues to have wetlands characteristics according to some delineation procedures.

Generally, those who seek a permit for wetlands filling must demonstrate to the satisfaction of the regulatory authorities that they have considered all "practicable" alternatives to avoid the wetlands and that the activity proposed for the filled wetlands is water dependent. And, when a permit is granted compensation for the filled wetlands in-kind and on-site, if at all possible, is expected. Taken together, these are termed the "sequencing" rules.

Over time the geographic scope of wetlands regulations and sequencing has expanded from riparian areas to isolated wetlands and to—possibly—areas where water may seldom reach the surface of the soil. The expanding geographic scope catches more land in the regulatory net and highlights three related concerns about wetlands regulations: inflexibility, economic burden, and environmental loss.

What is meant by inflexibility? In the sequencing review there is little concern for the costs of the foregone development opportunity to the applicant, the region, or the nation. And, no matter how degraded the wetlands, or no matter how isolated they are from a larger watershed, the current regulatory program insists on avoidance for all activities not deemed to be water dependent.

Inflexibility leads to economic burden and, perhaps, the undermining of the public consensus that has developed in support of wetlands management. To be blunt, the sequencing and compensation requirements of current wetlands permitting are implicit taxes on land development, since all wetlands development bears a compensation cost for the functions lost. Of course, it pays a far greater cost if the permit is denied, since some share of the development value is lost.

This implicit "tax" and the reduction of development value are most politically acceptable when the public interest gains from wetlands protection are the most clear. Hence the regulatory program was able to maintain support when riparian areas and certain isolated wetlands with obvious wetlands functions were the target of regulation. But as the geographic scope of the program expands, whatever the scientific merit of delineating areas as wetlands, the land subject to this implicit tax and development value reduction increases and the social consensus for the current permit program weakens. What was perceived initially as protection of critical, but limited, areas of the environment appears to have become a national land settlement regulation and taxation policy through the back door of wetlands regulation.

The inflexibility of sequencing can also work to the detriment of environmental improvement. There is little attention paid to the fragmentation, isolation, and functional degradation of the wetlands preserved or compensated for by in-kind and on-site creation and restoration. Commercial and residential development winding among so-called protected wetlands is the product of the regulatory rules which stress wetlands avoidance. Wetlands in the midst of concrete parking lots are the product of on-site compensation requirements.

The effect of this development—whether or not the product of the permit process—has often been to diminish the ecological functions of wetlands by polluted runoff, by changes in hydrologic regimes, and by the fragmentation of the landscape which isolates the wetlands from the surrounding uplands, waters, and biological resources of the watershed. These functional effects, which occur away from the wetlands site, are uninventoried and escape regulation. As a result, in many areas wetlands exist, but their functions in the watershed are so degraded that their contribution to watershed processes is insignificant.

To move beyond the current regulatory program and its problems, the nation needs a wetlands management program, as distinct from a wetlands regulatory program. Wetlands management must be part of a total landscape perspective which recognizes two realities. First, wetlands protection must be part of a total land settlement policy which resets market signals. And, also, wetlands per se are not the concern. Concern is for the role wetlands play in support of watershed ecosystems.

I will comment on land settlement only in passing, although it may be the more significant of the two points. In the not-too-distant past, markets did not allocate wetlands as we desired—they weren't being drained rapidly enough. We set about to make policy that encouraged drainage. These policies were a resounding success, since this rigged market induced landowners to drain over 50 percent of the nation's wetlands, mostly for agriculture. Today, we have a new understanding of what we think of wetlands and these market outcomes are deemed to be undesirable.

Deregulation markets in the broadest sense may save wetlands more effectively than more regulation. To illustrate, the 1985 "Swampbuster" reforms and the 1986 Tax Reform Act eliminated the incentives to conversion in the tax code. The results—in my view—have been to slow and indeed stop wetlands loss to agricultural conversion.

Where do we go with this story now? Throughout the nation, the urban development pressure on nontidal and coastal wetlands is determined by the way people seek to settle the land. This land settlement has been described as sprawl. It seems to me—and I could elaborate—that government policy, more than the so-called free market, is at work in sprawling settlement over the landscape with one consequence being development pressure on wetlands. What policies am I talking about? Exclusionary zoning such as large lot subdivision rules, local government fiscal policy, failure to maintain the habitability of central cities and close-in suburbs, gasoline pricing policy, tax policy toward real estate, and many more. Reform these policies to let market forces work and sprawl will be diminished, much as reform of agricultural and tax policy to let the markets work has taken pressure off wetlands from agricultural development. Having said this let me return to the more mundane—reform of current wetlands regulation.

The second message from landscape thinking is that the functional value of an existing wetland, in a given location, is established by its contribution to a larger aquatic system. We have to recognize that existing wetlands are an accident of the development process and do not necessarily bear any relationship to the optimal configuration of those wetlands within the landscape. We should be thinking about reintegrating wetlands that have been lost or degraded into ecologically optimal locations. Wetlands regulation should acknowledge this watershed perspective. Instead, there remains a too strong tendency in the current regulatory program to protect the status quo and not look for opportunities to advance environmental improvement at the watershed level through wetlands creation and, more realistically, wetlands restoration.

So how do we get there? Imagine an application to fill a wetlands area where the foregone development values of permit denial are exceptionally high and the environmental benefits of avoidance are questionable. Under current inflexible sequencing rules, neither the foregone development value nor environmental outcomes of permit denial would be considered. And if for some reason the permit is granted, compensation would focus primarily on in-kind and on-site replacement. The economy and the environment stand to lose. We need to turn wetlands regulation to a broader goal, by creating markets for wetlands functions and by overcoming the inflexibility that creates high economic and environmental costs.

How do we do that? By recognizing that a market-based policy is the next generation of reform beyond mitigation banking. The mitigation bank is a tool to make off-site compensation for wetlands losses which are permitted in the regulatory program. But there are limitations to the current ideas about banking. First, compensation ratios when a permit is granted seek no net loss of functions. Restoration should achieve a net gain where more than one unit of credit is expected in return for each unit of permitted loss. Also, the mitigation bank relies on the wetlands developer to undertake restoration or creation as the deposit to the bank. For most permit applicants, this is financially unworkable. For the watershed, the wetlands compensations required are too small to realize the scale economies that might be achieved by larger scale restoration. And placing the responsibility for successful restoration and creation on people who have neither the expertise, experience, nor long-term interest in wetlands and watersheds dooms many restorations to failure.

A market-based policy begins with a recognition: the applicant wants a permit, but the regulatory agency wants to protect and restore the ecological functions of watersheds. These incompatible objectives have the potential for deal making, which is the essence of markets. A market-based permitting program will separate the decision on the granting of a permit from decisions about where and when to restore wetlands.

A market-based approach includes a permit review process whereby the magnitude of development value is considered in granting a permit. A share of that development value is then captured by the agency and put toward the benefit of the watershed. The system works through the exchange of money and permits in order to support scientifically sound and well-managed wetlands restoration programs, toward the goal of net-gain. The recipient of a wetlands development permit makes the money payment either to the permitting agency or to a private firm which restores wetlands and sells the credits directly to wetlands developers.

I expected to hear opposition to market-based approaches, so let me anticipate two of the arguments. Some in the development community might be opposed to a share-the-gain rule for setting compensation ratios and fees. Yet for the society at large to be willing to move beyond the current sequencing rules there must be some perceived opportunity to be environmentally better off with-versus-without any given permit being issued. When a permit is granted with a no-net-loss regulatory goal, all of the net economic returns accrue to the applicant. A share-the-gain approach could secure some of that return for wetlands programs. There must be a willingness to share gains—not claim extortion or a taking. As noted earlier, the current regulatory program already implicitly imposes a development tax. This proposal simply makes the tax explicit.

The wetlands protection establishment also will stand in the way. Its concern is that degraded wetlands can never be restored to their previous condition. Skepticism about wetlands creation is even more widespread. This concern is based on past experiences with restoration and creation which have often not been successful. Unfortunately, critics of restoration and creation fail to distinguish between failures of the science and failures from poor application of the science. Most failures are probably attributable to unclear goals, inadequate expertise in doing the restoration, and an absence of monitoring to make modifications to the projects over time. These are institutional failures which must be addressed with policy and program reform, but should not be used as an excuse to reject the possibility of successful restoration and creation.

All of the preceding comments lead me to the subject of classification, because the market-based approach depends on classification. Wetlands management to serve the larger purpose of watershed restoration would begin by initiating a planning process of watershed re-design to establish the sizes, types, and locations of wetlands/uplands complexes that will have the potential for long-term survival as functioning ecosystems. This could be accomplished in the SAMP (Special Area Management Plan) process under the Coastal Zone Management Act, in the Advanced Identification Program under §404, or as part of a separate watershed planning authority under state or regional authority.

Existing wetlands might be classified into three types based on the following criteria. Criterion one would consider the magnitude of the ecological value to the watershed of the site proposed for development if the permit is denied. This is a critical notion because the criterion acknowledges the possibility of degradation, isolation, and fragmentation even if the wetlands site is saved. The second criterion is the difficulty and cost of restoring or creating lost functions if the permit is granted. The third criterion is the magnitude of the development value to the landowner that will be realized if the permit is granted. The more the development value, the more gain there is to share.

With these criteria three classes of wetlands follow: Class I would be those wetlands of exceptionally high ecological value, with functions that are costly or difficult to replicate and for which development values are likely to be low. Avoidance is the best management strategy for these wetlands areas and only the most obvious water-dependent and high-value development would be even considered for a permit.

Class II wetlands are where the wetlands site now has modest functional value to the watershed, or where the current value will be compromised even if the permit for filling is denied. These should also be wetlands where cost-effective restoration of functions is possible and where development values may be high enough to achieve the net-gain goal. Some flexibility in sequencing is expected as particular circumstances dictate. Class III wetlands would be areas where a fixed development fee might be established with only limited permit review being required.

General rules for classification can be established and maps that describe protected areas and the lower value—fee for development—areas might be depicted. However, the actual classification of any given site should be made only during a permit review. The criteria from permit to permit should be consistent, but the factors that will lead to a particular classification will change as development patterns change and as the state of restoration science changes. Also, rigid advanced classification will introduce questions of property value takings.

Let me conclude by saying that a nation unable to define wetlands and with no explicit policy defining the purposes and intergovernmental responsibility for regulation of the wetlands which are defined will be hard pressed to devise creative solutions to wetlands regulation challenges, including classification schemes. Indeed, the classification debate has often been intractable because we have not first come to grips with the goals and strategies for the regulatory framework. Thinking about reform in market-oriented terms will allow no net loss to give way to net gain. And the net-gain goal within the market-oriented strategy will clarify the meaning and purpose of classification.

A Work in Progress

Peter Matthiessen

In this passage from the next novel in the trilogy that began with *Killing Mr. Watson*, a grizzled swamp dweller ruminates on the sorry state of affairs in the Everglades. While Peter Matthiessen might not admire his protagonist, he shares some of his sentiments.

Matthiessen has eloquently documented the degradation of natural environments and native cultures in both fiction and nonfiction. A Matthiessen portrait of North American migratory birds begins on page 102.

Speck sat down and accepted a tin plate of food. "More fish on this plate than I seen all week. Never seen fishing so poor since the Red Tide. Them fish is just as fed up with the National god-damn Park as I am." To Whidden he said, "When your people first come here to Lost Man's, trout and snook and mullet was so thick right back in here that you could dance on 'em, it was a pure astonishment to the heart and eye. In this damned sorry day and age, a man can't hardly get enough to feed his cat."

He held his plate close under his nose, so that his eyebrows bristled over his food. "Us local people likes our fish, y'know. Local people don't eat shark or manatee, and ain't all of 'em will eat a turtle. Won't eat conch neither—call that nigger food. But over to Key West and the Bahamas, them people will eat conch and glad to get it. That's how come we call 'em Conches, I guess.

"Used to land one half-million pounds of good fish ever' year; by the end I was doing good to land one tenth of it. Now they won't let us commercial fish at all, that's how bad it is, and this was one of the great fisheries of the whole world!

"Yessir, when the Parks come in, they told us if we left our homesteads peaceable, we could set net out of Flamingo for the rest of our natural life. For some damn reason, I thought their word was good. Man is only as good as his word, we used to say, and this was the federal damn government!

"I never knew the U.S. government would tell a barefaced lie like that. If them damn bureaucrats and politicians can get away with it, they'll steal you blind. Hypocrites and liars, right up to the President, just tell the stupid-ass damn public any damn old thing to keep their ass covered! This is the greatest country in the world, it *hurts* me to speak bad about my country, but the truth's the truth." Speck gasped for breath. "Hell, I ain't *talkin'* to my own country, not no more. A man can't trust one word they say that ain't writ down in black and white, signed, sealed, and hand-delivered, and even then, it don't mean diddly shit, they'll find a way to screw you all the same. I got an idea now how them Injuns must of felt about all them broken treaties, bein' lied to and stole off of and generally fucked over for two hundred years!

"Weren't that the way you was brought up? To trust the government?" He spat into the flames. "Well, now they screwed up the whole Everglades, and they ain't no fish left anyway, so it don't matter.

"My granddaddy died in 1945, two years before they put in the damned park—he sure hit a lucky streak when he done that. That park coming in beat anything I ever saw. Told us we could live there at Flamingo and commercial fish right where we was at for the rest of our natural lives, and turned right around once they got in, just threw us out.

"We moved over to Homestead, that was 1951. Offered us two dollars an acre, got a little more—got seven, eight thousand for everything, take it or don't. Parks burnt our fish houses, hundred-foot dock and all—that hurt, you know, all that hard work wasted. You take fellers like us, fishing is all we ever done, or know to do. I don't understand how they could go and burn up all that hard hand work, I just don't understand the stupid waste of it. And then they raise up holy hell when us poor fellers went over to hunting crocs and gators in the park! Well, now them things is all died off for lack of good freshwater in the Glades, we're back to smugglin' just like our daddies done, and granddaddies, too—aigrette plumes and bottleg liquor, guns and gator flats, it just don't matter. The law can't catch us back here in amongst these mangroves and it never could.

"One time a feller from St. Augustine, got him a zoo, he paid me to hunt him up some crocs. Sure enough, he shows up at my house one evening—'Got muh croc-o-diles?'

"I says, 'Sure thing, they's sixteen right out back.' But when I poked my head around the house, all I seen out there was a Cadillac convertible. 'What in the hell you aim to *haul* 'em in?' I says.

" 'Muh car,' he says.

" 'Your *car*? Why, hell,' I says, 'I got one here that goes twelve feet, fill that whole Cadillac!'

" 'Twelve *feet*!?' he hollers. 'I want *that* 'un *now*!'

"So we jump on that croc and rassle him around, roll him up into a ball, got him humped some way into the trunk, that tail rung out like a dang mule in a tin stall. I fling the smaller ones in the backseat, they hit that velveteen just a-snappin' and a-crapping', and this croc fancier don't mind one bit. Takes off for St. Augustine bumping the ground with the load of crocs he's got in there, left a big 'ol ugly cloud of smoke right in my yard.

"Next time he showed up, he bought him a hen crocodile had a big hump on her shoulders, big as a coconut. Said, 'That 'un don't look so good, I'll give you ten down and twenty-five on top if she goes two weeks.' So he sent a envelope without no money into it, notified me she had upped and died. Well, the next year I was going through St. Augustine, stopped over to see him, and there was my humped-up crocodile, star of the show!

"So I says, 'My, my, that pretty little hen you got in there, damned if she don't look some way familiar!'" Speck nodded a little at the memory. "Well, you fellers know somethin'? I must've hurt that feller's feelings! 'Cause he hollered out, 'No, no, no, *no,* that there ain't your ol' hen at all!'" Speck nodded more. "That's the way we left it, 'cause I didn't have no brand on her nor pedigree nor nothin'." The old man sighed. "That feller had him a good head for the croc business, is what it was. That's how you get you one them Cadillac convertibles, I reckon.

"Used to be plenty of crocodiles down Florida Bay. I guess I could still find a few, but I'd have to hunt for 'em. When the Parks took over, anytime you showed me one crocodile east of the park, I could take you *in* the park and show you fifty. Today any crocodile you show me *in* the park, I'll take you outside and show you five."

Speck Daniels spat into the flames. "I told 'em, 'You're so worried about the crocodiles but you're the ones to blame, 'cause you go down there, go messin' with the nest. It's just like birds, you keep messin' with the nest, they're goin' to leave it.' Said, 'You went down there and caught them crocs, put beepers on 'em, electrical fuckin' apparatus to where you can follow 'em around two miles away. It's like a damn horse, you tie a kerchief to his tail, he'll run hisself to death trying to get rid of it. Can't find no crocs to hang beepers on no more, but you still got the guts to wonder what become of 'em!'"

Whidden poked the fire: "Bill Smallwood was telling me how back in the Forties, you could see lots of crocs from the Key West Highway if you knew what you was looking for."

"Well, to see one now, you got to organize a damn safari, and," Speck said, "even then, you got to night-light 'em, and even then, all you might get is a puff of mud or a little far-off ripple crost the water." He spat violently again. "'Cause they just *ain't* no crocodiles no more—them big old crocs are few and far between and they are by no manner of means the only old-time critters that are going. Look at your sawfish, sea turtle, your manatees! Your bears and panthers! Them things was common all around these rivers in my daddy's time! And them aigrettes, more scare today than what they was when every cracker in south Florida was a damn plume hunter! It's like I told Parks, 'If you go on like this, you'll have a big dead country on your hands, is all, just dead water and mud, sawgrass and mangrove.'

"Them bureaucrats admitted right in public that wild four-legged critters was down 70 percent, and the birds 95 percent. I said, 'You aimin' to wait until the other 5 percent is gone before you admit you don't know what you're doin'?'

"Cut the water comin' south from Okeechobee and just ruined the Everglades is what they done. Ruined one of the greatest fisheries, wrecked the most beautiful country in the world. It's just layin' out there now, no use to nobody."

Bay Country

Tom Horton

With a history of habitat modification dating back to colonial times, the natural state of Chesapeake Bay can only be a matter of speculation. This passage was excerpted from a chapter in which the author ponders the dual question: What is natural, what is right?

Tom Horton lives on the eastern shore of the Chesapeake and is a regular contributor to the *Baltimore Sun.*

It is winter in Harford County, and, crouched in a blind, I am watching, almost forgetting to breathe as dozens of bald eagles glide silently down the long shafts of setting sun to roost in the tall, dead trees. It is one of the largest concentrations of this magnificent and endangered species outside wild Alaska. Ah, wilderness! Well, hardly. The roost is downrange on the U.S. Army's Aberdeen Proving Ground, and there is scarcely a minute when the calm is not punctuated by the pounding of 120-millimeter howitzers. The eagles seem not to mind. Their numbers increase here with each winter.

It is summer at the Chincoteague National Wildlife Refuge, and I am marveling to a ranger at the eye-stretching sweep of pristine marsh, dune, and ponds. All about, a diverse population of migratory wildfowl is strewn like confetti. It is inspiring—also "100 percent managed," the ranger proudly replies. The dunes have been bulldozed up and stabilized with plantings of beach grass. The ponds were dug to catch fresh water, and equipped with floodgates to divert the annual coastal run of young eels into the impoundments as a food supply to hold the birds there. At night, floodlights attracted crab larvae to a nearby ocean cove, where a powerful pump sucked them through a pipe laid across a road and into one of the ponds, where crabbers would exclaim at nature's bounty in months to come.

It is fall at Horsehead Farm, a waterfowl preserve in Queen Anne's County, and a photographer friend is remarking at the frosted, natural beauty of dawn light illuminating the feathery plumes of tall reeds that surround us. I tell him the reeds are phragmites, an introduced species despised as a weed by all card-carrying environmentalists, because it out-competes the indigenous bay grasses and offers little food value to wildlife.

What is it we mean anymore by the "natural environment"? The closer we look, the harder it seems to know. The forestry ecologists sneer at reporters who throw around terms like *virgin forest*. There probably aren't ten acres of a really unaltered climax forest ecosystem in the state anymore, they say. Meanwhile a peregrine falcon, symbol of all that is fierce and untamed and free, hatches eastern North America's first chicks (called *eyases*) in the wild in thirty years—hatches them in downtown Baltimore, on a granite ledge of the United States Fidelity and Guaranty Building's thirty-third floor. Cities, it turns out, concentrate pigeons and rats, candy to peregrines, better than nature ever could.

It is often said by managers in environmental agencies that the hardest step in saving the Chesapeake Bay, or any ecosystem for that matter, is deciding what kind of environment we want to preserve. As natural an environment as possible, you say—but how to define that? We lament the vanishing of fish and animal habitat before civilization's march, but any wildlife expert will tell you there are far more deer in Maryland, and in most of the nation now, than ever existed in the days of the Indians. And consider wild geese, whose numbers around the bay have grown from a few thousand in the 1930s ("you could get your picture in the paper for shootin' one then," a Cambridge resident told me), to nearly one million nowadays. Likewise, although we have become so alarmed about the decline of the state fish, the rockfish, as to place a moratorium on catching them, the bay's crab population is booming, and total production of fish in the estuary quite possibly has never been higher. If pollution is killing the bay, it seems awfully selective.

What else can we say about the "natural" state of things?

We learned, during five days in June 1972, that events occurring in nature can be so catastrophic as to overwhelm our best efforts at pollution control. Tropical Storm Agnes so accelerated the natural sedimentation processes that are gradually filling in the bay, it was said to have "aged" the estuary many decades in less than a week. Another century of enforcing the state's sediment pollution laws on every developer and farmer scarcely will offset Agnes.

The natural state of things can also be overstated, and come to represent an impossible goal. Legislators, watermen, and even scientists who should know better often cite the fifteen million–bushel oyster harvests of a century ago as an example of the bay's prepollution productivity. But that Everestian peak of harvest (current ones are about one million bushels annually) was mostly indicative of uncontrolled rape, as huge steam vessels scraped the bottom bald with their gaping dredges, taking shell and undersized oysters along with the adults. It was a harvest rate insupportable for more than a few years by the most pristine bay that ever existed.

Another example: some knowledgeable fisheries experts have speculated that the capacity of the bay to produce large numbers of rockfish may well have been greater in the mid-twentieth century than in the days of Captain John Smith. True, the explorer's party described rock so thick one could nearly walk on their broad backs, and that was probably not too far-fetched, because there was very little harvest pressure, and the fish can live for several decades. But as for the *rate* of reproduction, the betting is that up to a point (perhaps now exceeded) our injection of more nutrients into the system, via sewage and farm fertilizers, probably grew far greater supplies of microscopic aquatic life whose supply is critical to how many baby rockfish survive each year.

What, then, are we to make of our conventional image of human beings as spoilers—numbers of people up, pollution up, and environmental quality down? How do we interpret environmentalist urgings not to manipulate or intervene with nature when *natural* seems such an elusive quality, and sometimes not what we'd like it to be? I would be suspicious of anyone who claimed to have all the answers, but a few guidelines suggest themselves. You must be wary of using any single species as an indication of natural quality. There are at least a couple reasons why deer are more abundant now than in Indian days. We have killed off all the big predators, cougar and wolf and the like; and our massive forest-clearing activities, while polluting streams and destroying habitat for many deep-woods species, have nonetheless created lots of what game biologists call *edge habitat,* or areas where forest debouches on field or pasture. It just happens that such junctions favor deer, especially when one side includes a cornfield.

It is the massive proliferation of corn-growing since World War II that has led to the abundance of wild geese. Ironically, our expanded grain agriculture resulted in a huge increase in fertilizer, washed by rains into the bay in such unremitting quantities that it has killed the submerged grass beds. And these grasses were the prime food of ducks like the canvasback, which will not feed in the cornfields. So we have more geese, but few canvasbacks. The trade-off is more than geese for ducks. It is a loss of balance and diversity, which are pretty good indicators of health and resilience and stability in natural systems. The submerged grasses also were critical in absorbing pollutants from sewage, and in harboring dozens of aquatic species during one stage or another in their life cycle.

As for the paradoxical health of crabs even as their fellow bay dwellers, the rockfish, have declined, it is misleading to treat them equally as indicators of pollution just because we find them in the same waters as adults. Rather, look to where each species spends its most vulnerable, larval stages. The crab spawns in the clean, oceanic environment of the bay's mouth, whereas the rock, and virtually every other species that is reproducing poorly—shad, herring, yellow and white perch—spawn in the streams and rivers close to the polluting influences of civilization. Again, we have a natural system that, in terms of gross seafood landings, seems booming right along, but is seriously out of kilter. You must look at all the parts, and their relations to all the other parts. Only then can you begin to judge what is natural.

Of the eagles at Aberdeen, it was in retrospect a happy accident, the army's sealing off eighty thousand acres of open field, forest, marsh, and water on Harford County's bay shore during World War I. Given the ferocity of development that has consumed so much of the surrounding natural waterfront, it seems likely nothing less than the fire power of an army division could have kept Aberdeen Proving Ground sacrosanct. It is profoundly humbling that constant cannon fire has been far less destructive to the environment than the condos and suburbs and marinas; and that our national symbol, the eagle, would rather endure the sounds of war than the sight of human settlement.

The havoc wrought by natural catastrophes like Tropical Storm Agnes often is used by the unthinking or the unscrupulous as an excuse not to bother with environmental protection. Don't worry about more control of a certain air pollutant, they say; one eruption of a volcano can dwarf our manufactured quantities of it. I prefer the Boy Scout philosophy—leave the campsite as you found it, if not better, for you are just passing through. The only responsible course is to do whatever we can to put the least possible burden on the environment, because we cannot predict the frequency of a volcano or an Agnes, which some feel was at least a once-in-500-years storm. It is intriguing to reverse the natural-catastrophe argument and ask: Has anyone ever stopped developing the Ocean City beach front because at some point a hurricane is likely to offset our efforts?

What is natural? What is right? Here are some absolutes. Curves are natural. We grow up hearing so often that a straight line is the shortest distance between two points that we end up thinking it is also the *best* way to get there. A river knows better—it has to do with how it dissipates the energy of its flow most efficiently; and how, in its bends, the sediment deposited soon turns into marshes and swampy islands, harboring all manner of interesting life, imparting charm and character to the whole waterway. I would defy you to find a river on this planet that prefers to run straight, unless it has been taught so by the U.S. Army Corps of Engineers. People do exist who seem to prefer the straight line to the meander, the ditch to the creek, but it is mostly a failure of education that they are so unaware of the natural beauty and values of the curve.

Changelessness, or at least the diligent pursuit of it, is a good. Many environmentalists and ecologists feel that precisely because it is so hard to know what is natural, we should, in any decision affecting the environment, consider first how *not* to change the existing order. Aldo Leopold once wrote: "If the biota in the course of eons has built something we like but don't understand, then who but a fool would discard seemingly useless parts. To keep every cog and wheel is the first premise of intelligent tinkering." Of course, the "no-build" alternative is a required consideration of all federal Environmental Impact Statements nowadays, but we seldom accord it the seriousness it deserves. When we do, the results can be gratifying. A California law requires a power company proposing say, a $1 billion power plant, to first calculate whether the same billion, spent on conservation, solar power, storm windows, and so forth, could not save more energy than the new plant would generate. The law has avoided several new plants. I wish every schoolchild in Maryland could be allowed to hike, hunt, fish, swim, and breath the clean air at some of the sites in rural Maryland reserved by the state and by utility companies for future power plants. It would do much to make them lifelong advocates of energy conservation.

At the extreme in promoting changelessness are some Indian tribes who hold certain lands so numinous they have made them holy places. I make no such pretensions, but it is true that one of my favorite fishing spots, on the remote Honga River in Dorchester County, has not yielded a fish for me in years. I go there for the view of pine and salt marsh and bay; it is one of the few places to have remained just the same as in my boyhood memories. I suspect mine is not an isolated or silly sentiment. It may be one reason that close to one million fishermen a year keep coming back to the bay even though, according to state creel surveys, more than a third of all their trips produce no fish at all. They must be hooking into something else, something natural and deeply satisfying, and it may have to do with changelessness.

Finally, I would propose the quality of *wildness* as a valuable aspect of what is natural. Yes, it can be partly a created thing, like the lovely, constructed scene at the Chincoteague Refuge; but there we have only provided a setting, a way station. Crab, osprey, canvasback duck, great blue heron, and migrating eel—all bear witness that larger natural systems, far beyond our ability to concoct, still survive. There is considerable energy being expended these days around the Chesapeake Bay to build hatcheries to produce more rockfish, resurrect the American shad, and repopulate the bay with waterfowl. It would only be to augment depleted natural populations until we can turn the environment around to let them come back naturally, the hatchery proponents say. But the concept has such power, you can see the undercurrent of their thinking—if worst comes to worst, don't worry, we can just hatch our fish and birds for our sport; and if the migratory flights of the herons and ospreys should ever flag, well, a small hatchery tucked away in the pines at Chincoteague, one supposes, could supply the ponds indefinitely. If it worked, why knock it? A heron is a heron is a heron.

But that is to confuse nature with zoos. A wild trout implies a whole watershed still forested enough, still enough removed from human pollution, to maintain a clean, cold, constant flow in its streams. A canvasback duck, as it plops down on the bay's surface one fall morning, brings with it the certitude that some of the vast, lovely prairie pothole marshes of Saskatchewan, its nesting and summering grounds, remain inviolate. A hatchery trout or a hatchery duck would be just as beautiful, but something natural would be missing, something would not seem right. The author and Maryland native John Barth, in a discussion on the bay's future, once speculated that perhaps, just perhaps, our technologies could succeed in keeping the waters clean and productive even as we ringed the estuary with "wall-to-wall Glen Burnies." We would still have oysters, crabs, and rockfish, but we would not have the bay, he said. "The spirit," he said, "would have gone out of it."

The River Always Wins

Ted Williams

In early 1993 the great rivers of America's midsection reasserted themselves over much of the Mississippi Basin. In the aftermath of the flood, some of the area's residents are rebuilding their levees and their lives on the floodplain; others are pulling out. Government agencies, for their part, are compensating some to stay, others to leave.

Ted Williams writes on environmental issues for various periodicals. This piece was excerpted from an article that originally appeared in *Audubon* magazine.

Strapped into the shotgun seat of the Missouri Department of Conservation's Cessna 182, I inspected the stone revetments that were supposed to have shackled the Mississippi River's biggest tributary, the Missouri. Now, on the ides of March 1994, they were under sand and under water. Everywhere the floodplain was cratered with scour holes, as if it had been saturation-bombed by B-52s. Some are 50 feet deep and 200 yards across; even the Army says it can't afford to fill them in.

Still, the Corps is trying to repair its flood-containment array, which, throughout the Mississippi Basin, includes 30 super levees it built itself and 1,500 private levees, most of which were engineered to its specifications and funded four to one with federal dollars. By the time you read this, all the federal levees and about half the private levees will be up again.

Three thousand feet below me, in a scene from an ant farm, bulldozers crawled over cropland reclaimed by the river, pushing silt into failed levees and making new ones around the upland shores of scour holes. Sand covered former corn, wheat, and soybean fields up to four miles back from midchannel. It had drifted to 10-foot depths, burying boat ramps and silos, buckling the sad, broken husks of houses and barns where nothing lives now save lonely cottonwoods planted by families who thought the river had been defeated. There was sand in front of us, sand in back of us, sand as far as I could see.

On the ground at Grafton, Illinois, where the Mississippi collects the Illinois River coming down from Chicago, I stopped for lunch at Beasley's Fresh Fish. Jim Beasley nets the river; his wife, Deborah, does the cooking. The water had lapped the bottom of their sign four feet above my head, but they'd gotten everything out in time, and the cement walls had held. Other people weren't so lucky. The road along the river was lined with abandoned houses waterstained to the eaves, some leaning with the flow. A piece of flotsam hung from a telephone wire.

Tired of rebuilding, the citizens of Grafton have voted to move a third of the town out of the river and up onto dry land. In all, about 200 Mississippi Basin communities from southern Missouri to Wisconsin will make major retreats from floodplain living, at a total cost to U.S. taxpayers of $500 million. "If you know anything about the history of the Midwest, you know that people who came here were going to cling to the land regardless of what they could get out of it," says Scott Faber of American Rivers, a nonprofit conservation organization. "This is *unheard-of*."

I stopped at the café in Hartsburg, Missouri, but it was closed and won't reopen. Lots of the residents aren't going to rebuild. The town was lonely and silent, save for the procession of dump trucks hauling dirt down to the ruptured levee. The four-foot-high banks of dry river mud along the streets had been plowed up like snow. Broken sandbags surrounded broken neighborhoods. Houses slumped windowless beside rubble-filled dumpsters. A tilted sign with two letters missing said: HARTSBURG THANKS EVER ON. HELL OF A TRY.

Standing in one of the levee breaks was levee-district president Orion Beckmeyer—hazel eyed, steel haired, leather skinned, a farmer since 1961. Now farmers in Hartsburg and elsewhere are considering pulling their operations out of the river. Under the Soil Conservation Service's $100 million Wetlands Reserve Program, they can convert qualifying acreage to wetlands by selling easements to the government. But if the farmers do that, they can't gouge dirt from the wetlands to fix their levees.

"It's taking a man's property use without paying for it," laments Beckmeyer, who is thinking about selling wetland easements on 30 of his own acres now covered with thigh-deep sand. "I don't know where that leaves this country. God gave us these resources, and we need to use them. We need to feed the world."

Three hundred miles north, in Louisa County, Iowa, ice lingered in the Mississippi's backwater puddles left from the big flood, and the red-winged blackbirds, old news in Grafton and Hartsburg, had just arrived. Now they were flashing their red epaulets and shouting from every snag. They were seeing a different sort of spring. The U.S. Fish and Wildlife Service flew me over one of its metal water-inlet structures in the Mark Twain National Wildlife Refuge. The dike that used to be level with it wasn't broken—it was *gone*, sheared off at ground level. Now what remains just stands there, a monument to river power and human impotence.

Slightly downstream and a little way up the Iowa River, we orbited over 3,000-acre Levee District Eight while an adult bald eagle orbited below us. Maybe it was hunting fish in the recharged, reclaimed oxbow lakes. Sealed from the river by the levee, the oxbows had silted in, and their fish had died out. But now the river had returned as it would return each spring through the hopelessly ventilated flood barrier, scouring out the silt, collecting young fish, spreading spawners. This is how rivers used to work before the engineers "improved" them, to use their word. Here, at least, the Mississippi and its ecosystem were breathing again.

Later that day I inspected the blown-out levee with Tom Bell, Wapello District manager for the Mark Twain Refuge. The sun was warm on our necks, the air cool and scented with old fish and new mud. Crows jeered at a red-tailed hawk. Shovelers cut V wakes on the oxbow lakes. Mallards burst out of flooded timber. Gulls caroused over gizzard shad stranded in a year-old puddle. A redheaded woodpecker played peekaboo with us from behind a pin oak. To our left the Iowa River had cleansed a field of corn, leaving driftwood and stubble sticking up through sand. New wetlands were everywhere; and the only sounds were made by wildlife.

The river at Levee District Eight had been trying to tell people something. Eighteen times over the past 66 years it had busted up the levee, and 18 times humans had fixed it. The 1990 repairs had taken so long that the farmers didn't get a crop the next year. Crop-insurance premiums were going up; payments, based on crop yield, were doing down. Still, when the river busted up the levee in 1993, the Corps prepared to plod ahead in its war with Mother Nature. The big levees the Corps builds itself. But if you sign up for its private-levee program and do your bulldozing to government standards, you can chase the retreating water almost to the bank, and the Corps will pay 80 percent of the repair cost each time the river breaks your levee. The only catch is that the alleged benefits have to outweigh the costs, usually not a problem.

Had the farmers come up with their 20 percent ($160,000), the Corps would have replaced its Maginot Line around Levee District Eight yet again. But this time even the farmers had had enough, especially now that they had a chance to sell out to the Fish and Wildlife Service. The service couldn't put its hands on the cash, so it turned to the National Fish and Wildlife Foundation—an eight-year-old organization hatched and partly funded by Congress. The foundation put up a no-interest emergency loan of $250,000 and arranged a matching loan from a private group called the Conservation Fund. The Iowa Natural Heritage Foundation pledged $10,000 and agreed to do the actual land transactions, and the Soil Conservation Service provided $1.7 million. "This is the first time anything like this has been attempted," declares the National Fish and Wildlife Foundation executive director Amos Eno, "and we're going to be doing a lot more of it."

Game Wars

Marc Reisner

To combat the lucrative black market trade in wildlife, the U.S. Fish and Wildlife Service employs undercover agents who can think like—and sometimes strike deals with—poachers. In this excerpt from Marc Reisner's firsthand account of how undercover game wardens operate, the central figure of the book talks about his philosophy of conservation.

Marc Reisner is a San Francisco–based writer with a particular interest in water resources and wetland environments.

A pair of geese make a racket. A few thousand geese make a very loud racket. We pulled over, rolled down the windows, and the cacophony was electrifying. The landscape was boringly flat—a bleak panorama of lone trees and marshes and stubbly fields—but the geese in their numbers made it mesmerizingly wild. There were ducks, too, hundred of them, swimming and dabbling in the irrigation canals. Most were pintails, which are beautiful, elegant ducks; the males have a long pointed tail and a mottled feather pattern like walnut burl. But they were reduced to nonentity status by the crowds of shrieking, braying geese.

Dave Hall began to drive again. He was hunched forward, steering with his elbow, peering through the upper windshield at a swarm of geese that had just funneled like smoke out of a nearby field. Then he was driving with a pair of binoculars trained on the geese. "More speckle-bellies," he said. "We got quite a few this year."

"Dave, do you still hunt geese?"

"Yup."

"Do you eat them?"

"Sure."

"Is a white-fronted goose good to eat?"

"It's the best. A speckle-belly tastes like a great big pintail."

"You love waterfowl more than anything in the out-of-doors."

"Sure. That's right. I am a duck and goose freak."

"But you eat them."

"Sure I do."

"Isn't it like eating your kids?"

"What do *you* eat?"

"Many animals are executed for my dining pleasure. I just have a hard time eating ducks and geese anymore."

"If it wasn't for waterfowl hunters, we'd hardly have any ducks *or* geese anymore. It's the users of the resource who have done the most to protect them. How many anti-hunters do you see buying up a couple million acres of Canadian marshland for nesting refuges? Does Ducks Unlimited do that, or do the Friends of Animals do that?"

"I've talked to some game wardens who won't hunt anymore. Or at least some have told me they won't hunt waterfowl until the populations go back up."

"I've heard that kind of bullbleep from a lot of game wardens, too. If I quit hunting, man, I'd probably turn into one of these antis who want to close it all down, too. But you wouldn't stop *poaching*. And if I quit, I'd be no good at my job. If you're a game warden, you've got to hunt to understand how a goose thinks. Then when you've got goose hunters around, you know what they're doing because you know what the geese are doing. Then you can get to the right place at the right time, and if the hunters have got overlimits you can nail their ass. You show me a game warden who's so correct he won't hunt and fish anymore, and I'll show you he ain't worth a damn at the job. Those are the same kind who're ineffective as undercover wardens. They hate the outlaws so much they can't even associate with them. You can't be an undercover agent if you aren't willing to associate with a lot of riffraff. Ivory poachers, goose creepers, drug pushers—they're all alike. Riffraff."

We passed a sign announcing that we had entered the Lacassine Refuge. The rice fields reverted instantly to marsh. We were still hearing geese, but now most of them were hidden by the tall water grasses that blanketed the refuge. The road became dirt, then rolled up onto a levee and rolled off again, at a small cluster of wooden buildings on a couple acres of lawn, overshadowed by huge willows. One of the buildings said REFUGE HEADQUARTERS.

The three people inside seemed relieved to see us. Two were employed by the Fish and Wildlife Service, graduate-level Eagle Scouts dressed in government brown with bronze name tags pinned to their chests. The third man was older, perhaps thirty-five or forty, with a walnut-oil complexion and thick, curly black hair. He was wearing new Levi's, a checkered flannel shirt, and a brown cotton jacket. He was handsome, with an air of quiet dignity in repose, but there was something sinister underneath—it was a brutally handsome face. The body was formed to match—five feet eight, close to two hundred pounds, a small running back with explosive speed.

Dave Hall had become prickly and a little gloomy in the car. Now he was suddenly animated.

"Hey, A.J.!" he said to the older man.

"How you doon, Dave?"

Dave Hall turned to the two wardens. "How you fellows today?"

"We're fine," said one.

"You been talking to old A.J. about his outlawin days?"

A.J. shuffled and stared at the floor. The wardens smiled faintly but said nothing.

"My friend's a writer," said Dave Hall. "He's gonna interview A.J. about alligator huntin. How many gators do you suppose you killed on the Lacassine Wildlife Refuge, A.J.?"

A.J. looked curiously at me, then back at his feet. "I doan believe I ever did outlaw on the Lacassine Refuge."

Even the Eagle Scouts had to laugh. A smile flickered across A.J.'s solemn face and disappeared. "Ask me no questions and I'll tell you no lies."

"How many, really?" persisted Dave Hall.

A.J. shrugged.

"A.J., then, dammit, what is the *most* alligators you ever killed in one night?"

"Hundred fourteen."

"Hundred fourteen," echoed Dave Hall. "Figure it. Back then you're getting . . . what? . . ."

"Bout eight dollars a foot."

"Eight dollars a linear foot. Say the average gator is five feet. Forty dollars a gator times a hundred fourteen is . . ."

The two young refuge wardens were wide-eyed.

". . . is four thousand five hundred–plus dollars for one night's outlawin."

"Maybe that's high," said A.J. "I doan recall puttin that kinda money in the bank."

"The *bank!*" Dave Hall laughed. He turned to the wardens, then to me. "You see now why we had such a hellacious time shutting these old gator poachers down? It was the best money on the bayou. It was a whole hell of a lot better than working some old oil rig, don't deny that, A.J. A hunter who was good and diligent could make more money than the president of the local bank!"

"Unless he embezzles or somethin, a bank president doan go to jail," said A.J.

Dave Hall grinned. "A.J., you know I never put you in jail, though I'd have loved to. I took you *out* of the Cameron Parish jail."

"You done that. You know I'm grateful for it."

The Eagle Scouts seemed more puzzled than ever. Here was perhaps the best-known game warden in the United States swapping stories with one of the most audacious alligator poachers in Louisiana history. What was this about Dave Hall getting Caro *out* of jail?

"A.J. used to wade chest-high through the marshes with a .22 rifle on his back and his arms flat by his side so they didn't end up in some gator's mouth," said Dave Hall. "He'd zonk them gators and skin them in the marsh. *You* try skinning a gator in the middle of a swamp at night. Then he'd drag a thousand dollars in hides back to camp. Isn't that right, A.J.?"

"Right," said A.J. "Always keep your arms by your sides."

Wetlands or Just Wet Lands?

Gordy Slack

The San Francisco Bay Area is home to some of the world's most expensive real estate, as well as some of the most adamant environmentalists, who are acutely aware that much of the Bay Area's development has taken place on filled salt marsh habitat. Hence, when the owner of a huge tract of vacant bayside land wanted to go the route of development, it touched off a precedent-setting legal action.

Gordy Slack is associate editor of the California Academy of Sciences magazine, *Pacific Discovery*. This story was originally published in 1991 and was updated in 1995 for this anthology.

Next time you fly into San Francisco International Airport from the south, ask the person next to you what's in those huge blue, green, and pink geometric patches of water that dominate the South Bay. I've heard them described as fisheries, pharmaceutical plants, and bacteria farms. Even an airline pilot who flies over the ponds half a dozen times a week didn't know what they were. "Down below, you see San Francisco's sewage treatment plants," the pilot informed his passengers.

In fact, those multi-colored squares are concentrating and crystallizer ponds used by the Leslie Salt Company to produce nearly one million tons of salt a year. They occupy approximately 30,000 acres of bay coastal lands—more than half of the bay south of the San Mateo Bridge. Although they aren't pristine wilderness, they certainly aren't sewage. The salt ponds are saltier than the bay (the colors are produced by the different microorganisms that can survive the various levels of salinity), but they still provide crucial wildlife habitat to fish, shrimp, burrowing owls, and some endangered species. The ponds are also extremely important to the 200,000 wintering shorebirds and 75,00 wintering waterfowl that depend on them each year.

In 1978 Leslie Salt was purchased by Cargill, one of the largest privately owned companies in the U.S., spurring fears among conservationists that the Minneapolis-based company would divide the property and sell it for development at high bayside real estate prices. Though most of the property comes squarely under the protection of federal laws against development of wetlands, the legal status of thousands of acres of Leslie's land, primarily that used or once used in the final, crystallization, stage of salt production, is less clear.

Wetland activists want to see all of Leslie's property remain in salt production, see it restored to tidal wetlands, or protected as seasonal wetlands. Leslie executives, however, insist that though they have no major development plans, they retain the right to sell their land to the highest bidder. They fear that its value will plummet if it is classified as wetlands and therefore falls under federal jurisdiction.

"Leslie is not publicly stating that it wants to develop these lands, but there is no doubt in my mind that they plan to," says Marc Holmes, a program director of Save San Francisco Bay Association, an Oakland-based non-profit organization. "Will they let 40,000 acres [In addition to their 30,000 South Bay acres Leslie owns 10,000 acres on San Pablo Bay in Napa and Solano counties] of prime real estate go down without trying to make a profit? . . . It's just a matter of when," Holmes says.

A recent court ruling on a 153-acre tract of Leslie's land, currently being appealed to the U.S. Supreme Court, illustrates the complexities of the controversy. The majority of the contended land, called the Newark Coyote Tract, is a retired salt pond once used in the final stage of Leslie's salt production process. Leslie admits they want to sell this particular plot of land to developers. The U.S. Government says they can't. At loggerheads in this case are the well-established right of property owners to develop and sell their own lands, and the recently mandated responsibility of the government to halt and reverse the destruction of wetlands.

The outcome of the case may decide the fate of much of what Leslie calls its "developable" property: "About ten percent of our total holdings," says Leslie's property manager Robert Brown. If the government can legally claim jurisdiction over Leslie's property, it may have gained new and powerful tools for adding to and protecting one of the nation's most endangered habitats. For this reason, the case has drawn the attention of environmentalists and land developers around the country. If the court accepts the government's case, says Leslie's attorney Edgar Washburn, "that could involve millions of acres in the United States."

The controversy over the Newark Coyote Tract began five years ago when Leslie started digging drains in the property in preparation for its sale to developers who would construct a business and light industrial park there. In the dry season the tract doesn't look like much—just a large barren field with little vegetation. It is especially bleak compared to the lush salt marsh across the road. Yet this marsh was once a crystallizer, too. Its transformation began in 1979 when it was acquired by the San Francisco Bay National Wildlife Refuge.

The refuge chose a site nearby for their headquarters and if the Newark Coyote Tract were developed, "it would be like putting a McDonald's at the visitor center of the Grand Canyon," says Paul Kelly, wildlife biologist at the California Department of Fish and Game. Not only would it be an "esthetic disaster," Kelly says, but "the loss of the habitat itself, and dangers and stresses it would put on the refuge, would also be very significant."

When the U.S. Army Corps of Engineers discovered Leslie's preparations for development, it issued a cease-and-desist order on the grounds that the area had taken on some "aquatic" characteristics and was therefore under Corps jurisdiction according to Section 404 of the 1972 Clean Water Act, a provision requiring owners of wetlands to apply to the Corps before filling or developing them.

Leslie filed a suit contesting the Corps' right to interfere, arguing that most of the area was not wetlands. Furthermore, Leslie contended, whatever wetland characteristics were present resulted from government actions on or adjacent to Leslie's property.

In the early 1980s Caltrans, the California highway authority, constructed a sewer line and public roads on and around the Newark Coyote Tract. The construction created ditches, road beds, and culverts that hydrologically connected Leslie's land to the nearby Newark Slough. Caltrans also breached a levy on the wildlife refuge adjacent to the property and destroyed a floodgate that had prevented tidal backflow from reaching the site. Leslie also maintained floodgates on refuge land which a Fish and Wildlife Service employee propped open to inundate refuge property, unaware that he might have been letting bay water onto the Leslie site. All these events could have created the "aquatic" features, Leslie asserts, but that was not the salt company's fault. In essence, Leslie argues, the government was seizing their property by turning it into wetlands and then citing the Clean Water Act to gain jurisdiction over it.

The Corps countersued, claiming it had the right to regulate the land's use under the Clean Water Act, that the endangered salt marsh harvest mouse used that property as habitat, and that migratory birds used the former crystallizer for feeding and resting during the winter and spring when they were flooded by seasonal rains. The Corps argued that how the salt pond came to be wetlands was irrelevant. If Leslie wanted to sue Caltrans, they could. But it was the Corps' job to protect wetlands where they found them.

To establish a property as wetlands, according to federal guidelines, the Corps must demonstrate the presence of three primary indicators: water (an area has to be wet long enough to support wetland vegetation); hydric soils, a condition defined by the soil's ability to become and remain saturated; and characteristic wetland vegetation.

If was easy to demonstrate the presence of water. The crystallizer was designed specifically to hold water pumped from briny salt ponds adjacent to the bay. Even after it was retired from salt production in 1959, seasonal rain collected in the crystallizer area and remained there through the winter and spring.

The presence of wetland vegetation was more difficult to establish. "The salinity in crystallizer ponds is so high that nothing grows in them, nothing can live in them," says Bill Britt, Leslie's vice president in charge of the company's land holdings.

It takes five years for Leslie to turn bay water into salt. First they pump it into condenser ponds, where the water evaporates and the salinity increases. The brine is moved into increasingly saline ponds over the production process. Finally, when it is nearly ready for "harvesting," the brine is pumped into crystallizer ponds where the salt crystallizes, the remaining brine is siphoned off, and the final product is extracted. When the water is removed the crystallizers are covered with hard, jagged salt crystals: not a hospitable habitat for most wildlife, though birds do sometimes rest on the ponds; "possibly because they feel safe from predators," says Leslie's Robert Douglass.

In its nearly 30 years of retirement, however, the Newark Coyote Tract has become more hospitable. Although it is hardly lush, it does support some seasonal wetland vegetation such as annual pickleweed.

When the Northern California District Court heart the case in 1988, Leslie's witnesses portrayed the former crystallizer pond as a "biological wasteland" with "no wildlife values whatsoever." The government witnesses, on the other hand, stresses the biological importance of the litigation site, despite its lack of characteristic vascular wetland vegetation. Paul Kelly testified that on the site he had found hundreds of three-spined stickle-backs, a small estuarine fish that inhabits the upper sloughs and estuarine areas of the bay. They must have been transported onto the site by tidal water from Newark Slough, perhaps through the open culverts, Kelly says.

Kelly also stressed the importance of the seasonal standing water in the former crystallizer pond. At this point nontidal rainwater wetlands may be even more important to the wetland ecosystem than tidal salt marsh—not because it plays a more important ecological role, but because there is so much less of it in the Bay Area. Since most of the nontidal marsh has been lost, shorebirds have few places to feed during high tides or to find protection during storms. The abandoned crystallizer pond in the litigation site is one such place. Dowitchers, sandpipers, and gulls, among other birds, all feed here on brine flies, brine shrimp, and water boatman, Kelly says.

The restored salt marsh on the other side of the road is incontestable evidence of the litigation site's wildlife *potential*. Rick Coleman, refuge management of the San Francisco Bay National Wildlife Refuge, describes what he could do with the Newark Coyote Tract if it became part of the refuge.

"I envision it as a complex of open mud flats, interspersed with cordgrass and pickleweed, maybe clapper rails, definitely harvest mice, snowy plover, and least terns. It would provide public viewing and environmental education opportunities. It would look like the one hundred acres across the road that the refuge acquired in 1979. They provide habitat for 20–40,000 birds at one time. Pickleweed and cordgrass are growing vigorously. Shorebirds use them at high tide when they become optimum feeding and loafing habitat. We could do exactly the same restoration on the other [Leslie] complex."

Even Judge Charles A. Legge, who presided over the district court hearing, acknowledged the wildlife value of the site when he wrote his decision: If it were the court's function to decide what *should* be done with the property, "this court would probably say that the San Francisco Bay Area has too much development and that more land should be left undeveloped."

But that was not how the court saw its function. Rather its duty was to "define what powers the Corps has been given by Congress and by the regulations, and to apply those definitions to the evidence which the court has heard about the property." In other words, the judge had to decide if the crystallizer ponds were wetlands under the strict federal definition, not whether they would be a beneficial addition to the refuge.

On October 3, 1988, the court ruled in favor of Leslie on all grounds. The great majority of the site did not satisfy the requirements for wetlands. Though they were wet enough of the year, the soils on most of the property were not considered hydric. The judge also denied that there was the requisite vascular wetland vegetation growing on the former crystallizer. Finally, although the court conceded that parts of the site had become wetlands, it disqualified them from Corps jurisdiction because they resulted from government actions; even the areas which had become *biological* wetlands were not to be considered wetlands from a *jurisdictional* point of view.

Conservation groups saw the decision as a major setback and feared it would open the door to the development of Leslie's crystallizer properties and other "artificial" wetlands across the country.

When the U.S. Government decided to appeal the decision, the National Audubon Society and Save San Francisco Bay Association joined the case as interveners, meaning that the case could not be settled without their agreement.

Having failed to gain jurisdiction over the property by proving it to be wetlands, the government took a new tack. This time, in its appeal to the Ninth Circuit Court of Appeals, the defendants stressed the "other waters" provision in the Corps' EPA-mandated guide-lines, arguing that the property's use by migratory birds that cross the state lines brings it under Corps jurisdiction.

The government's approach relied on a technicality in the Environmental Protection Agency's guidelines for Corps jurisdiction over waters crucial to "interstate commerce," classifying them as "other waters of the U.S." The EPA criteria, stated in a regulatory guidance letter, directs that waters are to be so considered "which are or would be used as habitat by birds protected by Migratory Bird treaties; . . . or other migratory birds which cross state lines; or which are or would be used as habitat for endangered species. . . ."

The record showed that migratory birds (including many protected by Migratory Bird treaties) and at least one endangered species used the property as habitat.

On February 6, 1990, the Ninth Circuit Court of Appeals overturned the district court's decision, granting the Corps jurisdiction over the property. In addition to agreeing that the abandoned crystallizer fell into the category of "other waters," the three appeals court judges also overruled the lower court's decision on the wetland areas that had been created by Caltrans construction and other government activity. How the areas became wetlands was irrelevant as long as the Corps did not intentionally create them to gain jurisdiction over them, the judges ruled.

Leslie's vice-president, Bill Britt, calls this use of the Clean Water Act "novel" and "probably not constitutional" because it depends on a regulatory guidance letter from the EPA rather than any spelled-out provision in the Clean Water Act itself.

"We were shocked by the ruling," Britt says. "If this opinion is upheld, it will have a tremendous impact across the country. We've already seen the Corps asserting jurisdiction where it has never asserted it before. . . . We're not just talking about the Newark Coyote

Tract. This isn't just important for Leslie, but for anyone who has property on or near water."

Leslie has appealed the case to the Supreme Court of the United States. The Court should decide whether to hear the case by the end of January. While it decides, the winter rains will flood the Newark Coyote Tract, birds will land there for food and sanctuary, the harvest mouse will scurry along, protected by the what-ever-you-want-to-call-it from predators and high tides.

ADDENDUM

In 1991 the U.S. Supreme Court refused to hear Leslie Salt's appeal, and remanded the case back to the Ninth District Court, instructing the judge to designate which parts of the Newark-Coyote site were wetlands, which parts were "other waters of the United States," and which parts were neither. Judge Legge ruled that of the 153 acres on the site, ten acres were wetlands and twelve acres were "other waters." These twenty-two acres would fall under the jurisdiction of the Army Corps of Engineers. The remaining 131 acres were designated "developable." Leslie (now called Cargill Salt) has proposed consolidating the twenty-two acres of designated land (it is currently spread in patches throughout the property) and rezoning the remaining area for an industrial park. In 1994, the City of Newark passed a resolution accepting that rezoning proposal and stating their commitment to seeing the property developed. Though Cargill has begun preparing parts of the property for construction, before development begins the Corps must accept the consolidation proposal.

When the Government Tinkers with Wetlands Policy, All of Alaska Is Affected

Kim Fararo

More than two-thirds of the total acreage of U.S. wetlands is in Alaska, patchily distributed over half the entire area of this vast, largely unpopulated state. Practically every development project in Alaska must deal with wetlands regulations, so it's not surprising that pressures to bend the rules there are strong.

Kim Fararo is a business reporter for the *Anchorage Daily News*, where this article originally appeared.

The federal government recently issued its latest guidelines for how wetlands development should proceed in Alaska.

Who should care? Anyone who wants to build a home in a marshy area, any developer who wants to build a subdivision, any Anchorage resident who favors building new softball fields, not to mention any fisherman who wants his favorite fishing hole to remain well-stocked and anyone who cares about migrating birds or merely about preserving open land in a city.

You should care because building in wetlands almost always requires government permission and because the state of Alaska is covered with wetlands of every type. Because too much fill in too many wetlands can cause flooding and help dry up the underground aquifers that feed water wells. Because too little fill can slow development of everything from oil fields to growing cities that want to build schools.

First, what exactly is a wetlands?

It's basically a wet place that serves some purpose in the ecosystem, from feeding aquifers to feeding fish. And they come in all shapes and sizes. Popular Potter Marsh is a wetlands. But so are the many tiny ponds that dot the North Slope and the bogs scattered throughout Anchorage.

Next, why are regulators fiddling again with the wording of wetlands policy?

This latest round of debate on wetlands is meant to clear up the uncertainty created here when former President Bush declared the United States would have "no net loss" of wetlands. The country, he said, already had developed many of the lands and was paying the environmental price. After a storm of protest from Alaskans who felt they were suffering for the sins of more developed states, Bush proposed granting an exemption to the 49th state.

The proposal would have allowed Alaskans to fill in wetlands without much regulation until the state had used 1 percent of those lands. The plan raised another storm of protest, this time from environmental groups fearful Alaska would make the same mistakes as other states.

That argument held sway with President Clinton, and he threw out Bush's proposal. Instead, he said, regulators in Alaska should sit down with those most affected by wetlands rules and see how the government could better serve them.

The policy that emerged May 13 [1994] from those discussions includes few major changes, in good part because the regulators involved say they never forced Alaska to live up to the strict "no net loss" standards applied elsewhere. Those regulators, including the U.S. Environmental Protection Agency and the Army Corps of Engineers, say they have rarely asked builders to create or restore wetlands to replace the ones they destroyed, as often mandated in the Lower 48.

The regulators said they will continue that practice under the newly announced policy. They also will continue to insist that the "footprint" on the land be as small as possible and to ask developers, cities and companies to prove that they couldn't build somewhere less damaging.

In some cases, meeting those requirements is relatively easy. In others, it can be time-consuming and expensive.

The new policy also has clarified some issues, for instance, putting in writing the EPA's oft-stated assurances that the Clean Water Act allows regulators to be flexible in deciding whether builders must replace wetlands.

That cheered pro-development groups, because it is expected to help builders in lawsuits over construction that is considered inevitable.

The federal agencies have also vowed to complete wetlands reviews for individual permits in 90 days, rather than the average 106 days they now take.

The agencies say they can meet that goal if they hire more people, which might not happen. In the meantime, they'll attempt to speed up by creating more time-saving general permits for wetlands they deem low value or for activities they consider low impact.

If you're building in an area covered by a general permit, you don't need to submit to a separate review for your project, but you do need to follow the rules set out in the general permit. Anchorage had a general permit, but it expired.

The following are summaries of conversations about the changes with some people who advised the government on wetlands revisions:

Henry Mitchell, executive director, Bering Sea Fisherman's Association
Mitchell had two competing goals when he served on the wetlands task force. As a representative of fishermen, he wanted to ensure

wetlands rules were strong enough to protect streams where fish spawn. As a representative of many Native fishermen who live in villages built mainly on wetlands, he tried to make sure building reviews are quicker.

Mitchell likes the idea that the agencies are going to pay more attention to explaining the wetlands program to Native communities and to trying to work out compromises that make sense for building in remote regions.

He is worried, however, that without more staff, the agencies won't live up to their promises to do more explaining and to do it more quickly.

"All this is wonderful if, in fact, the money is available to have the personnel to basically conduct it," he said.

Becky Gay, executive director, Resource Development Council
RDC represents people who want to use the state's resources to better their economic lives. It includes miners, oil companies, developers and some cities.

Gay says she is disappointed with the government's policy because it doesn't go far enough. It doesn't, for instance, clearly say that Alaska is exempt from the "no net loss" nationwide policy. This could leave all construction open to court challenges from environmental groups. It also says developments that are expected to cause minor impact shouldn't have to do extensive reviews, but doesn't define "minor impact."

Gay supports more general permits being written, but is not encouraged many will be. She cites Juneau's experience. The city has been trying for years to get such a permit. The Corps recently agreed to give it something akin to a general permit on a trial basis, but the National Wildlife Federation has threatened to sue the Corps over it.

In general, Gay said, she would like the state's wetlands to be classified by their value, then have the rules for using the least valuable ones made simpler and more consistent.

"Tell us what wetlands we can use," Gay said. "We know kind of what you want us to avoid, but we don't know what we can use."

Tony Turrini, counsel for the National Wildlife Federation in Alaska
Turrini is mainly pleased with the wetlands policy because it doesn't further weaken a program he feels is already too lenient.

Turrini wants to see more replacement of wetlands, but isn't sure it will happen. The regulators say they may begin requiring North Slope oil producers to replace some of the many acres of wetlands they've filled in over the past three decades. But the EPA's Al Ewing said the policy doesn't mandate such replacement.

Turrini said the Wildlife Federation has notified the Corps it will sue over Juneau's proposed permit, because the Corps wants to allow the city to administer the permit. Turrini says the Corps can't cede its responsibility for wetlands protection granted under the Clean Water Act.

"While the Corps doesn't always do the greatest job, the local governments tend to be far more susceptible to political pressures brought to bear by development interests," Turrini said.

Peter T. Hanley, supervisor of permitting for BP Exploration (Alaska) Inc.
"BP was pleased . . . [with] the flexibility in the regulations. However, the report still does not really clarify how these will be applied in Alaska, which were the major concerns of most of the Alaska stakeholders. The report basically states that the no-net-loss goal will not be applied on an individual permit basis. It has also not fully recognized the difficulties, if not impossibility, of requiring [the creation of new wetlands] in the state, especially in rural Alaska. BP and

many stakeholders indicated that the national goal of no overall net loss of wetlands, applied to Alaska, was unworkable and unwarranted due to the abundance of wetlands in the state, the minimal loss of wetlands in Alaska and the general lack of restoration sites."

The Desert Smells Like Rain

Gary Paul Nabhan

Is human presence necessarily detrimental to wetland environments? Ethnobiologist Gary Paul Nabhan has found evidence at two oases in the Sonoran Desert—one on either side of the Mexican-U.S. border—that sometimes the human touch might actually be beneficial. Nabhan is project manager of the Southwest Traditional Crop Conservancy Garden and Seed Bank.

In this lake there lived a monster, much larger than a man,
who hated people, and killed them when they came for water.
   The Monster of Quitovac

A cloudless sky, a bone-dry road. After miles of eating dust on a drive parallel to the border, we had arrived at what seemed an apparition—a little pocket of greenery in an otherwise harsh grey habitat.

Soon my old Pagago friend Remedio had found his way down the trail to the pond. The next thing I knew, he was crawling on his hands and knees out onto the trunk of a cottonwood tree that reached over the water. He hung one arm down and scooped up a drink.

"Sure is *sweet* water. What do they call this place?"

"Depends on who you talk to," I mumbled, glancing across at an Organ Pipe Cactus National Monument placard. "Well, the Park Service calls it Quitobaquito, after the Mexico *Quitovaquita*. And three hundred years ago, Padre Kino christened it *San Seguio*. But all I ever heard your people call it is *A'al Waipia*."

"A'AL WAIPIA? This is it?" He was stunned for a moment. "In all of my life I never thought I would get to see this place where we are standing! I just thought we were going to another place because those signs didn't say *A'al Waipia*. So this is where those little waters come up from the ground!"

Those little springs, which the Pagago call *sonagkam*, flow into a modest pond touted as one of the few authentic desert oases on the continent.

Out in the stretch of the Sonoran Desert where any sources of potable water are few and far between, *A'al Waipia* has been more than just a curious landmark. It is a critical *watermark* that has literally served and saved thousands of lives over the centuries.

Listen to the crusty explorer Karl Lumholtz soften under its touch around 1910:

. . . The little stream of crystal clear spring water at Quitovaquita is smaller than a brook, but it seemed much alive as it hurried on in its effort to keep the dam full. As I had been long unaccustomed to seeing running water, and for twenty days had drunk it more or less brackish, the tiny brook seemed almost unreal and was enchanting in its effect. It was also a delight to indulge in my first real wash for nine days.

Where a spring bubbles up in the desert, water-loving plants cuddle around it. Thus *A'al Waipia* has been an ecological oasis, a spot of lush riparian growth. As such, it attracts vagrant and migrant bird species from the seas, seldom seen in the arid interior.

And that's what the Park Service plays on—they offer us a cool, shady sanctuary where we can sit and watch birds, and ponder over a little pond filled with endangered desert pupfish.

But, unfortunately, *A'al Waipia* is no more than a shadow of what it once was. To sense its historic significance, one must go to another place. Off the beaten track. A true Sonoran oasis, thirty miles to the south of Organ Pipe Cactus National Monument, in old Mexico. *Ki:towak.*

My pickup truck bounced along over the washboard road. Amadeo, Remedio, and I pointed out plants to each other as we went— the bristle-topped senita cactus, heavy-trunked ironwood trees, and odorous, yellowish-green croton shrubs.

We edged over a rise, and all of a sudden the desert was whisked away—palms and cottonwoods reached above the horizon, and teal splashed up into the air. Amadeo grabbed his field glasses—a white-faced ibis down on the mudflats of the pond, and a couple of pigs foraging in the saltgrass.

Remedio sighed, knowing that this place was the place he had heard of: "*Ki:towak.*"

We parked the pickup beneath a towering California palm; then Remedio and I walked over toward an old Papago house sitting almost on the edge of the pond. Amadeo took off in the other direction to survey birds—he would sight twice as many species that afternoon as we has seen at *A'al Waipia* in the morning.

A lean old Papago quietly greeted us as we approached his house made of saguaro ribs and organ pipes. Luis Nolia had been born nearby and was now the oldest living resident of the Papago settlement. A descendant of the semi-nomadic Sand Papago, he had as a child gathered the sweet underground stalks of sandfood in the dunes to the west, and eaten them like *carne machaca*. His family's women had crushed mesquite pods in bedrock mortars, and the men had transformed themselves into animals by wearing the fur masks and hoods of the *Wi'igita* ceremony.

Decades ago, Luis himself had been lured to the U.S. by wages to be earned picking cotton. After his wife died and his sons had grown up and settled in Arizona towns, he became lonely for the old ways and returned to Sonora. Now he grows summer field crops, keeps an orchard and a few animals, and is knowledgeable about the many medicinal plants with which the oasis springs are blessed.

Luis too blesses the oasis, for his work keeps it healthy. He is proud of the way the springs flow unencumbered by debris—he has dug out the fallen sediment so that the streamlets run clear from their source. Every summer, Luis plants squash, watermelon, beans, and other vegetables. His plowing and irrigation encourage at least six species of wild greens which he harvests at various times. Various medicinal plants and Olney's tules (for which *Ki:towak* is named) grow in the irrigation ditches.

Luis is appreciative of trees, too, and his plantings literally rim the oasis and field edges of *Ki:towak*. The willow cuttings that he stuck into the pond bank grew quickly into saplings and now stabilize the earth. He harvests willow branches to make leafy crosses that hang on the walls of every Papago household at *Ki:towak*, but keeps his own supply alive. Elderberry, salt cedar, date, and California palm are planted near his house to provide shade. Wolfberry, mesquite, and palo verde form a hedge on his field edge, and thorny brush is piled between the shrubs to discourage stray cattle from entering.

He has dug fig and pomegranate shoots from the base of ancient, abundantly bearing trees, and transplanted them out to more open areas in the orchard where they can thrive. He offered Remedio and me a bag of figs and a few white-seeded, rusty-shelled pomegranates to savor.

Earlier, in the day, walking on the west side of *A'al Waipia,* Remedio and I came upon a sight that made him sick inside. There were fruit trees—or the remnants of them—still putting out a few leaves (but no fruit) in an overgrown mesquite bosque. At least five pomegranate shrubs were dead, and another eighteen were dying. Just a few rangy, unpruned figs were left.

"Poor things, such old trees left with no one to help them!" Remedio lamented. He wondered if they could be dug up and given to a family who would care for them.

They were a reminder that until 1957, *A'al Waipia* had been a *peopled* oasis just as *Ki:towak* is today. Looking down at the foot of the dying fruit trees, we saw irrigation ditches running along in much the same pattern as those which still function in the field/orchard at *Ki:towak.*

For *A'al Waipia* was formerly a Papago settlement too, with six-and-a-half acres of crops, and more of orchards.

Geographer Ronald Ives put it simply: "It is reasonable to believe that this settlement, situated at a perennial spring, has been continuously occupied since man came to the area."

The archaeological record bears out the suggestion of long inhabitance—seven distinct prehistoric and historic sites have been found on the U.S. side of the *A'al Waipia* area, and at least two major ones south of the border fence.

From the 1830s onward, there are records of the names of Papago inhabitants who lived at the oasis. After 1860, Mexicans and Americans came to stay at *A'al Waipia* too, some even intermarrying with the Sand Papago there. At least eight adobe houses were raised, a store and a mill were built, the pond deepened, and the ditches improved. But while visitors and buildings came and went, two Papago were patriarchs of the place for well over a century: Juan José and José Juan Orosco.

Juan José lived at the springs off and on from the 1860s until at least 1910, when Karl Lumholtz reported that he was well over a hundred but still in command of his faculties. José Juan Orosco, famous both as a medicine man and hunter, followed the older man as patriarch of *A'al Waipia* for several more decades. After Organ Pipe Cactus National Monument was established in 1937, Orosco's grazing rights were recognized, and he used them until his death in 1945.

The Park Service and the Papago disagree about what happened after that. The more-or-less official story is that José Juan Orosco's son Jim agreed to let the Park Service "condemn" his holdings in Organ Pipe Cactus National Monument, including "his" place at *A'al Waipia*. In return for the land and improvements he claimed by way of squatter's rights, Jim Orosco was given $13,000.

Some of the Papago tell versions of an altogether different story. One version claims that Jim Orosco never actually had exclusive rights to the place; he simply stayed there with the real caretaker, an old man called *S-Iawuis Wo:da*—Worn Out Boot—who was being paid by descendants of Juan José. The tellers of this version insist that *A'al Waipia* wasn't Jim Orosco's to sell: legally, all descendants of the two patriarchs should have been consulted. A great-granddaughter of Juan José lamented, "The old people knew it was wrong, but they didn't say too much when it happened."

Whether or not Jim Orosco could legally surrender Papago rights to *A'al Waipia*, it is clear that at the time the Park Service did not look upon the resident Papago as assets to the Monument. Orosco is reputed to have gone on drinking binges, and at one time, there was a Park Service sign on the road to the springs that said, "Watch Out for Deer, Cattle, and Indians."

The Papago farmland in the Monument was condemned without Congressional order, and without consultation with the Papago Tribe. By 1962, the National Park Service had destroyed all sixty-one structures remaining at *A'al Waipia* and the Growler Mine, wiping away most of the signs of human history in the Monument.

Bob Thomas of the *Arizona Republic* later commented on the Park Service's superficial commitment to its mandate of preserving ". . . various objects of historic and scientific interest." In a 1967 article entitled "Price of Progress Comes High," Thomas wrote:

. . . Near Quitobaquito on the Organ Pipe National Monument a few years ago a government bulldozer knocked down the home of the late José Juan, a Papago Indian who lived there all his life. In doing so, workmen churned up the only known stratification of human habitation between Ajo and Yuma.

He added that the Papago:

. . . distrust the government's promises to protect the park's treasures. In the past, the government has unknowingly or unfeelingly destroyed historic and prehistoric artifacts in the area.

By this destruction, the Park Service gained a bird sanctuary to provide tourists with a glimpse of wild plants and animals that gather around a desert water source.

Or so they thought. For an odd thing is happening at their "natural" bird sanctuary. They are losing the heterogeneity of the habitat, and with it, the birds. The old trees are dying. Few new ones are being regenerated. There are only three cottonwoods left, and four willows. These riparian trees are essential for the breeding habitat of certain birds. Summer annual seedplants are conspicuously absent from the pond's surroundings. Without the soil disturbance associated with plowing and flood irrigation, these natural foods for birds and rodents no longer germinate.

Visiting *A'al Waipia* and *Ki:towak* on back-to-back days three times during one year, ornithologists accompanying me encountered more birds at the Papago village than at the "wildlife sanctuary." Overall, we identified more than sixty-five species at the Papago's *Ki:towak,* and less than thirty-two at the Park Service's *A'al Waipia.* As Dr. Amadeo Rea put it, "It is as if someone fired a shotgun just before we arrived there. The conspicuous absences were more revealing than what we actually encountered."

When I explained to Remedio that we were finding far fewer birds and plants at the uninhabited oasis, he grew introspective. Finally, the Papago farmer had to speak:

"I've been thinking over what you say about not so many birds living over there anymore. That's because those birds, they come where the people are. When the people live and work in a place, and plant their seeds and water their trees, the birds go live with them. They like those places, there's plenty to eat and that's when we are friends to them."

I think that Remedio would even argue that it is natural for birds to cluster at human habitations, around fields and fence-rows. I'll go even further. It's in a sense natural for desert-dwelling humans over the centuries to have gathered around the *A'al Waipia* and *Ki:towak* oases. And although they didn't keep these places as pristine wilderness environments—an Anglo-American expectation of parks in the West—the Papago may have increased their biological diversity.

So if you're ever down in Organ Pipe Cactus National Monument and visit the Park Service wildlife sanctuary of Quitobaquito, remember that an old Papago place called *A'al Waipia* lies in ruin there. Its spirit is alive, less than forty miles away, in a true Sonoran Desert oasis. There, the irrigation ditches are filled with tules, and they radiate out from the pond into the fields like a green sunburst. *Ki:towak.*

Glossary

Cowardin, Lewis M., et al. (1979). "Classification of Wetlands and Deepwater Habitats of the United States." U.S. Department of the Interior.

ACID. Term applied to water with a pH less than 5.5.

ALKALINE. Term applied to water with a pH greater than 7.4.

BAR. An elongated landform generated by waves and currents, usually running parallel to the shore, composed predominantly of unconsolidated sand, gravel, stones, cobbles, or rubble and with water on two sides.

BEACH. A sloping landform on the shore of larger water bodies, generated by waves and currents and extending from the water to a distinct break in landform or substrate type (e.g., a foredune, cliff, or bank).

BRACKISH. Marine and Estuarine waters with Mixohaline salinity. The term should not be applied to inland waters.

BOULDER. Rock fragments larger than 60.4 cm (24 inches) in diameter.

BROAD-LEAVED DECIDUOUS. Woody angiosperms (trees or shrubs) with relatively wide, flat leaves that are shed during the cold or dry season; e.g., black ash (*Fraxinus nigra*).

BROAD-LEAVED EVERGREEN. Woody angiosperms (trees or

shrubs) with relatively wide, flat leaves that generally remain green and are usually persistent for a year or more; e.g., red mangrove (*Rhizophora mangle*).

CALCAREOUS. Formed of calcium carbonate or magnesium carbonate by biological deposition or inorganic precipitation in sufficient quantities to effervesce carbon dioxide visibly when treated with cold 0.1 normal hydrochloric acid. Calcareous sands are usually formed of a mixture of fragments of mollusk shell, echinoderm spines and skeletal material, coral, raminifera, and algal platelets (e.g., *Halimeda*).

CHANNEL. An open conduit either naturally or artificially created which periodically or continuously contains moving water, or which forms a connecting link between two bodies of standing water.

CHANNEL BANK. The sloping land bordering a channel. The bank has steeper slope than the bottom of the channel and is usually steeper than the land surrounding the channel.

CIRCUMNEUTRAL. Term applied to water with a pH of 5.5 to 7.4.

CODOMINANT. Two or more species providing about equal areal cover which in combination control the environment.

COBBLES. Rock fragments 7.6 cm (3 inches) to 25.4 cm (10 inches) in diameter.

DECIDUOUS STAND. A plant community where deciduous trees or shrubs represent more than 50% of the total areal coverage of trees or shrubs.

DOMINANT. The species controlling the environment.

DORMANT SEASON. That portion of the year when frosts occur (see U.S. Department of Interior, National Atlas 1970:110–111 for generalized regional delineation).

EMERGENT HYDROPHYTES. Erect, rooted, herbaceous angiosperms that may be temporarily to permanently flooded at the base but do not tolerate prolonged inundation of the entire plant; e.g., bulrushes (*Scirpus* spp.), saltmarsh cordgrass.

EMERGENT MOSSES. Mosses occurring in wetlands, but generally not covered by water.

ESTUARINE. Occurring where rivers meet the sea.

EUTROPHIC LAKE. Lakes that have a high concentration of plant nutrients such as nitrogen and phosphorus.

EVERGREEN STAND. A plant community where evergreen trees or shrubs represent more than 50% of the total areal coverage of trees and shrubs. The canopy is never without foliage; however, individual trees or shrubs may shed their leaves.

EXTREME HIGH WATER OF SPRING TIDES. The highest tide occurring during a lunar month, usually near the new or full moon. This is equivalent to extreme higher high water of mixed semidiurnal tides.

EXTREME LOW WATER OF SPRING TIDES. The lowest tide occurring during a lunar month, usually near the new or full moon. This is equivalent to extreme lower low water of mixed semidiurnal tides.

FLAT. A level landform composed of unconsolidated sediments—usually mud or sand. Flats may be irregularly shaped or elongate and continuous with the shore, whereas bars are generally elongate, parallel to the shore, and separated from the shore by water.

FLOATING PLANT. A non-anchored plant that floats freely in the water or on the surface; e.g., water hyacinth (*Eichhornia crassipes*) or common duckweed (*Lemna minor*).

FLOATING-LEAVED PLANT. A rooted, herbaceous hydrophyte with some leaves floating on the water surface; e.g., white water lily (*Nymphaea odorata*), floating-leaved pondweed (*Potamogeton natans*). Plants such as yellow water lily (*Nuphar luteum*) which sometimes have leaves raised above the surface are considered floating-leaved plants or emergents, depending on their growth habit at a particular site.

FLOODPLAIN. A flat expanse of land bordering an old river.

FRESH. Term applied to water with salinity less than 0.5 ‰ dissolved salts.

GRAVEL. A mixture composed primarily of rock fragments 2 mm (0.08 inch) to 7.6 cm (3 inches) in diameter. Usually contains much sand.

GROWING SEASON. The frost-free period of the year (see U.S. Department of Interior, National Atlas 1970:100–111 for generalized regional delineation).

HALINE. Term used to indicate dominance of ocean salt.

HERBACEOUS. With the characteristics of an herb; a plant with no persistent woody stem above ground.

HISTOSOLS. Organic soils.

HYDRIC SOIL. Soil that is wet long enough to periodically produce anaerobic conditions, thereby influencing the growth of plants.

HYDROPHYTE. Any plant growing in water or on a substrate that is at least periodically deficient in oxygen as a result of excessive water content (plants typically found in wet habitats).

HYPERHALINE. Term to characterize waters with salinity greater than 40 ‰, due to ocean-derived salts.

HYPERSALINE. Term to characterize waters with salinity greater than 40 ‰, due to land-derived salts.

LACUSTRINE. Occurring in association with lakes.

MACROPHYTIC ALGAE. Algal plants large enough either as individuals or communities to be readily visible without the aid of optical magnification.

MEAN HIGH WATER. The average height of the high water over 19 years.

MEAN HIGHER HIGH TIDE. The average height of the higher of two unequal daily high tides over 19 years.

MEAN LOW WATER. The average height of the low water over 19 years.

MEAN LOWER LOW WATER. The average height of the lower of two unequal daily low tides over 19 years.

MEAN TIDE LEVEL. A plane midway between mean high water and mean low water.

MESOHALINE. Term to characterize waters with salinity of 5 to 18 ‰, due to ocean-derived salts.

MESOPHYTE. Any plant growing where moisture and aeration conditions lie between extremes. (Plants typically found in habitats with average moisture conditions, not usually dry or wet.)

MESOSALINE. Term to characterize waters with salinity of 5 to 18 ‰, due to land-derived salts.

MINERAL SOIL. Soil composed of predominantly mineral rather than organic materials.

MIXOHALINE. Term to characterize water with salinity of 0.5 to 30 ‰, due to ocean salts. The term is roughly equivalent to the term brackish.

MIXOSALINE. Term to characterize waters with salinity of 0.5 to 30 ‰, due to land-derived salts.

MUD. Wet soft earth composed predominantly of clay and silt— fine mineral sediments less than 0.074 mm in diameter.

NEEDLE-LEAVED DECIDUOUS. Woody gymnosperms (trees or shrubs) with needle-shaped or scale-like leaves that are shed during the cold or dry season; e.g., bald cypress (*Taxodium distichum*).

NEEDLE-LEAVED EVERGREEN. Woody gymnosperms with needle-shaped or scale-like green leaves that are retained by plants throughout the year; e.g., black spruce (*Picea mariana*).

NONPERSISTENT EMERGENTS. Emergent hydrophytes whose leaves and stems break down at the end of the growing season so that most above-ground portions of the plants are easily transported by currents, waves, or ice. The breakdown may result from normal decay or the physical force of strong waves or ice. At certain seasons of the year there are no visible traces of the plants above the surface of the water; e.g., wild rice (*Zizania aquatica*), arrow arum (*Peltandra virginica*).

OBLIGATE HYDROPHYTES. Species that are found only in wetlands—e.g., cattail (*Typha latifolia*) as opposed to ubiquitous species that grow either in wetland or on upland—e.g., red maple (*Acer rubrum*).

OLIGOHALINE. Term to characterize water with salinity of 0.5 to 5.0 ‰, due to ocean-derived salts.

OLIGOSALINE. Term to characterize water with salinity of 0.5 to 5.0 ‰, due to land-derived salts.

ORGANIC SOIL. Soil composed of predominantly organic rather than mineral material. Equivalent to Histosol.

PALUSTRINE. Pertaining to freshwater wetlands not associated with lakes or rivers.

PERSISTENT EMERGENT. Emergent hydrophytes that normally remain standing at least until the beginning of the next growing season; e.g., cattails (*Typha* spp.) or bulrushes (*Scirpus* spp.).

PHOTIC ZONE. The upper water layer down to the depth of effective light penetration where photosynthesis balances respiration. This level (the compensation level) usually occurs at the depth of 1 % light penetration and forms the lower boundary of the zone of net metabolic production.

PIONEER PLANTS. Herbaceous annual and seedling perennial plants that colonize bare areas as a first stage in secondary succession.

POLYHALINE. Term to characterize water with salinity of 18 to 30 ‰, due to ocean salts.

POLYSALINE. Term to characterize water with salinity of 18 to 30 ‰, due to land-derived salts.

RIPARIAN. Pertaining to the bank of a river, pond, or small lake.

RIVERINE. Occurring in association with rivers.

SALINE. General term for waters containing various dissolved salts. We restrict the term to inland waters where the ratios of the salts often vary; the term haline is applied to coastal waters where the salts are roughly in the same proportion as found in undiluted sea water.

SALINITY. The total amount of solid material in grams contained in 1 kg of water when all the carbonate has been converted to oxide, the bromine and iodine replaced by chlorine, and all the organic matter completely oxidized.

SAND. Composed predominantly of coarse-grained mineral sediments with diameters larger than 0.074 mm and smaller than 2 mm.

SHRUB. A woody plant which at maturity is usually less than 6 m (20 feet) tall and generally exhibits several erect, spreading, or prostrate stems and has a bushy appearance; e.g., speckled alder (*Alnus rugosa*) or buttonbush (*Cephalanthus occidentalis*).

SOUND. A body of water that is usually broad, elongate, and parallel to the shore between the mainland and one or more islands.

SPRING TIDE. The highest high and lowest low tides during the lunar month.

STONE. Rock fragments larger than 25.4 cm (10 inches) but less than 60.9 cm (24 inches).

SUBMERGENT PLANT. A vascular or nonvascular hydrophyte, either rooted or nonrooted, which lies entirely beneath the water surface, except for flowering parts in some species; e.g., wild celery (*Vallisneria americana*) or the stoneworts (*Chara* spp.).

TERRIGENOUS. Derived from or originating on the land (usually referring to sediments) as opposed to material or sediments produced in the ocean (marine) or as a result of biologic activity (biogenous).

TREE. A woody plant which at maturity is usually 6 m (20 feet) or more in height and generally has a single trunk, unbranched to about 1 m above the ground, and a more or less definite crown; e.g., red maple (*Acer rubrum*), northern white cedar (*Thuja occidentalis*).

WATER TABLE. The upper surface of a zone of saturation. No water table exists where that surface is formed by an impermeable body.

WOODY PLANT. A seed plant (gymnosperm or angiosperm) that develops persistent, hard, fibrous tissues, basically xylem; e.g., trees and shrubs.

XEROPHYTE, XEROPHYTIC. Any plant growing in a habitat in which an appreciable portion of the rooting medium dries to the wilting coefficient at frequent intervals. (Plants typically found in very dry habitats.)

Bibliography

Adam, Paul. *Saltmarsh Ecology*. Cambridge: Cambridge University Press, 1990.

Archie, Michele. "The Wetlands Issue: What Should We Do with our Bogs, Swamps and Marshes?" Washington, D.C.: North American Association for Environmental Education, 1992. Environmental issues forum.

Barnes, R. S. K., and K. H. Mann. *Fundamentals of Aquatic Ecosystems*. Boston: Blackwell Scientific, 1980.

Briuer, Elke. *The Young Scientist's Introduction to the Wetlands*. Vicksburg, Miss.: Wetlands Research & Technology Center, U.S. Army Engineer Waterways Experiment Station, 1993.

Buist, Henry. *Wetlands Protection Policy*. Agricultural Information Bulletin 664–18. Washington, D.C.: Government Printing Office, 1993.

Burgis, Mary, and Pat Morris. *The Natural History of Lakes*. Cambridge: Cambridge University Press, 1987.

Caduto, Michael J. *Pond and Brook: A Guide to Nature Study in Freshwater Environments*. Englewood Cliffs, N.J.: Prentice-Hall, 1985.

"Classifying wetlands for regulatory purposes." Working paper, Association of State Wetlands Managers, Berne, N.Y., 1992. Conclusions and recommendations from the National Workshop conducted March 25, 1992, Washington, D.C.

Cole, Gerald A. *Textbook of Limnology*, 3rd ed. St. Louis: Mosby, 1983.

Cowardin, Lewis M., et al. *Classification of Wetlands and Deepwater Habitats of the United States*. Vol. FWS/OBS-79/31. Washington, D.C.: Government Printing Office, 1992.

Cox, Kenneth W. *Wetlands: A Celebration of Life*. Sustaining Wetlands Issues Paper 1993:1. Ottawa, Ontario: North American Wetlands Conservation Council, 1993.

Cvancara, Alan M. *At Water's Edge: Nature Study in Lakes, Streams and Ponds*. New York: Wiley, 1989.

Davis, Steve M., and John C. Ogden, eds. *Everglades: The Ecosystem and Its Restoration*. Delray Beach, Florida: St. Lucie Press, 1994.

DeWitt, Calvin B., and Eddie Soloway, eds. *Wetlands: Ecology, Values and Impacts*. Madison: Institute for Environmental Studies, University of Wisconsin, 1977.

Dugan, Patrick. *Wetlands in Danger*. London: Reed Consumer Books, 1993. A Mitchell Beazley World Conservation Atlas.

Errington, Paul L. *Of Men and Marshes*. Ames, Iowa: Iowa State University Press, 1969.

Finlayson, Max, and Michael Moser, eds. *Wetlands*. Oxford, U.K. and New York: International Waterfowl and Wetlands Research Bureau and Facts on File, 1991.

Fisheries, Wetlands and Jobs: The Value of Wetlands to America's Fisheries. Oakland, Calif.: Campaign to Save California Wetlands, 1994. (Prepared for the Campaign to Save California Wetlands by William M. Kier Associates; assisted by Clean Water Action et al.)

Frost, Jane Rubey. *Designing Wetlands Preservation Programs for Local Governments: A Guide to Non-regulatory Protection*. Olympia: Washington State Department of Ecology, 1992.

Glaser, Paul H. *The Ecology of Patterned Boreal Peatlands of Northern*

Minnesota: A Community Profile. FWS Biological Report 85–7 (7.14). Washington, D.C.: Government Printing Office, 1987.

Goldman, Charles Remington, and Alexander J. Horne. *Limnology.* New York: McGraw-Hill, 1983.

Goodwin, Richard H., and William A. Niering. *Inland Wetlands of the U.S. Evaluated as Potential Registered National Landmarks.* Natural History Theme Studies No. 2. Washington, D.C.: National Park Service, 1975.

Heimlich, Ralph E., and Linda L. Langner. *Swampbusting: Wetlands Conversion and Farm Programs.* Agricultural Economic Report vol. 551. Washington, D.C.: Government Printing Office, 1986.

Hutchinson, G. Evelyn. *A Treatise on Limnology.* New York: Wiley, 1957.

Interagency Committee on Wetlands Restoration and Creation: *A National Program for Wetlands Restoration and Creation: Report of the Interagency Committee on Wetlands Restoration and Creation to the Policy Coordinating Group, Interagency Task Force on Wetlands.* Washington, D.C.: Government Printing Office, 1992.

Johnson, Charles W. *Bogs of the Northeast.* Hanover, N.H.: University Press of New England, 1985.

Kantrud, Harold A., Gary A. Krapu, and George A. Swanson. *Prairie Basin Wetlands of the Dakotas: A Community Profile.* FWS Biological Report 85 (7.28). Washington, D.C.: Government Printing Office, 1988.

Kirby, Ronald E., Stephen J. Lewis, and Terry N. Sexson. *Fire in North American Wetland Ecosystems and Fire-Wildlife Relations: An Annotated Bibliography.* FWS Biological Report 88(1). Washington, D.C.: Government Printing Office, 1988.

Kusler, Jon A., and Mary E. Kentula, eds. *Wetland Creation and Restoration: The Status of the Science.* Covelo, Calif. and Washington, D.C.: Island Press, 1990.

LeCren, E. D., and R. H. Lowe-McConnell, eds. *The Functioning of Freshwater Ecosystems*. International Biological Programme vol. 22. Cambridge: Cambridge University Press, 1980.

Leopold, Aldo. *Round River: From the Journals of Aldo Leopold*. Edited by Luna B. Leopold. New York: Oxford University Press, 1953.

Lodge, Thomas E., and Marjory Stoneman Douglas. *The Everglades Handbook: Understanding the Ecosystem*. Delray Beach, Florida: St. Lucie Press, 1994.

Lyons, Janet, and Sandra Jordan. *Walking the Wetlands: A Hiker's Guide to Common Plants and Animals of Marshes, Bogs and Swamps*. New York, Wiley, 1989.

McKinnon, Christopher. *The Value of Wetlands*. Rural Information Center publication series no. 26. Beltsville, Md.: Rural Information Center, U.S. National Agricultural Library, 1993.

Meanley, Brooke. *Swamps, River Bottoms and Canebrakes*. Barre, Mass.: Barre Publishers, 1972.

Mitsch, W. J., ed. *Global Wetlands: Old World and New*. Amsterdam: Elsevier, 1994.

Mitsch, William J., and James G. Gosselink. *Wetlands*. New York: Van Nostrand Reinhold, 1986.

Moss, Brian. *Ecology of Fresh Waters: Man and Medium*, 2nd ed. Boston: Blackwell Scientific, 1988.

National Wetlands Working Group. Coordinated by C. D. A. Rubec. *Wetlands of Canada/Terres Humides du Canada*. Montreal: Environment Canada/Polyscience Publishers, 1988.

Niering, William A. *Wetlands*. New York: Knopf, 1985. The Audubon Society Nature Guides.

Odum, Eugene Pleasants. *Basic Ecology*. Philadelphia: Saunders College, 1983.

———. *Freshwater Ecosystems*. Philadelphia: Saunders College, 1983.

Odum, William E., et al. *The Ecology of Tidal Freshwater Marshes of the United States East Coast: A Community Profile*. Vol. FWS/OBS-83-17. Washington, D.C.: Government Printing Office, 1984.

Sather, J. Henry, and R. Daniel Smith. *An Overview of Major Wetland Functions and Values*. Vol. FWS/OBS-84/18. Washington, D.C.: Government Printing Office, 1984.

Sims, Daniel H. *Reclaiming Forested Bottomlands in the South Through the Conservation Reserve Program*. Forest Management Bulletin R8, vol. 37. U.S. Forest Service, Southern Region, 1989.

Steinhart, Peter. *Tracks in the Sky: Wildlife and Wetlands of the Pacific Flyway*. San Francisco: Chronicle Books, 1987.

Thomas, Bill. *The Swamp*. New York: W. W. Norton, 1976.

Thompson, Gerald, and Jennifer Coldrey. *The Pond*. Cambridge, Mass.: MIT Press, 1984.

U.S. Environmental Protection Agency, Region V, and Eastern Energy and Land Use Team, U.S. Fish and Wildlife Service. *The Ecological Impacts of Wastewater on Wetlands: An Annotated Bibliography*. Vol. EPA-905/3-84-002. Chicago: USEPA, Region V, 1984.

Van der Walk, Arnold, ed. *Northern Prairie Wetlands*. Ames, Iowa: Iowa State University, 1989.

Weller, Milton Webster. *Freshwater Marshes: Ecology and Wildlife Management*, 2nd ed. Minneapolis: University of Minnesota Press, 1987.

The Wetlands. Written and produced by Jonathan Donald. 60 min. Pittsburgh: WQED, 1988. Videocassette. Conserving America series. Includes a 12-page, illustrated resource guide.

Wetlands Deskbook. *Environmental Law Reporter*. Washington, D.C.: Environmental Law Institute, 1993. An ELI deskbook.

Wetzel, Robert G. *Limnology*, 2nd ed. Philadelphia: Saunders College, 1983.

Wharton Charles W., et al. *The Ecology of Bottomland Hardwood Swamps of the Southeast: A Community Profile.* Vol. FWS/OBS-83/37. Washington, D.C.: Government Printing Office, 1982.

Windell, John T., et al. *An Ecological Characterization of Rocky Mountain Montane and Subalpine Wetlands.* FWS Biological Report 86(11). Washington, D.C.: Government Printing Office, 1986.

Winger, Parley V. *Forested Wetlands of the Southeast: Review of Major Characteristics and Role in Maintaining Water Quality.* Resource Publication Vol. 163. Washington, D.C.: Government Printing Office, 1986.

Yellowlegs, Eelgrass and Tideflats. Produced by Scott Cossu and Peter Randlette. Written by Michael McCallum and Sara Williams. 29 min. Olympia: Washington State Department of Ecology, Wetlands Section, 1987. Videocassette.

Permissions

The editors gratefully thank the following for permission to reprint copyrighted material:

William A. Niering, "Wetlands of North America" from *Wetlands of North America*, © 1991 Thomasson-Grant Publisher, text © 1991 William A. Niering.

Marjory Stoneman Douglas, "The Everglades: River of Grass" from the book *Everglades: River of Grass*, revised edition copyright © 1988 by Marjory Stoneman Douglas. Used by permission of Pineapple Press, Inc.

Allen Chesser, "Turtle Ways" reprinted by permission of Delma E. Presley.

Bland Simpson, "The Great Dismal" from *The Great Dismal: A Carolinian's Swamp Memoir*, by Bland Simpson. Copyright © 1990 by The University of North Carolina Press. Used by permission of the publisher.

John and Mildred Teal, "Life and Death of the Salt Marsh" reprinted by permission of Mildred and John Teal.

Aldo Leopold, "Clandeboye, Manitoba" from *A Sand County Almanac and Sketches Here and There*, by Aldo Leopold. Copyright 1949, 1977 by Oxford University Press, Inc. Reprinted by permission.

Paul Gruchow, "Journal of a Prairie Year" from "Journal of a Prairie

ABOUT THE EDITORS

Sam Wilson is an environmental consultant who participates in the design and implementation of wetland mitigation projects. He also writes on environmental subjects and is a research associate at the California Academy of Sciences in San Francisco.

Tom Moritz is a professional librarian and information specialist who has worked in the fields of natural history and natural resources for over 20 years. He is currently Academy librarian at the California Academy of Sciences.